GLORY, DEATH & DAMNATION

A TALE OF THREE CAPTAINS

JIM CURRIE

authorHOUSE

AuthorHouse™ UK
1663 Liberty Drive
Bloomington, IN 47403 USA
www.authorhouse.co.uk
Phone: UK TFN: 0800 0148641 (Toll Free inside the UK)
      UK Local: (02) 0369 56322 (+44 20 3695 6322 from outside the UK)

Published by AuthorHouse 03/15/2022

ISBN: 978-1-6655-9733-3 (sc)
ISBN: 978-1-6655-9734-0 (hc)
ISBN: 978-1-6655-9732-6 (e)

Print information available on the last page.

Any people depicted in stock imagery provided by Getty Images are models,
and such images are being used for illustrative purposes only.
Certain stock imagery © Getty Images.

This book is printed on acid-free paper.

Because of the dynamic nature of the Internet, any web addresses or links contained in
this book may have changed since publication and may no longer be valid. The views
expressed in this work are solely those of the author and do not necessarily reflect the
views of the publisher, and the publisher hereby disclaims any responsibility for them.

CONTENTS

PART 3

PART 4

PART 5

PART 6

PART 7

PART 8

PART 9

PART 10

PART 11

DEDICATIONS

I dedicate this effort as follows:

First: In memory of my incredible, sweet, darling wife Anne. Who, for over 60 years of married life and until her recent untimely death, stood by me and our children throughout my time on land and at sea. Who, for many years after I discovered *Titanic,* suffered my interminable rantings about "The Big Boat with the four chimneys". Who was taken away from me long before her time and before this was finished.

Second: To the memory of all those brave sailor-men and women who gave up their precious lives in an attempt to save the lives of others less able.

Third: To the memory of all those innocents - rich or poor - men, women and children - who lost their lives on that terrible morning of April 15, 1912.

Last - but not least: To the memory of those men who carried out their duties as they were trained to do and who were condemned and are still -to this day -condemned by the ignorant for doing so.

> *Our race of existence is run!*
> *Thou grim King of Terrors; thou Life's gloomy foe!*
> *Go, frighten the coward and slave;*
> *Go, teach them to tremble, fell tyrant! but know*
> *No terrors hast thou to the brave!"*
>
> Robert Burns

PROLOGUE

This is the true story of three Sea Captains who were born as far from the sea as the width of the English Midlands would allow.

Two were from the town of Bolton in the County of Lancashire, and the third was from Hanley in Staffordshire.

The oldest was from Hanley and he was born in 1850.

Of the two Bolton lads; the oldest was born in 1877 and the other was born there, eight years later. - 1885.

In the middle of the nineteenth century, Staffordshire was a thriving pottery area, while Bolton had a booming textile industry. Consequently, you would be forgiven for thinking that these lads would have followed careers in the Textile or Pottery trades, however fate decided otherwise.

From humble, beginnings, all three became world famous Sea Captains who are spoken of to this very day.

When they first went to sea, they served in sailing ships - eventually, all three gained the highest qualification of Master Mariner in sail. However, the age of steam was rapidly changing the world, and it did not bypass shipping. Consequently, all three of our captains moved with the times and upgraded their Master Mariner Certificates to that of Extra Master (Steam).

Despite the similarities between these men, it was not until the early morning of April 15, 1912, that their lives became inextricably intertwined. That morning, the brand new White Star liner RMS Titanic sank with an horrific loss of human lives - a death toll which, during peacetime, and thankfully to this day, has still to be surpassed.

As with almost every human tragedy, the *Titanic* disaster and subsequent Inquiries into it have produced a plethora of information.

Since those fateful hours between April 14 and 15, 1912 and right up to the present day, individuals have been queuing-up to pontificate, praise and condemn. Sadly, too many of them, including many historians and would-be historians, have given-way to a delicious temptation to dig-up conspiracy theories. Some have even gone as far as to manipulate and manufacture situations to fit the then, popular beliefs. A few have been almost plausible, while others should rightly be condemned to the twin realms of fantasy and distortion. Unfortunately for historic record, in doing so, they have created an almost impenetrable fog which hampers those of us who simply seek the truth.

If you are looking for a juicy story - forget it. As it has often been said, "there is nothing new under the sun". However, if, like me, you have had it up to the back teeth with the Eureka! moments, such as mirages, moving but stationary ships, burning ships, replacement at birth ships, magnetic storms and aliens, and speculative manipulation of evidence, then this book is most certainly for you. Because, as we progress, I will point-out to you enough, factual evidence of conspiracy, manipulation, deceit and down-right-lying which should be more than enough to satisfy a healthy appetite for the truth.

Basically, I think it is time the truth was exposed, warts and all. Not for my pleasure in doing so, but to make an honest attempt to see justice finally allocated where it is due. Many who embark on this voyage will be confronted with ideas that make them feel uncomfortable - so be it! The truth can often be a hard sea-biscuit to swallow

In the past, and until now, many prominent individuals and organisations have pottered with the idea of obtaining justice for those less than fairly dealt with by the authorities and the general public back in 1912. However, during the intervening years, the twin powers of gossip and scandal and their offspring, downright lies, have reigned supreme. These same years have spawned numerous movies, many of which are undoubtedly excellent works of the movie-maker's art, but they have universally been based on a recipe of poetic license, death, romance and incompetence. Fighting the movie-goer is a daunting task at the best of times. Fighting to rebuke a source of income is even more difficult.

Among those tasked with finally putting part of this story to bed was no less than the august body known as the Marine Accident Investigation Branch of the UK Ministry of Transport.

The M.A.I.B. was founded in 1989 by the then Secretary for Transport, a Conservative MP named Cecil Parkinson.

Around 1991, The Secretary was petitioned by a man named Leslie Harrison to re-examine the case of one of our captains - Captain Stanley Lord. Harrison was a private individual who had at one time been General Secretary of The Marine and Mercantile Services Association, a Trade Union for ship's officers and precursor of the present day Nautilus UK.

In 1992, after a false start, during which, the task was farmed out to a retired Govrnment Marine Inspector, the MAIB produced a report which took one step forward. However, of necessity, it was a cautious, political, baby step, not the giant leap forward expected by Harrison.

True to form, and like all material which in any way changed the status quo, it seems to have been ignored and promptly buried.

In the initial pages of this work, I will not attempt to praise, condemn or minutely dissect any thing or the actions of any individual or individuals. Instead, using all available evidence and my skills and experience gained as a Mariner, Marine Surveyor & Marine Accident Investigator, I will set the scene in the form of a word- picture.

In the main, the words I put in the mouths of the characters are mine. However, they are developed from verbal descriptions of actual happenings given under oath by surviving witnesses and from having personally performed many of the duties described by them.

I will take you onto the decks of the three vessels which, for want of a better description, were the leading players in the *Titanic* tragedy. These were, in order of appearance:

The Cunard vessel RMS Carpathia, commanded by Captain Arthur Rostron from Bolton - the White Star Line vessel RMS Titanic, Commanded by Captain Edward J. Smith from Stoke on Trent, and - the Leyland Line vessel, SS Californian which was, at that time, commanded Captain Stanley Lord who was also from Bolton.

The early years of these three men are well documented so I leave that part of their story for others to elaborate upon.

I should add that during this voyage of discovery, you will read about a ship named *Mount Temple*. While this vessel was not a principal player, the part she and her Captain played in the story is important enough for her to be included as a vessel of special interest.

After setting the scene, I will remind you of the most popular, most believed versions of the tragedy. Having done that, I will offer you a personal summary regarding the conduct of our three captains and where appropriate, the conduct of members of their respective crews.

Finally, in the last part, I will systematically destroy the silliest, basically false versions of the *Titanic* story which readers have been fed since that fateful day of Monday, 15th April, 1912. I will do so, not for the sake of smug superiority, but for historical accuracy.

It is my sincere hope that you enjoy what you are about to read and that after doing so, will close the back cover with a mind cleared of *Titanic* nonsense.

Let the wind of truth blow the mists of myth from your eyes and let your mind behold the truth.

Captain Jim Currie. -
Glasgow, - February, 2022

INTRODUCTION

Courses toward Destiny.

Shortly after Noon (5 pm GMT - April 11), the Cunard Liner SS Carpathia, cast off her tugs and headed down-river for the open sea. She had recently left her berth at Pier 54.Manhatten, New York.

For the next couple of hours, she would traverse New York Bay, through the Verazanno Narrows and down the Ambrose Channel. At the outer end of that channel, marked by the Ambrose Channel Light Vessel, the New York pilot would disembark to the pilot Cutter SS New York - the *Carpathia* would then be ready to start her return journey across the North Atlantic toward the Mediterranean.

In doing so, she would follow a prescribed route known as "The Southern Track'. *Carpathia* would first head south of east in a straight line. This was designed to keep her well clear of the danger of colliding with vessels coming toward New York from the east. Then she would head eastward for 1042 miles until she met with the 47th Meridian. From there, she would follow a long, curving track which would bring her to a point off Cape St Vincent, in Portugal and thereafter along the coast to the British Protectorate of Gibraltar. Thereafter, she would continue eastward, into the Mediterranean - heading for the Italian ports of Genoa, Naples and Trieste. Her final destination was the Adriatic port of Fiume. According to the evidence given by *Carpathia's* captain to the members of a US Senate Committee tasked with inquiring into the cause of the disaster; he had about 325 crew and 745 passengers amounting to at least 1070 souls in his care when his ship left New York.

Far away to the eastward - across the North Atlantic Ocean, the brand new White Star liner RMS Titanic was off the southwest tip of Ireland. She had left Queenstown earlier that afternoon. Now, after passing along the beautiful south coast of Ireland, she had the Fastnet Rock lighthouse on here starboard beam and was starting a long curving, 1618 miles long, track across the North Atlantic.

This part of the voyage would take her to an unmarked position in mid-Atlantic known to Western Ocean men as *The Corner*. From there, she would make straight for her destination - New York - "The Big Apple".

At the moment *Carpathia* was disembarking her New York Pilot, *Titanic* was over 50 miles to the west of Ireland and well on the way to meet her fate.

According to the findings of the British Inquiry into the disaster, *her* Captain, Edward J. Smith had a total of 1,770 souls in *his* safe keeping.

* * *

The Leyland Line steam ship *Californian* had left Tilbury Docks, London on 5th April without passengers but loaded with a cargo destined for the US port of Boston Ma. Her captain, Stanley Lord had the souls of 54 crew members in his safe keeping. Around the same time as *Carpathia* disembarked her pilot, *Californian* was well into her voyage and had covered just under 6 days of her 11 ½ day voyage.

* * *

The Canadian Pacific Steamship Company passenger vessel SS Mount Temple had left the Belgian port of Antwerp on April 3, bound for the port of St John. New Brunswick . As with the *Titanic* and the *Californian*, she would take, more or less, the same track across the Atlantic to *The Corner* before turning directly for her destination. Her Captain, James Moore had 1640 souls in his safekeeping.

At the time *Carpathia* left New York, the *Mount Temple* had completed 7 days of her voyage.

In the following pages, I will tell you about each vessel, and then take you aboard them shortly before the world learned about the *Titanic* disaster.

PART 1

CHAPTER 1

FULL AWAY ON PASSAGE

RMS Carpathia. National Archives
PIC 1

The RMS Carpathia was a passenger ship owned by the Cunard Line. Her 'as built' speed was 14 knots (16.1 mph) so she was not exactly what you might call an *ocean greyhound*.

By 1912, she was 9 years old and in steamship terms, becoming a mature, sedate "old lady".

Originally *Carpathia* had been built for the North Atlantic trade -running between Liverpool, Queenstown (Cove-Ireland) and Boston. However, at the end of her first year in service, her run was modified, and her final destination was changed from Boston to New York during the summer months only. In the winter, she ran between New York and the Mediterranean ports of Gibraltar, Genoa, Naples, Trieste and Fiume in the Italian Adriatic.

Carpathia's Captain, Arthur, Henry Rostron had taken command of her on the 18th of January of that year of 1912 - less than twelve weeks before the *Titanic* disaster. He was doubly rewarded, because on that very same day, the Royal Navy had promoted him to the rank of Commander in the Royal Naval reserve. Little did he know that it would be the day that his luck would improve and continue to improve beyond his wildest dreams.

First *Carpathia* would head south and eastward to avoid meeting vessels arriving at New York from Europe and farther a field. Once well clear, she would heads due east until reaching a jumping off position where she would follow a pre- determined, track which would bring her to the entrance to the Mediterranean, but near enough to the Azores where there was a coaling station should she need it.

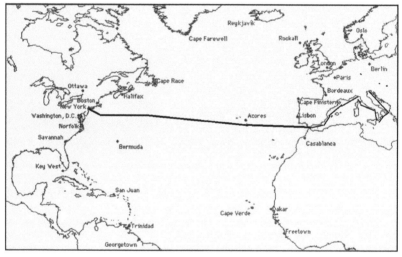

J. Currie 2022

We join *Carpathia* as she is about to start the first leg of her voyage eastward across the wide Atlantic - as she starts that memorable voyage that would be etched forever onto the memories of every living soul on board her.

Her young 4th Officer has just taken a bearing of the Anbrose Lightship at the entrance to the channel leading up to the great city of New York.

"That's the Light vessel abeam now sir."

Captain Rostron was standing on the port (left) bridge wing, he had just waved farewell to the New York Pilot. On hearing the junior officer's advice he quickly walked to the exact centre of his enclosed bridge and stood there staring ahead arms spread and hands resting on the window ledge.

He had been waiting for that very moment. Without turning, he gave a crisp, loud, order to his Fourth Officer who, in anticipation of what was to come, had stationed himself beside the helmsman.

"Bring her head round to East, Mister."

The young Officer acknowledged the order, then in a quieter tone passed it on to the Quartermaster who repeated it and at the same time, expertly spun the steering wheel four complete turns to the left - turning it until it could turn no further. The man then watched the needle of his steering compass. At first, it stayed steady, then, almost reluctantly it began to move left - to follow the fixed line in front of it which represented *Carpathia's* bow. Thereafter, it moved left at an ever-increasing rate; eventually catching up with the fixed line - the Lubber-line

However, at that very first sign of movement, the Quartermaster had eased-off the steering wheel and within seconds, the ships bow reached a steady swing-speed to the left. The Quartermaster returned the wheel to the mid-ship position and intently watched the graduations on the steering compass dial spin steadily under the fixed lubber line as the bow came round in a smooth turn - first Southeast, then East-south-East.

As the spinning compass direction of East by South past beneath the lubber line of the compass, he deftly spun the wheel hard over in the opposite direction. Years of experience had taught him the exact moment when to do this - to compensate, using the rudder to check and finally stop the swinging bow of a ship.

The speed of the leftward swing of the bow quickly slowed as the compass symbol "East" slowly approached the lubber line. In no time at all, the Quartermaster had her steadied on course.

"Due East she is, sir." He confirmed to the Fourth Officer, who in turn, passed-on the fact to the captain in front of them. "Very well Quartermaster." responded

Rosron in a quiet, superior tone. "Steady as she goes."

"Steady as she goes it is, sir." came back the acknowledgement.

Having given that order and seen it carried out; Rostron then strode to the engine room telegraph, grabbed the handles, and gave a double ring Full Ahead. This was and still is to this day in manned engine rooms, the universal signal indicating *Full Away on Passage*. The voyage had begun.

Deep down below in the main engine room,the engineer on the control platform was expecting the "Full Away" telegraph signal and immediately acknowledged it by giving the engine control platform a double ring ahead, thereby copying Rostron's signal. As Rostron noted the reply indication on the bridge telegraphs. his Fourth Officer noted the ship time and Greenwich Time in his Movement Book. The Wheelhouse clock showed 2 pm, local New York time and the ship's Chronometer which always showed the time at Greenwich, England, read 7 pm. These times would later be transcribed into the Official Log Book.

As he wrote down the times, it crossed the young man's mind that although the sun outside the wheelhouse was high in the sky, it would already be on the horizon back home at Greenwich and the gas mantles of the street lights would soon begin to glow.

Once settled on her course, Captain Rostron stepped out onto the exposed bridge wing and joined the two uniformed officers standing there.

The Watch of his First Officer had ended at 2 pm that afternoon and he was in the act of handing over *to Carpathia's* Chief Officer

The latter had been on duty much longer than normal, He should have been below for the previous 8 hours, but because the ship had sailed from New York at Noon, he and the ship's Carpenter had remained on the forecastle head, right up forward at the bow since the ship had left her berth until the Pilot had disembarked. This was standard practice on ships when navigating narrow channels. The two men were stationed there in case the ship lost power and an anchor needed to be dropped. They would only leave their post when the anchors had been secured for sea and the Pilot had disembarked.

The forward crew of sailors who had let go the bow ropes and tugboat lines had long since gone below.

"Right Gentlemen!" the captain announced expansively.That's her on the course for the next alteration. I have decided that we will first follow the east-bound southern track to Longitude 70°West in the Latitude of 41 degrees 10 minutes North. If we make our usual 14 knots, we should be there in just over 13 hours. After that, we'll head due East to 47 degrees

West where we'll head for the Medi. Oh by the way! Just to spoil your day, I hope you've both remembered that since we're now heading East, we'll all be loosing a little sleep each night. We will be advancing the ships clocks."

"Have you worked out the necessary clock change sir?" asked the First Officer.

"I have." Rostron laughed and added " and I almost forgot about that extra 5 minutes of Eastern Standard Time we added to New York Time when we arrived at New York. I reckon we will be at the Longitude of about 67 degrees, 30 minutes West by Noon tomorrow so we need to advance the clocks a total of 30 minutes tonight. The Second Officer can put them forward 15 minutes at 10 pm and as usual, we will add the remaining 15 at Midnight. That means that allowing for the change, we should be at the alteration position at about quarter to four tomorrow morning. After that, it looks like we'll be advancing them about 28 minutes each day."

Rostron was a happy man. He was almost 43 years of age and here he was, in command and on the bridge of his second passenger ship. He had taken 6command of the *Carpathia* a little over 12 weeks earlier, on the 18th of January to be exact. For all of the previous year of 1911, he had been captain of the Cunard passenger ship SS Pannonia. Before that, the Cunard Company had only trusted him with command of cargo vessels. In fact, by the time he reached 40 years of age, he was beginning to think he was doomed to cargo ships for the rest of his sea-going life. For sure, *Carpathia* was not one of the Company greyhounds; she was 9 years old and starting to show her age. On a good day, she might still average her original service speed of 14 knots. No worries now though, he was on the way up. Yes! He was indeed a happy man.

He decided to leave the bridge.

." That's it then! I can see I'm not needed up here." He turned to the Chief Officer; "She's all yours Mister. If you do need me you know where to find me. I'll leave instruction in the Night Order Book later on."

With these few words Captain Rostron went below, leaving the two senior officers to complete the change-of-Watch ritual. Thick black smoke poured from *Carpathia's* single funnel, gradually streaming out astern as she picked up speed. She was on course for her appointment with history.

* * *

The ship settled down to he cruising speed; all aboard her being resigned to her long, slow journey across the North Atlantic

As we have learned, she would first sail on her present course until 3-45 am the next morning, 12th April. Then the course would be altered in the direction of her jumping-off point where she would start the long, curving, Great Circle track for the Straights of Gibraltar; the gateway to the Mediterranean.

In 1898, a number of trans-Atlantic liner companies entered into a non binding agreement, that they would follow prescribed tracks that would separate eastbound and westbound traffic and keep them well clear of iceberg in the iceberg season beginning in the spring of each year. These tracks were not binding on other ships crossing back and forth.

In April, 1912, ships making their way westward from the UK and Europe followed the Northern Track. This consisted of a long curving course to an unmarked position aptly known to North Atlantic men as *The Corner*. On reaching that position, they would turn and head in a straight line for their respective destinations. Ironically, as earlier mentioned, this track had been designed to take ships southward of the danger from icebergs during the spring and summer months.

CHAPTER 2

CARPATHIA - APRIL TWELVE TO FOURTEEN

Just before 9am the next morning of April 12, the Second and First Officers were out on the starboard side of *Carpathia's* bridge wing to perform the ritual of Morning Sights. This was standard practice on every ship at sea when out of sight of land. It was a beautiful spring morning; just a few high clouds to mar the otherwise clear blue sky and a cold breeze was blowing from the North. The sun was brilliant in the east and the horizon below it, clean and clear-cut, like the edge of an unblemished ruler. It was in fact a navigators' dream morning. Both men had their personal sextants at the ready and were about to find out just how far to the eastward *Carpathia* had progressed since she had left the coast of America. The Fourth Officer was in the chart room, bent over the chronometer, pencil in hand and the Sight Books of each officer open at a new page. He was listening intently for the word 'TIME ', shouted by each of the men out on the bridge wing.This would be the moment when the height of the sun above the horizon was measured.

The first to shout was the First Officer. After a pause, to allow the fourth Officer to note the GMT in days, hours, minutes and seconds, the procedure was repeated for the Second Officer. When that was over, the first, physical part of the ritual was completed. The two senior officers then came into the Chart Room where they performed complicated calculations to determine *Carpathia's* Longitude at that time.

The results showed that *Carpathia* seemed to be making her normal service speed of 14 knots. However, this would not be verified until mid day when the sun was due south and a latitude could be obtained to cross with an up date of the longitude obtained at 9 am sights. At that time, another ritual known as "Noon Sights" would produce a fixed position for the ship.

At a few minutes before 12 o' clock, Noon, the officers once again assembled on the bridge for Noon sights. This time they were accompanied by Captain Rostron.

Once again the sun measurement and timing ritual was performed. The results produced two things - a fixed position for the ship and the exact time difference between ship time and Greenwich Mean Time. They also showed that the Captain's predictions were correct; the ship was indeed making her service speed of 14 knots and her clocks did not require any adjusting. Consequently, the amount to advance the clocks each day would be 28 minutes.

Carpathia's eastward passage was uneventful. As Rostron had anticipated, she maintained her service speed of 14 knots until she passed the longitude of 65 degrees West, thereafter, she began to 'feel' the Gulf Stream, and her speed picked up to close to 16 knots.

The weather was clear and perfect, and although the north wind continued to blow there was little or no cloud cover by day and the evening and nights were clear, with stars setting right on the horizon. - and so, the navigator's dream continued.

With their sextants, *Carpathia's* navigators were able to plot the ship's location and course with an accuracy unusual for that part of the world where westerly gales, 100% cloud cover and rain were the normal order of the day (and night).

At Noon on 14th April, the sights placed the ship near to the Longitude of 52 degrees, thirty minutes West. At that time, Captain Rostron predicted that with the help of the Gulf Stream his ship would be at the Longitude of 45 degrees 19 minutes West at Noon on the 15th. He therefore instructed that the clocks should be advance a total of 29 minutes during the coming night. He, and the men with him on the bridge at that time, as well as everyone else on board *Carpathia,* was blissfully unaware that in a space of less than 24 hours, their lives would be changed for ever

At dusk that same evening, the wind dropped off completely. The sky was clear and the horizon was, once again, perfect for celestial observations. Stars could be seen setting on the horizon. Consequently, *Carpathia's* 2nd Officer Bisset was able to obtain a first class fix by star sights. This included a sight of the Pole Star for Latitude which would have told him that *Carpathia* was making a course to the northward or southward of her intended track. The Longitudes calculated also confirmed that the ship was making a better-than-average speed, which was usually the expected bonus in that part of the ocean.

* * *

Carpathia was equipped with wireless supplied by the Marconi Company. The equipment was manned by a single Wireless Operator also supplied and paid for by the same Company. By then, the equipment was vintage, and had a maxim range of 250 miles at night

The Operator, whose name was Cottam, did not have any specific hours of duty; consequently he was on call as required. However, he tried to restrict his office hours to the hours of daylight and up until Midnight each day. In fact, it was better at night, because darkness favoured wireless signals.

In 1912, the benefits of wireless were not well understood and more ships were sailing without such equipment than those who had it. Then, the principal means of communication between ships at sea were flags and heliograph by day and a Morse signalling light during the hours of darkness.

Much like our modern phones; Wireless was not considered primarily as a life-saving tool but as a means of communicating. Consequently the main uses of wireless at that time were inter-ship gossip, passing personal messages and navigation information. However, its receiving capabilities were much greater than the transmitting ones, and very often, an Operator would hear but be unable to respond.

At about 7pm that evening of April 14, Wireless Operator Cottam had exchanged information with the west-bound White Star liner *Titanic* and received a message from one of her passengers addressed to one of *Carpathia's* passengers. Thereafter, Cottam kept a listening Watch up until 11-45 pm ship time.

Earlier that day, Cottam had been in contact with the Leyland Liner *Parisian* and was waiting for a reply from him before his normal routine of shutting down his station and making his end-of-Watch report to the bridge. After that he planned to go to his room and get some sleep.

It should be noted at this point, that Marconi Wireless Operators did not work in ship time, but worked in either the Greenwich Mean Time kept at London or Eastern Standard Time kept at New York.

Due to the limited range of ship wireless in those days, Marconi Operators on British Ships which were west of the Longitude of 40°West noted the times of sending and receiving in terms of New York Time. However, before reaching longitude 40° West, all times were noted in term of Greenwich Mean Time.

Now back to our story.

At about 10 pm New York Time that evening Cottam was contemplating going to bed. The ship's clock told him it was nearing Midnight, so he tidied his desk, collected copies of the day's messages and took them to the bridge.

On his return to the wireless room, the young Operator did not immediately make ready for bed, but removed his bridge coat and sat by the Operator's desk; he was still hoping to receive a reply from the *Parisian* before he finally shut down. He donned the earphones and listened.

The air waves were silent and he was bored, so he decided to tune into the Long Distance Shore Station at Cape Cod, a wireless station on the US Eastern seaboard, located 50 miles south east of the city of Boston, Massachusetts. He knew that at that time, the station would be transmitting world news for liner passengers at sea.

So; crouched over his work desk with his earphones in place and lead pencil poised in hand, Cottam listened. He was planning to take down the latest news broadcast. Although he was not officially tasked to do this, it gave him something to do during the quiet times. His translation of the stream of dots and dashes into neat legible print would subsequently end up on the Purser's typewriter and eventually appear on the passenger notice board. He knew the service would be appreciated by the passengers when they saw his efforts displayed for everyone to read.

However, in this instance, and for some unknown reason, Cottam did not write anything down but simply listened until the news bulletin was finished. He continued to listen because he also knew that after transmitting the news, it was the normal practice of the Cape Cod Station, to transmit messages for ships at sea. They would do this by first sending a string of the call sign letters of ship's they had messages for. On hearing his ship's particular call sign letters, a listening Operator would know there was a message or messages specifically for him. He would wait until Cape Cod had finished transmitting, and then call them to retrieve the message, or messages in question.

Cottam was listening for *Carpathia's* call sign which consisted of the Morse letters MPA: Dash-Dash...Dot-Dash-Dash-Dot...Dot-Dash. Or if you prefer...dah,dah - dit,dah,dah dit - dit,dah.

He waited in vain. However, he heard the call sign "MWL" and immediately recognised it as the call sign for the RMS Titanic.

Cape Cod had four messages for *Titanic* and when they had finished transmitting, Cottam switched his equipment to transmit and began by sending *Titanic's* call sign three times, followed by the call sign of *Carpathia*.

Titanic responded almost immediately and Cottam asked her Operator if he knew that Cape Race was sending a batch of messages for him. To his surprise, the *Titanic* Operator responded with an urgent request *"Come at once - it is a distress message CQD."* and gave *Titanic's* distress position as Latitude 41 degrees 46 minutes North, Longitude 50 degrees. 14 minutes West.

As a matter of confirmation, Cottam asked the *Titanic's* Operator if he wished this request to be passed to Captain Rostron. He received an answer in the affirmative. Immediately, the young Operator took the transcribed message to First Officer Dean who was in command of the bridge Watch thereafter, the two of them headed for Captain Rostron's Cabin.

CHAPTER 3

APRIL 15 - A RUDE AWAKENING

Captain Rostron had just got into his warm bunk. He snuggled down, closed his eyes and prepared for a contented sleep. Suddenly there was a loud knock on his door. Before he could answer, the door opened an in rushed his First officer and Wireless Officer Cottam. Rostron glanced at his bedside clock and saw that it was 12-35am. Inwardly he thought, *this had better be good.* "

"Yes?" Rostron was barely able to keep the annoyance out of that curt inquiry.

Cottam ignored his captain's tone; unable to contain his excitement, he spoke with a rush. "I've just received a distress call from the new White Star liner *Titanic* sir."

Roston was immediately alert.

"Distress call? Are you sure? No mistake?"

"Absolutely sir! Her operator sent me a CQD then told me that they had hit ice and needed immediate assistance."

"Was that all?"

Cottam thought about giving his captain the full story culminating with his contact with *Titanic* then decided against it. "No sir, he also let me have her position."

It was then Dean's turn to speak.

"I have that position here sir." As he spoke, Rostron had risen from his bunk, thrown a dressing gown over his pyjamas and gone over to an Admiralty Chart of the North Atlantic which lay open on his chart desk.

"Right then Mr. Dean, let's have it".

Dean read out the coordinated of *Titanic's* distress position and Rostron jotted them down on the margin of the chart.

"Did you work a DR for us Mr. Dean?"

"Yes sir. I calculate that we are at about forty one, ten North, and forty nine, thirteen West."

As Dean dictating the DR position, Rostron marked it on the chart. Then he scribbled beneath it, the words *Titanic's distress position.* Quickly he performed a little sum, then reached for his bookcase and brought down a heavy book of nautical tables. After briefly flipping from table to table he straightened-up and spoke.

"Are you sure about our estimated position Mr. Dean?"

"Absolutely sir! We had really good sights at dusk last night so we know exactly where we were at that time. That DR position can't be too far out after a five hour run-up since then."

"What speed did you use?"

"15.5 knots sir".

Rostron thought for a moment. "With the push we're getting from the Gulf Stream, that seems just about right to me."

He continued speaking. "OK! I reckon we are about 58 miles away from *Titanic* at this moment. The true course from here to her distress position is North 52 degrees West". He turned and headed for his bathroom. "Bring her round onto that immediately Mr Dean. I'll get dressed and be up on the bridge shortly."

"Will I call all hands sir?" asked Dean.

"No - not yet. Tell the Bosun to stop the Deck Watch doing whatever they are doing and get them up onto the boat deck to uncover our boats and empty them of spare gear including masts and sails. You never know, our boats may be needed. Tell him they must work quietly so as not to alarm any of our passengers. Also send a man with my compliments to the Chief Engineer and the heads of all departments, I need them up here as soon as possible." He turned to Cottam.

'Sparks, contact *Titanic*, give them our position and tell them we are on our way. Keep in contact with her and inform me of any new information. By the way, have you heard of any other vessel going to her aid?"

"No sir, I haven't. There are other vessels in the vicinity but I would guess that most of the single Operator ships have shut down for the night. Do you wish me to try and contact any of them?"

Rostron thought for a moment then answered. "No Sparks that'll do for the time being. We don't want to clutter the air waves with unnecessary chatter. If I need you to do any more, I will send for you. In the meantime, just keep a listening Watch and if you hear anything you think I need to know, let me know immediately."

Once the door closed behind Cottam, Captain Rostron got dressed, sat by his desk and commenced to outline a course of action on his scrap pad. Before he did so, he spent a brief time contemplating the possibilities of Salvage. Like every other ship master, he knew that if he successfully saved a ship, her cargo and those on board her during a distress, he and his crew would be lawfully entitled to salvage money. He could almost retire on his share of any salvage money due from saving a ship like *Titanic,* and that did not include the undoubted boost to his career that would come from such a rescue.

Since very early times, every shipmaster has been morally bound to go to the rescue of a vessel in distress. The rule in 1912 dictated that "The master in charge of a vessel shall render assistance to any individual found at sea in danger of being lost, so far as the master can do so without serious danger to the master's vessel or individuals on board".

That Rule has now been enshrined in International Maritime law.

Rostron had just completed his notes when the Chief Engineer arrived. The captain brought him up to date on the situation then ordered him to call out an extra team of firemen and do whatever thought necessary to get the firemen to work flat out. "I need you to get these old engines of yours working harder than they have ever done before…I want speed, Chief, and as much of it as you can safely give me". The Chief promised to do his best. As the Chief Engineer was leaving, the remaining Department Heads arrived in Rostron's cabin. These included the Chief Steward and the English Doctor.

The captain brought the newcomers up to date and gave each a list of his orders for preparation to receive survivors if this became necessary. Once they had all left, he donned his bridge coat and headed for the bridge. He could feel the excitement rising within him.

CHAPTER 4

APRIL 15 - *CARPATHIA* TO THE RESCUE

Just before 1 am, *Carpathia* was settled onto her new course of North 52 West and Rostron was fully dressed and back on his bridge, then the preparations began.

Like every other ship's captain, Rostron was very much aware of the danger from icebergs. The fact that he was going to the assistance of a vessel which had hit one, sharpened his anxieties. He immediately substantially increased his lookouts. Earlier, in the wireless room, Cottam had been in contact *with Titanic* once more. He gave them *Carpathia's* position which Rostron had provided for him and told them the ship was on it's way to help them and would be there about four thirty am. The time on *Carpathia* was then near 00-45 am on the morning of April 15, 1912.

At 1 am, Rostron sent a message to Captain Smith on the *Titanic,* confirming that he would be with him in three and a half hours. Shortly after that Cottam arrived back on the bridge with the news that *Titanic's* sister ship, RMS Olympic, was responding to *Titanic's* call for help and that the latter had told *Olympic's* captain to have his boats ready. So Rostron knew he had competition.

As the old *Carpathia* charge through the night, every rivet, beam and bulkhead vibrating with the extra effort demanded of her. Her deck crew were on maximum alert. There was a Lookout high in the Crows

Nest and two more lookouts right forward on the bow. Captain Rostron and two officers were up on the ship's exposed upper bridge - six pairs of anxious eyes strained to penetrate the black night ahead of the ship. Not only did they know they were looking for a ship in distress, but they also knew that the ship in question was in trouble because she had hit an iceberg. Now, here *they* were, on another ship, charging at maximum speed directly toward exactly the same danger. To emphasise this; although the atmosphere was crystal clear and the sea was flat calm, the air temperature was neat zero and the ship-generated wind was razor-sharp.

Around 1-45 am, Durrant heard the *Titanic* Operator telling someone that there was flooding in the engine room. He passed this information to the bridge.

Less than an hour later and about two hours into the rescue mission, a bright florescent green light was seen low on the horizon, a little over 5 degrees left of the direction in which *Carpathia's* bow was then pointing. Rostron recognised it as part of the White Star Line's night signal. He checked his compass, found the ship was on the desired course and had the helmsman bring the bow around to the left until the green light was dead ahead. His first thought was *she must be still afloat!* Then he though again. *How on earth can this be? When we started off, we had 58 miles to steam and we have been running at full speed for no more than 2 hours. Our speed at the very, very best cannot be more that 15 and a half knots, so we should still have at least 27 miles to go until we get to the distress position. Perhaps the distress position was wrong? Or maybe my First Officer miscalculated our starting off point?*

He then had another idea. *If I can see them, they can see me. AT 3 o'clock, I'll send up one of my rockets every 15 minutes and let off a Company signal after it. These'll give them comfort and tell them that we're can see them and that we will be with them soon".* He immediately gave the order.

However, Rostron had no time to ponder his latest moves because his deliberations were rudely interrupted by the ringing of the forecastle bell. He raised his binoculars and made out the dark silhouette of an iceberg to the left of the direction in which he had seen the green light…it was too close for comfort, so he altered course to the right and gave it a wide berth. Ten minutes later, there was a whoosh and a loud bang follows by a bursting cascade of white stars high above the ship - the first rocket had been sent up.

This was immediately followed by the Cunard night signal and *Carpathia's* bridge was immediately illuminated by a bright blue roman candle - all of which temporarily blinded the "anxious eyes".

Immediately thereafter, four more ice bergs were seen and they had to zig-zag around them.

At 3 am the Lookout gave a single ring of his bell. Immediately, all binoculars were trained out on the starboard bow. This time, it was not ice they saw, but two white steaming lights of a vessel a little over 2 points on the starboard bow. The lower of these was to the left, indicating that the vessel showing them was either crossing ahead or heading in much the same way as they were, and should also be showing her red sidelight. In fact, one of Rostron's officers swore he could see that red sidelight. Perhaps *Carpathia* had competition?

Very soon, it became obvious that the green signal they had seen was not from *Titanic* herself, but from another source and *Carpathia* was heading straight for it. It was being shown at intervals but the ship's heading was frequently changing due to the ice bergs, so every time it was seen, Rostron would adjust his course to keep it dead ahead.

At 4 am, Rostron reckoned he was almost up to the source of the green signals; he had by then, ascertained that the source was not *Titanic* herself, but was in fact, a lifeboat.

As is so often the case at the end of a flat calm night, the wind had started to rise and the sea was now being disturbed by a breeze from the north, consequently, Rostron decided to bring his ship up wind, and stop her to the north of the lifeboat, thus providing shelter for its occupants. Just as he stopped his engines and was about to carry out his plan, the lookout frantically sounded three bells, indicating something was dead ahead. Raising his binoculars, Rostron saw yet another ice berg right in his path - between *Carpathia* and the lifeboat. It was too close and there was imminent risk of collision. He therefore gave a hard left rudder order and left the berg on his starboard side. Unfortunately the manoeuvre thwarted his plan to place his ship between the wind and the lifeboat. Not only that, but he had to throw his engines Full Astern to prevent overshooting the mark.

Finally, *Carpathia* was dead in the water, with the lifeboat in plain sight up wind on the starboard side. It was illuminated by the ship's lights which had all been switched on. From his position high on the starboard wing of *Carpathias* bridge, and in the growing light, Captain Rostron and his officer could see that the source of the green lights they had been heading for was a small wooden cutter, about 25 feet long. It was occupied by a large number of people wrapped in blankets and warm clothing. They could also see that the boat was commanded by a single individual wearing an officer's cap and had a single sailor at the bow. Rostron raised his megaphone and called to the officer.

"Ahoy there, the boat; if you can, come alongside by the side door which you can see is open, we will bring you and your passengers aboard".

The occupant in the officer's cap yelled back. "You need to stop; I have only one sailor on board." The time on *Carpathia's* clock was 4-10 am.

By 4-30 am, the survivors from the boat were safely on board *Carpathia*. Dawn was not too far away and by the rapidly increasing light, they found themselves in a vast ice field which stretched back in the direction from which they had come all around the southerly and westerly horizon and stretching out of sight to the horizon in the North West. To the south east, there was more open water dotted with numerous large icebergs - the ones they had so recently threaded their way between. The nearest of these was less than half a mile away and abeam to starboard. It was the one he had so frantically had to avoid just before stopping. Not only that, but there was a low lying chunk of ice a few hundred yards astern to port. The sea was relatively clear to the north. However, about three and a half miles to the west of where they were stopped, there was a solid, seemingly impenetrable, barrier of ice stretching from the North West to the south west, and as far as the eye could see.

It was very low, but had a few large ice bergs locked in its grip at its northern end

In the relatively ice-free area between *Carpathia* and the ice barrier, many other lifeboats could be seen.

Meantime, the officer in charge of the boat with the green flares had made his way up to the bridge and reported to Rostron.

"Good morning sir, my name is Joseph Boxhall and I was the Fourth Officer on the RMS Titanic. My boat is *Titanic's* number two port side Emergency Cutter and besides myself, I had survivors on board her". Boxhall continued. "I regret to inform you sir that *Titanic* sank at 5-47 am

GMT this morning. Unfortunately, many are still missing". He gestured around the sea in the direction of the ice barrier - "As you can see, we managed to get most of our boats away before she went down."

Rostron and the young officers around him were dumfounded by what they were hearing.

Rostron finally found his voice. "My God! man. How many are missing?"

"Unfortunately I cannot tell you that sir, we will not know until we recover all the boats." As the young officer spoke, Rostron could see that the lifeboats of *Titanic* were now converging on his ship.

Out in front of them, and nearest *to Carpathia,* there was a lifeboat with her sail up and towing another boat behind her. It looked like it would arrive alongside very shortly.

"Right then, Mr Boxhall, thank you for your report, get yourself below into the warmth and let my people look after you." He turned to his officers, "Now, gentlemen, it looks like we are going to be busy. I want the derricks (booms) rigged fore and aft to recover these lifeboats after we embark the survivors.

Inform the Chief Steward and Purser we are going to have a great many visitors very soon."

PART 2

CHAPTER 5

RMS TITANIC - 9-45AM-APRIL 14

PIC 2
National Archives

The Royal Mail Steamer "Titanic" was owned by the white Star Line of Liverpool. She was the second vessel of her class and was designed and built by Harland & Wolff Ltd, Belfast, in what is now Northern Ireland. When she finished her sea trials and was handed over to her proud owners, she was the biggest vessel ever built anywhere in the world.

After hand-over, on April 3, 1912, *Titanic* arrived in the early hours of the following day, April 4, at the port of Southampton in southern England. She stayed there for the next six days and during that time, took on supplies and coal for the voyage.

April 10, 1912, *Titanic's* final day at Southampton, dawned full of promise; the weather could not have been more favourable for anyone embarking on a voyage of hope and discovery. The sunrise was ablaze with glory, with only a few high fair weather clouds occasionally daring to briefly interfere in its splendour.

Titanic's first fare-paying passengers and the remaining balance of her crew were embarked by 11-30 am and at Noon that same day of April 10; with a deep baritone salute from her steam whistle, she cast off her last mooring rope for the very last time and, with the help of tugs, cleared the berth and proceeded down-river on the first leg of her first voyage to the New World.

The new ship's destination after Southampton was the French port of Cherbourg. That first leg was of very short duration, consequently she arrived at Cherbourg in the early evening of April 10 and dropped anchor. During a stay of a few hours, she embarked more passengers. Thereafter, she sailed for Queenstown (Now known as Cove) in the south of Ireland.

Titanic anchored off the entrance to the port of Queenstown at 11-30 am local time on the morning of April 11.(Ireland was then 25 minutes SLOW of GMT).

During her time at anchor, a few passengers disembarked, but many joined her there.

Two hours later - at 1-30 pm -she weighed anchor and half an hour after that, at 2 pm, she past Daunt Rock west of Queenstown and her engines were rung 'Full Away on Passage'. Unknown to those on board; this was the official start of her first and final brief voyage to the bottom of the ocean.

From the south of Ireland *Titanic* followed a long curving, pre-determined track to an unmarked point in the Atlantic known to Northern Ocean men as *The Corner*. From there she followed another pre determined track directly toward her intended destination of "The Big Apple" ...New York.

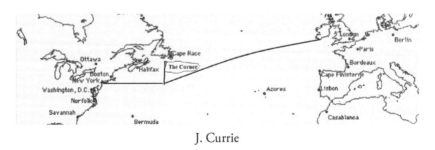

J. Currie

During the first three days out from Queenstown the weather had been totally unusual for the time of year. The North Atlantic behaved better than many of the old hands could remember. There were none of the inevitable fierce south-westerly gales bringing overcast skies. Even the steep sided ocean swells seemed to have taken a holiday.

As a new vessel, her engine room crew had followed the usual new ship practice of working up the engines to full speed.

There would be no attempt to break records or any of her brand new machinery. However despite these standard new-ship precautions, *Titanic* delighted those on board with her better-than-expected performance.

The fourth day out from Ireland was the best day by far. It was one of those very rare occasions on the North Atlantic run when there was an almost cloudless sky and a clear horizon. There was, however, a cold wind which earlier had been blowing strongly from the North West. Eventually, it had eased a little and veered round to blow from the north. Unfortunately, this cold wind had kept the passengers from enjoying the starboard side promenade decks. It had also prevented the usual Sunday morning fire and boat drill muster for the crew.

The date on the calendar showed that it was Sunday the fourteenth day of April in the year of 1912 and the ship's clock read 9-45 am.

Captain Edward J. Smith was on the bridge wing talking to the Officer of the Watch, Second Officer Charles Lightoller. They were discussing a wireless message which had been received from the Cunard passenger vessel SS Caronia, thirty minutes earlier. It read:

"Captain, 'Titanic.' - Westbound steamers report bergs, growlers and field ice in 42° N. from 49° to 51° W., 12th April. Compliments. - Barr."

When he received it, Smith had carefully read it, and reckoned that the position of the ice mention in the report would not be any threat to his ship. His experience of the area told him that it would be well to the north and east of the reported location when she got near to where it was last seen. Besides which, the track she was following was at least 10 miles south of the location where it had last been seen two days earlier

After showing the message to Lightoller, Smith left the bridge and entered the chartroom where he found junior Navigating officers Boxhall and Moody busy with their calculations. He addressed the senior of the two, 4th Officer Boxhall.

"Mr, Boxhall, I have received this message from the *Caronia,* it contains details of ice seen in the area. It looks to me that it will not be any threat to us, but please mark its location on the chart and when you are finished, pin the message to your notice board."

Boxhall took the message and quickly plotted it on the small scale chart entitled *North Atlantic -Western Sheet*. He circled the area in pencil and wrote the word "ice" next to it. Then he pinned the message to the notice board above the chart desk. Thereafter, the captain left the two young officers to their respective tasks.

About 11-55am, Captain Smith returned to his bridge for Noon sights. On arrival, he found his three senior officer's ready for action so he retrieved his sextant and joined them. Thus, just before midday *Titanic's* Captain and his three senior officers stood on the port side of her bridge wing, each man squinting through the telescope of a sextant. Very soon the sun would be directly south and they would each measure its height above the southern horizon. As they did so, Junior Navigating Officers would be in the ship's chart room nearby, waiting to note the shouted reading from each sextant and to note the exact moment of each sextant observation on the ship's chronometer. Thereafter, the same juniors would perform the task of calculating the ship's Noon position.

At the moment when the sun bore due south, the standby Quarter Master would sound the ship's whistle and ring 8 bells.an the bugler would exercise his lungs. Thus, every soul on board would know that the exact time was 12 o'clock Noon

The senior officers on the bridge wing, beside Captain Edward Smith, were Chief Officer Wilde, First Officer William Murdoch and 2nd officer Charles Lightoller.

Once the mid-day "sports' as they were affectionately described, were over, the calculations were made and the resulting Noon position was obtained. This enabled the Navigators to calculate the number of miles steamed from the previous, April 13 Noon position and the average speed attained between the two Noons. From the evidence given at the Inquiries into the disaster we know these were:

Noon: April 14, 1912
Latitude 42 ° 02'North, Longitude 44° 30'West.
Distance steamed 546 nautical miles.
Average speed: 22.1 knots.

These details were entered into the Log Book and a copy given to Captain Smith for eventual onward-transmission to the Company Office.

Thereafter, all but the Watch Keeping Officers on duty left the bridge and headed for the mess room and lunch. Not so Captain Smith - he had a few other things to do before eating. Consequently, he left the open bridge and went to his private chart room next to the main chart room.

As it happened; in the late afternoon of that day on April 14, *Titanic* would reach a specific turning point known to western ocean men as *The Corner*.

When it was reached *Titanic* would be turned onto a course which would take her to New York. Consequently, the exact time of course alteration was needed.

Captain Smith began his work. He had three calculations to make. These were as follows.

1. The distance and course to steer from Noon 14th until his ship would arrive at *The Corner* where he had to change directions.
2. The distance and course to steer from *The Corner* to where he estimated his ship would be at 12 o' clock Noon the next day - April 15. and...
3. Resulting from (2), the number of minutes by which the ship's clocks were to be altered so that Noon would occur at exactly 12 o'clock ship time the next day.

Smith was 62 years of age and had been travelling that route for very many years; consequently, he was very familiar with the conditions to be met. He expected that within a very short time after Noon that day, his ship would be slowed by what, in 1912, was known as the Gulf Stream. In that area, and at that time of year, Smith would expect to encounter a current of a little over one knot acting against his ship.

He also knew that *Titanic*, with her high superstructure and four closely placed funnels, was very much in profile like a giant sailing ship with four sails and that a wind of any appreciable force acting on her sides would affect her ability to steer a straight course, but the barometer was rising and the wind was dropping.

The Noon position just obtained showed him that he had about 124 miles to run before he would reach the position where he had to alter course - *The Corner*.

At that same time of Noon, it had been found that *Titanic's* course had to be altered a little to the right - to starboard - to line her up with *The Corner,* therefore it was altered to South 61.5 degrees West

As for an estimate of speed? - *Titanic* had averaged 22.1 knots for the previous day's run and he did not intend to increase speed before he turned.

Consequently, if she kept up that speed of 22.1, then by simple arithmetic, he estimated that she should be turning at about 5-36 pm. However, he factored-in the possibility of meeting that head current so estimated that his ship would only average 21.25 knots at best. Thus, he calculated that at 21.25 knots *Titanic* would need to be turned onto her next course at 5-50 pm.

The course to steer from *The Corner* to New York was a fixed one laid down by International agreement and designed to take west-bound vessels south of the danger of ice in spring time and to keep them fifty to sixty miles north of east-bound vessels following a similarly agreed eastward track.

Smith calculated that after turning *The Corner, Titanic* would be clear of the effects of the current and would once again, average a speed of 22 knots up until Noon, April 15. This would put her on the desired course line 414 miles west of *The Corner* at longitude of 56 degrees 15 minutes West.

Since the longitude at Noon that day was 44 degrees, 34 minutes West, this meant that *Titanic* would increase her westerly longitude by 11 degrees, 45 minutes between Noon April 14 and Noon April 15, which converted to time, was equal to 47 minutes. Consequently, Captain Smith rounded up the time change to a total of 47 minutes for the clocks to be set back in the coming 24 hours. These minutes of clock change would be shared by members of the 8 pm to Midnight and the Midnight to 4am Watches, meaning that the Watch-keepers would have to work an extra 24 minutes and 23 minutes respectively. However, they would be rewarded with a corresponding extra number of minutes in bed.

All other crew and passengers would get an extra 47 minutes in bed.

Having performed his task, the captain went into the main chart room and opened his Order Book at a fresh page. Then, in neat handwriting, he wrote the following:

> *"At 5-50 pm (8-48 GMT) a/c 265 True. Steady on course and ascertain compass error. Do so at frequent intervals thereafter.*

Obtain ship's position by celestial observation at dusk and report to me.

Clocks to be retarded a total of 47 minutes by 3-22am GMT -Midnight. Advise all departments.

Call me if in any doubt or there is any deterioration in visibility and/or the weather. R. J. Smith - Master".

After writing his orders, and before going for lunch, Captain Smith went out onto the bridge wing to have a quick word with his 2nd Officer Lightoller. The latter had taken over the bridge while Murdoch was eating lunch.

"Right then Mr, Lightoller, that's me finished with my work. It's a fine afternoon and I see we are on our own - nothing is sight. I have decided to retard the clocks 47 minutes tonight. I reckon we will be at *The Corner* at ten to six this evening. I expect I'll be on the bridge at that time, but in case I am held up, I have left the usual instructions in the Order Book for her to be turned onto the next course at that time."

Lightoller, felt a doubt in his mind concerning the timing, but instead of raising it with the captain, he decided to wait, and discuss it with Willie Murdoch when he came back on duty.

"Very well sir, I will draw Mr Murdoch's attention to it when he comes back from lunch".

"Do that, Mister Lightoller." replied Smith and with these few words, left the bridge.

At 1 pm prompt, *Titanic's* First Officer William (Willie) Murdoch was back on the bridge. He joined Lightoller out on the port wing, the two men leaned on the forward wing bulwark rail, sheltered from the north wind and enjoying the warmth of the sun. The horizon was sharp and clear all around and there was not a single vessel to be seen.

"Right then *two-oh*! Murdoch exclaimed expansively. Away you go below and get a bit of shuteye or something. I've seen the "Old man's" orders and signed them." Lightoller responded.

"What do you think of them, sir? Don't you think we should be turning earlier than that? I mean to say, we only had about a hundred and twenty five miles to go from Noon and she seems to be making the same speed as she did before Noon."

"Aye!" replied Murdoch in his soft, lowland Scots accent - looking back over his shoulder- "I noticed his time for the turn. However, our captain is a wily old bird and you can bet your sea boots that he has thought of everything down to the last dot. Besides, he knows this run better than the both of us put together. Away you go; get yourself below for a snooze. It'll work our fine, mark my words."

Lightoller took the advice and left the bridge.

Just after 2pm Captain Smith was in his chartroom, writing when his Fifth Officer, Jim Moody arrived with a message from the Wireless Room. It was a personal message from the captain of the White Star Line vessel *Baltic*. Smith thanked young Moody who respectfully stood back and waited for a reply. Smith opened the Marconigram envelope, took out the message and read:

> *"Captain Smith, 'Titanic.' - Have had moderate, variable winds and clear, fine weather since leaving. Greek steamer Athenai reports passing icebergs and large quantities of field ice to-day in lat. 41- 51' N., long. 49- 52' W.*

> *Last night we spoke German oiltank steamer Deutschland - Stettin to Philadelphia, not under control, short of coal, lat. 40° 42' N., long. 55° 11' W. Wishes to be reported to New York and other steamers. Wish you and 'Titanic' all success. - Commander."*

The Captain remembered the message he had received from the *Caronia* that morning, and that it had mentioned the longitudes of 51 degrees West and 49 degrees West. He noted the difference in coordinates between the two messages. He also noted that *Athenai's* captain had not given a position for the ice - just the position of his ship. There was no suggestion that it was anywhere near the intended track of *Titanic*. In fact, it looked to him as though the ice seen by *Athenai* was the western limit of the same field ice reported by *Caronia*. This suggested that it was moving more to the eastward at a rate of about 50 miles a day. Whatever it was doing, to his mind, it remained no threat to the *Titanic* and would be 25 miles farther north and east of her track when his ship arrived at 49 degrees West longitude. He checked a notation he had made earlier on his personal chart then quickly wrote a reply and gave it to Moody with instructions to take it to the Wireless Room.

After Moody had left, Smith folded the *Baltic* message and put it in his pocket. He would deliver it to the bridge later.

As mentioned before, the cold northerly wind had kept the passengers off the promenade decks; consequently those who were not in their cabins were in the ship's luxurious public rooms. Captain Smith had finished his writing and was now "socialising" - being seen around the ship.

On his travels, he spied the Managing Director of the White Star Company, Joseph B. Ismay; the man had boarded *Titanic* as a passenger on the maiden voyage.

Ismay was deep in conversation with two lady passengers - Mrs Thayer and Mrs Ryerson.

Earlier, the Managing Director and Smith had been discussing the progress of the voyage and the former had expressed his concern about the possibilities of delays from ice or weather. To allay his concerns, the captain had explained to him the benefits of wireless and the part it played in giving advance warnings of possible danger.

Smith was not in a hurry but at the same time did not wish to be delayed by a trivial conversation; he decided to let Ismay see this latest message containing a mention of ice, then make a quick exit. Consequently, he walked up the three ..

"Good afternoon to you sir and ladies - and if I may say so; a fine afternoon it is too." He turned to Ismay and handed him the message from the *Baltic*. "You may find this of interest, sir." then quickly added: "Please excuse me, -sir - ladies; much as I would prefer your conversation, I am unfortunately needed elsewhere; good afternoon." With these few words, Smith, respect fully saluted and left. He did not place much store by the message and would recover it later.

CHAPTER 6

THE CORNER

At 4 pm that Afternoon, the junior Navigators changed Watches. They did this every four hours throughout the voyage. Third Officer Pitman and Fifth Officer Lowe would go below and snatch some sleep. Now it was the turn of Fourth Officer Boxhall and Sixth Officer Moody. These two would stand the 'First Dog Watch' and would only work for 2 hours before going off duty again at 6 pm. At that time, Pitman and Lowe would return on duty and stand the Second Dog Watch until 8 pm. It was not a routine for the faint of heart.

Although all four of these young men were highly experienced, fully qualified Master Mariners; one of them - Fourth Officer Boxhall - had an Extra Master's Certificate.

Unlike the Chief, First and Second Officers, these four did not stand Watches on the bridge, but spent most of their time in the Chart Room behind it, or around the decks. As Fifth Officer Lowe put it:

> "*We Worked out things; worked out the odds and ends, and then submitted them to the senior officer. We are there to do the navigating part so the senior officer can be and shall be in full charge of the bridge and have nothing to worry his head about. We have all that, the junior officers; there are four of us. The three seniors are in absolute charge of the boat. They have nothing to worry themselves about. They simply have*

*to walk backward and forward and look after the ship, and
we do all the figuring and all that sort of thing in our chart
room."*

I think it important at this time to take a moment to mention that one
of the "things" two of the most junior officers were working on was a set
of what were known as *Propeller Slip Tables.*

These were tables which indicated the difference between actual distance
covered between two points on the water and the theoretical distance
between them obtained from the number of propeller revolutions. It was
normal practice to compile these during the maiden voyage of a steamship.

Propeller revolutions were obtained from a revolution counter in the
engine room. It was read at the end of each Watch period starting at Noon
each day and the result was then telephoned to the bridge.

However, as pointed out - these were theoretical distances which had
to be compared with a more accurate method of measuring distance.

'Slip' referred to the difference between propeller distance and actual
distance and was expressed as a percentage. However, an accurate difference
between the two was needed to produce an accurate value for 'Slip'. *Titanic,*
like all ships of her day, was supplied with a Patent Log which was also set
to zero at Noon every day, and was read every two hours thereafter and
the bridge notified of the result.

The Patent Log reading was an extremely accurate measurement of
how many miles and tenths of a mile the ship pulled the log 'gear' through
the water.

The 'gear' was a rotator, much like an elongated propeller, which was
towed behind the ship and revolved exactly 9000 times for every mile
it was pulled. Consequently, unlike the propeller which was part of the
ship - the Patent Log measured the true distance that the ship had dragged
it through the water.

Navigators in 1912 had mixed opinions as to what was the best means
of determining how far a ship had travelled in a given time and hence
her speed. Traditionalists favoured the Patent Log method while those
who believed themselves modernists, preferred more elaborate method of
speed by propeller revolutions. For this, they needed a reference able - a
'Slip Table'.

Just before 4 pm., Fifth Officer Lowe handed over to Sixth Officer Moody with the usual information regarding ship's position engine revolutions, course being steered and any relevant navigation information. Once he had left, Moody carried on with the development of the 'Slip 'Tables.

Fourth Officer Boxhall spent a little more time before *he* left. He had read Captain Smith's instructions about turning the ship and had immediately felt the same misgiving as had his superior had done earlier. He mentioned this to Third Officer Pitman who also expressed the same misgiving, adding that in his opinion *Titanic* would be at *The Corner* nearer to 5 pm in stead of 5-50 pm.

Inwardly, Boxhall did not think that the difference was as great, but agreed with Pitman that *Titanic* would run past her intended turning point before she did alter course onto her new track. Pitman then departed for his cabin.

"Right then Joe, she's all yours I'm off, enjoy *your* next two hours, I'll see you again at six."

At 5-45 pm, Captain Smith arrived on the bridge to supervise the alteration onto the final track for New York. He made his way out onto the port bridge-wing where he joined his Chief Officer Henry Wilde.

"Good evening Henry, anything around?"

"No sir." replied Wilde, gesturing around the horizon, "As you can see, we are all on our own."

As Smith had thought, the wind had dropped to a gentle breeze. There was not a cloud in sight and the horizon was like a knife edge. However it was cold with the promise of a chilly night to come.

Quarter Master George Rowe was standing behind the wheel in the wheelhouse behind the bridge. The window screens were still lowered but would be raised at dusk to enclose wheelhouse in darkness, save for the steering compass light and the little dim light that illuminated the course board in front of him. At that moment, the board indicated the course being steered South 85 degrees West.

Behind Rowe stood Standby Quarter Master Alfred Olliver and next to him, Sixth Officer Jim Moody.

All three were watching the Captain and his Chief Officer - waiting in anticipation -for the order to alter course.

At precisely 5-48 pm, the Chief Officer entered the enclosed bridge and stationed himself at the middle window. Two minutes later, after consulting his watch, the captain popped his head round the doorway to the bridge and in a measured, formal tone gave the order to alter course. "Bring her round to North 71 West, Mister Wilde". Wilde repeated the order and in a louder voice, passed it to Moody who in turn, passed it to QM Rowe. Thus, there was no mistake - everyone knew for certain the course to steer.

Rowe expertly spun the steering wheel to the right and watched his compass. Almost before he had the wheel hard over, he noticed the ship's heading start to change to the right; consequently, he eased off the wheel and let it return to mid-ship. As the lubber line neared the desired direction of North 71 West, he applied the wheel in the opposite direction. Within a few second, he had the ship steadied on her new course.

*"North 71 West she is sir" he advised Moody who had been watching the compass over Rowe's shoulder. "Very well, quartermaster" acknowledged the young sixth officer then confirmed then fact back through the chain of command to Captain Smith. *Titanic* was now on her final track for New York.

---

* The course of North 71 West was a compass course equal to a true course of S 85.5 West - the direction of the pre-planned track for New York.

CHAPTER 7

7·30 PM SIGHTS

Once his ship was settled on her new course, Captain Smith left her in the charge of his Chief Officer. Five minutes after that, Second Officer Lightoller, 3rd Officer Pitman and 5th Officer Lowe relieved the bridge and Lightoller took charge of the ship.

At 6 pm the quarter master on duty at the aft docking bridge phoned Fifth Officer Lowe and gave him the Patent Log reading; it was 125.7 nautical miles. At the same time, the engine room reported the engines had been turning at 75 rpm since Noon. Lowe would use these numbers to up-date the earlier mentioned Slip Table which was a work in progress.

Lowe divided the patent Log reading of 125.5 miles by five hours 50 minutes and got an average speed of just under 21 knots, which caused him to think.

This was his first trip across the North Atlantic, so he was unfamiliar with the idea of strong ocean currents. He knew from the recent handover of the Watch that the ship had not decreased engine speed. The wind had been from the north -therefore, there was no obvious reason as to why *Titanic* had slowed down a full knot from her pre-Noon speed of 22.1 knots. It dawned on him! -he remembered navigation School lectures concerning the Gulf Stream - *that was it!*

Then he considered the recent turn at *The Corner* - and the overheard conversation between Boxhall and Pitman concerning a turning point over-shoot. Now he was even more confused.

He did another calculation - this time using the average speed indicated by the Patent Log and the run time of five hours fifty minutes from Noon that day.

This indicated that *Titanic* had only covered a distance of 122.2 miles of the 124 miles she had to go from Noon to the turning point at *The Corner*. Something had slowed her down. It seemed that Captain Smith's timing for turning the ship had been vindicated.

Before the days of Satellite Navigation, the most accurate method of establishing a ship's position was by crossing multiple bearings of fixed objects on land. The next best method when out of sight of land was by using a sextant to measure the altitude above the horizon of celestial bodies such as stars, planets, the Moon and the Sun. However, for all such sextant work, a clear, sharp, visible horizon was an absolutely necessity. Unfortunately the only celestial body which is clearly visible during daylight hours is the sun. Consequently the ideal time to use the others was when they were visible at the same time as a clear horizon. As we all know, there are but two such times when the desired conditions occur in a day...Morning and evening twilight. That evening of April 14 was perfect for celestial observations. Consequently, Second Officer Lightoller planned to take celestial observations when he returned from his evening meal at 7-30 pm. Although he would physically perform the sextant work, the intricate calculations thereafter would be carried out by the senior Navigators, Pitman and Boxhall. The former would commence the work and the later complete it during the early part of the 8 to Midnight Watch. However before Lightoller returned, Pitman gathered all the necessary information needed.

First, he selected six suitable celestial bodies for the observations - three for Latitude one of which would be the Pole Star and three for Longitude. The results would produce and accurate fixed position.

As he would be taking the times for these observations, he opened his Sight Book at a new page and wrote down the names of each selected star. When the time came, he would take the chronometer GMT time and sextant reading of each star as Lightoller shouted it out and write the results against the appropriate star.

After the last sight was taken, he would start to calculate the ship's position.

Next, he calculated a DR position to be used with the sights. He would base it on his belief that *Titanic* should have turned *The Corner* at 5 pm instead of 5-50 pm, and that she was making 21.5 knots. In fact, he made two DR calculations these were:

1. DR for where he thought *Titanic* really was at 5-50 pm.
2. DR to be used with the evening celestial observations.

Having performed these preliminary tasks, all was ready for evening sights so Pitman completed his DR calculations by calculating an 8pm DR for the Scrap Log Book.

This was simply an extension of his DR to be used with the celestial observations. Itt was 41°-47.6'North, 48°-17.0'W.

At 7-30 pm Lightoller returned to the bridge. The First Officer had taken over the bridge to allow him to go for his evening meal. However, before he returned to his normal bridge duties and to relieve Murdoch, he opened his sextant box took out his sextant, noted the names of the selected heavenly bodies then made his way to the bridge wing. He left the doors to the wheelhouse and chartroom open so that Pitman could hear his shouted readings. Meanwhile, Pitman stationed himself at the chronometer box pencil in handed ready to note times and altitudes.

Since Lightoller was very familiar with the selected heavenly bodies, the operation to take all six sextant observation was over before 7-40 pm. After that, he relieved Murdoch and resumed his normal bridge duties, leaving Pitman to begin the lengthy process of calculating the evening position from the celestial observations.

Pitman had only time to ascertain that the ship was on her desired track before he had stop working and attend to the duties concerned with the end of Watch handover. Among other things, this meant filling-in the Scrap Log Book for the end-of-Watch handover. He also worked an 8 pm DR position which was an extension of the DR he used for sights and entered it into the Log Book space provided for it. Fifth Officer Lowe also worked an 8pm DR position for the captain. He scribbled the result on a bit of scrap paper, folded it and went into the captain's chart room and left on Captain Smith's chart.

At a few minutes to 8 pm, Boxhall and Moody arrived on the bridge,

"Here's a bunch of sights for you to work out old man" said Pitman when greeting Boxhall. The latter grimaced then smiled. "Thanks for nothing old man". Meanwhile Moody and Lowe exchanged the usual greetings and end of Watch information.

After things had quietened down, Boxhall sent Moody around the decks on "rounds". This was normal on a passenger ship. However, it being Sunday, the deck Watch were spending most of their time in the accommodation under the forecastle readi8ng or playing cards so this was simply a formality. After Moody had left, Boxhall settled down to his task…working the evening position.

Captain Smith made his way up to the bridge. He had just finished an excellent dinner in the company of the Ship's doctor, now it was time to check on his lads on the bridge. He needed to find out what was happening. The wind had gone completely; the sea was glassy-calm and the sky was crystal clear. Twinkling stars formed a dome overhead and down to the horizon all round.

Before going onto the bridge proper, the captain obeyed the call of nature and used the toilet facilities in his private suite of cabins behind the bridge. He then passed through his own chart room into the main chartroom where he found his Fourth Officer finishing the star-sights taken by Lightoller earlier.

"Good evening sir' Boxhall greeted his captain.

"Good evening Mr. Boxhall. What do you have for me?"

"I've just completed the evening sights sir"

"Splendid! Let's have them then, and I'll lay them off on my chart next door". Boxhall handed Smith a scrap of paper on which he had noted the latitude and longitude arrived at from calculating Lightoller's sights.

Smith turned back into his private accommodation where he had a smaller version of the ship's main chart room. Boxhall followed him but did not enter. Instead, he stood at the door opening and watched as the captain took a pair of brass- handles dividers and pricked-off the ships position indicated by the sights.

"Are you happy with this Mr. Boxhall? Looks to me like she's right on the track."

"Absolutely sir! Mr Lightoller took six star sights, three for latitude and the other three for longitude. As you know, they act as a check on each other and they all came in spot-on."

"That's fine then; thank you. If there's nothing else, I'll let you get back to your work and I'll go out and have a yarn with Mr. Lightoller. It's after nine o' clock and he'll be off Watch at ten."

Boxhall had nothing else to report so Captain Smith thanked him again then went out through the main chart room into the pitch dark, wheel house. There, in the faint glow from the steering compass light, he could just see Quartermaster Olliver standing behind the wheel.

"Evening, Quartermaster. How's she handling?"

Olliver who did not expect to be spoken to was taken aback for a moment but then replied in as few words as possible.

"Handling very well sir. About a degree either side."

"Very well Quartermaster'. Then, as if he needed proof, the captain bent over and looked at the compass. He noted with pleasure that his ship was right on course.

Having checked in the wheelhouse, Captain Smith then went out onto the covered bridge area which was in complete darkness. From there, the background of the lighter sky showed him the way out onto the exposed bridge wing, where he found 2nd Officer Lightoller pacing back and forward. Although Smith could not see them, he knew Lightoller would have a pair of night binoculars slung round his neck. Smith gave a discreet cough; he did not want to startle the younger man. At the sound of it, Lightoller stopped pacing. He knew exactly who had coughed.

"Good evening sir."

"A splendid evening it most certainly is Mr. Lightoller. This is what it's all about eh?"

"It is indeed sir." replied the Second Officer. "Although, to tell you the truth, sir, I would prefer a little wind and sea."

"Yes, I agree. This calm weather is all very well but we'll have a hell-of-a-job seeing any of the stragglers of this ice to the north of us which they're all talking about. When do you reckon we'll be up to it?"

"By the reports we've been getting, I thought we might meet-up with small stuff just after we crossed the 49th longitude"

"So when will that be then" asked Smith.

"Well, sir we are increasing our westerly Longitude by about a degree every 2 hours. We turned at the 47th meridian of longitude just before 6 pm so that would mean we would be up to the 49th four hours later; just before ten o'clock in fact. Young Moody assures me it'll be nearer 11 o'clock."

Thereafter the two men stood for a while discussing ice in particular and then the trip in general.

Just as Smith was about to take his leave, he cautioned Lightoller.

"Oh by the way Mr. Lightoller; just before I go, I think you should alert the lads in the Crow's Nest. Tell then that from now on, they're to keep a sharp lookout for small ice. We had a lot of wind from the north today. It wouldn't have much effect on the big bergs since they would be in the Gulf Stream, but some of the small stuff might have been wind-driven southward. Oh I know this is a big ship but even a little ice floe could do us a bit of damage, and we don't want to scratch our new paint, now - do we?" The captain finished the last remark with a chuckle.

"Very good sir. I'll see to that right away. Good night sir."

As soon as his captain had left the bridge, Lightoller had Moody call the Crow's Nest. Then, as a second thought, told him "Oh and Moody, make sure they pass-on the message to the men who will relieve them at 10 pm."

Titanic had six permanent Lookout men on duty night and day in the Crow' Nest when at sea. They worked in pairs on a basis of two hours on duty, six hours off. The Nest was located on the front of the foremast, forty feet above the bridge level. Besides the ubiquitous warning bell, it was equipped with the very latest in telephone communication with the wheelhouse However the latter was only to be used by the Lookouts in a dire emergency or-when, as in this instance, the bridge had to communicate orders to the Lookouts.

The Nest was also used as an additional conning position during ship passage along narrow waterways.

Immediately after the captain had left, 6th Officer Moody telephoned the Crow's Nest and delivered the warning about small ice to occupants Hogg and Evans; adding the caution that they were to ensure they passed it on to their reliefs at 10 pm.

CHAPTER 8

THE CALM BEFORE

After he left the bridge, Captain Smith retired to his private cabin. He partially shut the cabin door and hooked it about an inch open with the hook provided for that purpose. He then removed his heavy bridge coat and uniform jacket; hanging the former up and draping the latter over a chair. Removing his shoes, he lay down on his day bed which was really a settee in his day room designed for that purpose. He'd catch a little sleep.

Before shutting his eyes, he took out his pocket watch and turned the hands back 47 minutes. He did so, knowing that while he was asleep, the watch-keeping clocks on his ship would be put back for the planned clock change. If there was no emergency, the next time he woke-up, his watch would agree with bridge time. He planned to visit his bridge again when Chief Officer Wilde was to relieve First officer Murdoch. That would be at 2 o'clock the next morning.

Soon he was snoring gently. Although asleep, years of training had installed a trip-wire in his brain. The slightest thing amiss with his ship - even the change in engine vibrations, would have him instantly awake.

At 10 pm First Officer Murdoch was due on the bridge to take over the Watch from Lightoller. At the same time, two of the Quartermasters of the Watch would also change duties.

There were three QMs to a Watch and they operated on a rota. QM Rowe was stationed at the stern Docking Bridge for the entire Watch - from 8pm until Midnight. which included any planned clock change.

His job was to keep a lookout for anyone falling over the side. He also had to read the Patent Log recorder every two(2) hours and at the end of the Watch and report the readings to the bridge using the docking bridge telephone which was mounted on the aft end of the docking bridge rail.

The other two Quartermasters took turns at steering the ship. When one was not steering, he was stationed in the wheelhouse behind the one who *was* steering.

He was the bridge Messenger and Standby helmsman. He also had to call the Officers at one bell which was a fifteen minute warning designed to ensure that they turned up on time for duty.

Just before 10 pm, QM Olliver was steering and QM Hichens had just returned from taking the sea and air temperatures and making sure that the First Officer was awake and ready to come on duty.

Suddenly! the phone at the back of the wheelhouse buzzed and he answered it. It was Rowe, reporting the latest Patent Log reading. Hichens entered the reading into the appropriate record book. At the same time he noted that the ship had covered 45 nautical miles since the 8pm reading. Quick mental arithmetic told him the ship was now doing her best ever speed. He thought *twenty two and a half knots; the old girl really is steaming.* Thereafter, he exchanged places with QM Olliver and took over the job of steering the ship. At that same moment, Hogg and Evans in the Crow's Nest were relieved by Lookouts Fleet and Lee At a few minutes before 10 pm, First Officer Murdoch had arrived in the Chart Room, read and signed the captain's Night Order Book and then went out onto the bridge wing where he found Lightoller. The two men exchanged greetings and Lightoller formerly handed over the Watch. He remained there for a few minutes more until Murdoch's eyes adjusted to the darkness then headed for his bunk.

Four Bells were sounded, and the second half of the eight to Midnight Watch settled down. However, because the clocks were to be set back 47 minutes, they, being the junior Watch, would be getting an extra 24 minutes on duty.

The first part of the Midnight to 4 am Watch would get the remaining extra 23 minutes of duty.

As with all ships at sea, any clock changes were divided between the two night Watches. In the case of *Titanic*, the first half of the Log Book

Day from Noon, April 14 to Noon April 15 would 12 hours 24 minutes long, and the remainder Log Book day, from midnight to Noon, April 15 would be 12 hours 23 minutes long.

When the bridge clock read 12 o' clock Midnight for the first time, the GMT chronometer on *Titanic* would read 2-58 am and at that moment, bridge clock would be set back 24 minutes to read 11-36 pm, and the Master Clock would be stopped. When the bridge clock once again read 12 o' clock - midnight, it would be set back a further 23 minutes, which was the remainder of the planned clock change. When the bridge clock once again, and for the last time, read midnight, the change would be completed.

At 11-30 pm, 6th Officer Moody went out onto the bridge wing and rang seven strokes on the bell mounted on the bulkhead beside the door. He rang three sets of two followed by a single. Normally the Lookouts in the Nest would have copied his example by ringing the bell mounted on the fore part of the foremast above their nest. However, after 10 pm this was not the practice. Instead, they each shouted an acknowledgement with the cry "All's well - lights are burning bright" This told Moody, who could not see them, that they were awake and at their stations.

CHAPTER 9

ICEBERG RIGHT AHEAD, SIR

High above the bridge in the Crow's Nest, Fleet and Lee settled down for the remainder of the Watch. Their shift ended at 12 o'clock, Midnight, but although the bridge had sounded the 11-30 pm bells, they knew the clocks would be set back by twenty four minutes when it first read Midnight. Thus, they had another 54 minutes of sheer boredom staring ahead at an invisible sea in the direction of an invisible horizon before they were relieved. *What was it the officer said? Keep an eye open for small ice? They had to be kidding.*

Shortly after seven bells, the horizon became discernable. This was due to a faint lightening of it extending about twenty degrees from right ahead on either bow. Lee remarked *"Looks like mist ahead mate, if we see anything through that, it'll be a bloody miracle"*

Fleet inwardly didn't agree with him. He thought it was just another of the strange things seen at sea and dismissed it from his mind.

About thirty minutes later, Lee thought he could see a black shape low in the water, and right ahead. He felt the cold fear of adrenalin coursing through his body. "Christ! There's a bloody iceberg or something right ahead". His mate, Fleet, saw it almost at the same moment "Jeeezuz! So it is." He reached above and behind his right shoulder and found the bell toggle and swung the clapper against the bell violently three distinct times. This was the standard signal to the bridge that something had been spotted ahead or almost ahead.

Immediately the last stroke of the bell had been sounded - and because they were almost on top of the thing - Lee turned to his right and reached down into the corner of the nest where he knew he would find the nest telephone. He called the bridge and 6th Officer Moody answered almost immediately.

"What do you see"?

Fleet almost shouted down the mouthpiece "Iceberg dead a head sir".

The reply was simple and almost casual "Thank you".

Fleet replace the phone, and as he turned around, Lee, who had been staring at the approaching danger, excitedly remarked "Her head is starting to fall-off to port. The helm must be hard over already. I think we might miss it".

It had been a mere ten seconds since Fleet had first seen that dark shadow but already it seemed to be rising high out of the darkness and moving right at an agonizingly slow rate…becoming clearer as the *slow* seconds past. No doubt about it, it was a small iceberg, Barely the height of the forecastle Samson Post. *Would they miss it?*

Too late! There was a low, grinding sound as the ice contacted the ship's starboard *shoulder,* about 40 feet past the bow. At the same time, Lee imagined that the ship lurched imperceptibly to the right.

They could now see it clearly. It had a tall vertical side nearest to the ship - so near that the forecastle deck rail scraped powdered ice from it as it passed quickly along the starboard side.

As it went, it scraped the well deck bulwark rail, depositing light ice on the starboard side of the fore well deck. By the time it was level with the bridge, the Lookouts could see that although it was out from the ship's side, it was barely the height of the boat deck. Its shape reminded them of the Rock of Gibraltar - not the picture postcard view, but the view familiar to all sailors approaching it from the southeast.

Gibraltar from the Spanish mainland - tourist impression   Europa Pt.

PIC 3

Gibraltar from the southy east - Europa Point   *J. Currie 2022*

PIC 4

Europa Point from the South East.]

PIC 5

J.. Currie

PIC 5.5

This was confirmed on Day 2 of The UK Inquiry, by Able Seaman Joe Scarrott who told his questioners :" *Well, it struck me at the time that it resembled the Rock of Gibraltar looking at it from Europa Point. It looked very much the same shape as that, only much smaller.*"

Scarrott confirmed that it was almost mid-ship and out from the ship's side when he saw it. He also noted that as he watched, it began to close with the ship's side once again.

Down on the poop deck, at the stern Quartermaster George Rowe was leaning over the starboard side of the docking bridge rail when he felt a sort of heave or shudder of the ship. He looked forward and saw, faintly illuminated by the accommodation lighting, what he though was a sailing ship. However, his idea was shattered very quickly as he perceived an iceberg approaching his position. It wasn't touching the ship's side but it was getting damn close…less that ten feet off he reckoned. It occurred to him that they couldn't have missed seeing it on the bridge.

The iceberg passed astern into the darkness and he waited for a phone call - it didn't come. Suddenly, the present situation was more important. He looked at his watch. It read a few minutes after Midnight. *Damn! I was supposed to read the Patent Log at Midnight and pass the reading to the bridge.*

He went quickly to the port side of the docking bridge where the log registered was mounted. It read 260 nautical miles. He was about to phone the bridge with the reading, then he noticed that the log line was slackening off - indicating that the ship was slowing down. The line was beginning to point downward; soon it would be vertical and might catch in the propellers. He noted the reading in his book, then decided to bring the log line, governor and the rotator inboard until the ship moved ahead again.

Before all hell broke loose, First Officer Murdoch had been pacing up and down on the starboard wing of the bridge. Occasionally he would stop his pacing and sweep the horizon and intervening blackness of the sea with his binoculars.

Sixth Officer Moody was in the chartroom doing his *thing* and Fourth Officer Boxhall was sitting in his cabin. Having completed his rounds, he was enjoying a brief, unofficial time off to have a cup of tea and a puff at his pipe before the flurry of activity that always preceded the end of a Watch. However, just in case his boss, First Officer Murdoch, needed him and summoned him with his Officer's Call whistle, he had left his cabin door open on the hook.

He had also left the alleyway door onto the boat deck open for the same reason.

The helmsman - Quartermaster Robert Hichens, was encased in the darkness of the wheelhouse, intently watching his compass, his only source of light was from the compass card and the small light over the course board.

The last member of the Watch, standby Quartermaster, Olliver was off the bridge performing a standard duty. Except for the peaceful sound of the ship-generated wind passing through the rigging, and the monotonous shush-slap of the bow waves; it was an almost silent, perfect night.

First Officer Murdoch was on high alert. They were now in the area where they might encounter the odd patch of small ice, consequently, the sound of Fleet's three warning bells from the Crow's Nest had his immediate attention. He raised his binoculars and stared at the horizon ahead - did not see anything and then swept the area of sea immediately ahead of the ship and below the horizon. Instantly he saw it - dark menacing shape rushing toward him.- an iceberg!

In these fleeting moments, Murdoch saw that the berg had a high side which was nearest the ship, and tapered out to the right. To the left of it, there seemed to be clear water.

At the same moment he heard the telephone sounding in the wheelhouse. Years of training made him act instinctively. In a flash, he assessed and acted.

A. *He had to avoid the ice if possible and,*
B. *Since the danger was so close, be prepared to minimise any damage that might arise if the ship did contact the ice.*
   If (A) was unsuccessful, then he must stop the engines to avoid propeller damage and close the watertight doors.

Murdoch shouted a hard-a-starboard helm order to QM Hichens (In 1912 helm orders were given relative to a boat tiller I.e. in the opposite direction to the intended turn. - meaning that when the rudder turned the ship to the left, the tiller was turned to the right).

Within seconds, Murdoch saw the great ship's bow starting to turn to the left. However, with a sinking heart, he knew instinctively that it was too late. Seconds later he felt the ship start to tremble and knew they had hit the damn thing. Plan (B) was required. He rushed into the wheel house and gave a double ring to STOP on the engine telegraph, immediate followed with a double ring of FULL ASTERN. Then, without hesitating, he went to the Watertight Door control and activated the door closing lever, while at the same time pressing the warning bell.

Down in the cavernous bowels of the ship, the shrill alarm sounded, and the automatic doors separating the engine rooms and boiler rooms from each other began to descend to seal-off each compartment. This would take about 30 seconds, during which time, the warning bells would ring at each door would give the Firemen, Trimmers and Engineers on duty, time to keep clear of these giant metal guillotines as they descended inexorably into their sealed frames.

CHAPTER 10

WHAT WAS THAT?

Captain Smith was instantly awake. He consulted his watch; it was 11:16 pm. All hell had been let loose. He could feel the ship moving beneath his body in an unnatural way. Sounds of trilling telegraphs bells, shouting voices and the thump of feet could be dimly heard from out side his door. Smith was on his feet in seconds, grabbing and swinging-on his heavy bridge coat as he went. However he *did* take a moment to squeeze his swollen feet into his shoes. He was painfully ware that they weren't on properly. This made him hobble on one foot as he made a bee-line for the outer bridge.

The first person he met was First Officer Murdoch.

"What happened - what was that?"

First Officer Murdoch answered in a flood of words.

"We hit an iceberg sir. I tried to go to port around it but it was too late; it was too close - there was nothing else I could do. We hit it with our starboard bow. The helm's hard-a starboard and the engines are running full astern to stop her.

"Shut the watertight doors 'ordered Smith.

"I've already done so sir."

Almost 45 years of experience immediately began to pay-off. Smith's mind quickly sorted-out the situation.

Ok! The ship was or was not damaged. If she was damaged what was the extent of the damage? How will the weather conditions effect the ship's situation? Where are the nearest ships? Where are we at this moment?

To get the answers to all of these and many more questions, he needed to galvanise his crew into action. There were jobs to be done by specific individuals. Quartermaster Olliver who Smith had spoken to earlier had completed his 'trick' at the wheel and was now on standby to run messages. Boxhall and Moody were available for other duties and Murdoch was by his side.

"Mr. Murdoch; send Mr. Boxhall below to find out what's happening down there and send Olliver to find the Carpenter and get him to sound the tanks and compartments."

Murdoch looked around for Boxhall and was told by Moody that Boxhall was already down below decks having a look for damage, he therefore passed-on the captain's order to QM Olliver who left at the double to find the ship's Carpenter.

Between the engines running astern and the helm being hard-over, the ship had slowed to a halt. Smith ordered the engines to STOP. "Don't want her running backwards into that bloody iceberg again" was is excuse. Then he decided to save time.

"Mr. Murdoch; while the Carpenter and Boxhall are doing their inspections, I think we'll bring her back onto her course ready to continue once we get the all clear. I noticed she is off by 2 points to the southwest. How's the helm at the moment?"

"Still hard-a-starboard, sir." replied Murdoch.

"Right then, she'll need a little kick ahead to let the rudder work. Helm hard-a-port." He strode over to the engine telegraph and rank down Half Ahead on the engines.

"Helm's hard- a- port sir," confirmed Murdoch. Smith finished with "Steady her on S71W Quartermaster. Let me know when she is on that heading."

Almost immediately, QM Hichens, who was still on the wheel confirmed the helm was hard over the other way and a minute later, confirmed the desired heading of S71W. On hearing this, Smith stopped the engines. He was ready to continue on the voyage as soon as he received the expected all clear.

In the meantime, QM Olliver had returned from finding the Carpenter. By this time, the boiler were being blown down, and the noise of escaping steam made conversation impossible, so he was immediately sent with a message from the Captain to the Chief Engineer, requesting that something be done about the steam..

Once Smith was sure there was no more danger to the ship, he and Murdoch made their way onto the starboard bridge wing and looked aft. The offending bit of ice could be dimly seen off the ship' stern on the starboard side. As they looked, they were joined by Boxhall who had returned from his inspection trip below decks. He gave his report. "I've been right down as far as I can go without opening any compartments sir. I was unable to find any damage; not even a broken porthole".

The Captain's heightened anxiety slackened a little. "Thank you Mister Boxhall" then pointing "There's the blighter that caused all the trouble". Boxhall looked in the direction indicated but his night vision had been compromised due to his recent visit to the brightly lit accommodation. He couldn't be sure, but he though he could see a low-lying shadowy shape off the stern.

As he strained his eyes, he became aware that Captain Smith was speaking to him. "Sorry sir, I didn't quite catch that".

Smith repeated "You'd better get yourself back down there again mister. I have sent for the Carpenter, nip down and see if you can find him."

"Aye sir" replied Boxhall and headed below once again.

After Boxhall had gone, Captain Smith had a look over the starboard bridge wing dodger. Below on the forward well deck, he could dimly see many people. Not only people, he could also just make out a powdering of ice along the starboard side of the exposed deck. He drew his First Officer's attention to it.

"Look at that lot Murdoch! Must have been scraped off the berg. God! that was a close one.' Without waiting for Murdoch to comment he continued.

"Is it my imagination or are we taking on a bit of a starboard list?' He could feel the slight pressure of uneven weight on the soles of his feet.- his anxiety began to return.

On his way down from the bridge, on his second inspection trip, Boxhall met the Carpenter coming up.

The man was out of breath and red of face. "Where's the Captain Sir?"

Why? What's the rush?" The man was highly agitated and answered.

"I started sounding round as soon as I felt the bump. There's water coming in fast in...." He didn't get time to finish. Boxhall interrupted.

"Bloody-hell! The 'Old Man's on the bridge better report to him as soon as you can. I was down there earlier but didn't see anything. Then I was sent belowt o find you but here you are already. Well done! I'll carry on down and have another look."

The Carpenter hurried upward toward the bridge and Boxhall continued downward. A few seconds later he met a Postal Clerk. He too was highly agitated and asked where the Captain was.

Again, Boxhall wanted to know why the man needed the Captain.

"It's the Mail Room, sir; the water is pouring in there from somewhere and rising fast."

The Mail Room was on G Deck and Boxhall immediately knew this was serious news. He told the man he too would find the captain on the bridge. Thereafter, he went in the direction of the Mail Room to see for himself.

The Carpenter arrived on the bridge shortly before the Mail Room Clerk. He found Smith in the wheelhouse

"What have you got for me, *Chippy?*"

The Carpenter's face spoke of ghastly news and he verbally confirmed it.

"I am afraid she is taking on water fast in at least five compartments forward, sir."

Almost before the Carpenter had finished his report, the Mail Room Clerk arrived with his news of the Mail Room inundation. Within minutes, Boxhall returned from his second journey to the lower decks and confirmed the story

Captain Smith had heard enough; his worst scenario had arrived -he knew without question that his ship was in a desperate state and he needed help as soon as possible. He turned to Murdoch. "Mr. Murdoch, have all the officers called - call all the deck hands to stations and prepare the boats" He then strode quickly into the wheelhouse. Once there, he consulted device in front of the helmsman which indicated if the ship was upright or listed-over to the left or right.

Sure enough, it showed that she was listed over to the right; toward the starboard side; the side that had taken the brunt of the iceberg. Smith did not hesitate; he went immediately to the Chart Room, where he gathered the data he needed to calculate a distress position.

From the Scrap Log Book, he found the three times he needed: the 8 pm Dead Reckoning position - the time when the ship hit the ice, and the time when *Titanic* finally stopped. The DR for 8 pm was recorded as 41°-53'North, 47°- 19'West and the recorded times for collision and STOP were 11-40pm, 11-46 pm respectively.

However, Smith had another problem.

Normally the lapsed time between 8 pm and 11-40 pm would, by simple arithmetic, be 3 hours 40 minutes. However there had been a partial clock change before they had hit the berg. He looked at the chartroom clock, it read 11-52 pm. Then he looked at his watch, it read 11-29 pm. This puzzled him for a second them he remembered he had set his watch back the full 47 minutes before he lay down earlier. This meant that the run time from the 8pm DR was 4 hours 4 minutes, not 3 hours 40 minutes. Now for a speed.

The weather was perfect, so he decided to use an average speed of 22 knots. The result of his calculation was a Dead Reckoning position to which ships would head if he needed assistance it was at:

Latitude 41°- 44 minutes North, 50°- 24 minutes West.

Smith wrote this on a scrap oFpaper and headed for the Wireless Room.

CHAPTER 11

SAVE OUR SOULS

Normally, the Senior Marconi Operator Philips would have worked until 2 am the following morning. However, he had been much busier than usual during the previous day He had found and repaired a short circuit in the system and consequently, had lost much of his normal time off. As a result, Junior Operator Bride had agreed to relieve him 2 hours earlier than normal.

The ship-board Marconi station consisted of an operating room and adjacent sleeping quarters for the Operators

Bride had awakened of his own accord and noted that it was 11-45 pm. He also discovered that the ship was stopped and, through the open adjoining door, could see Senior Operator Philips was still at his desk. He got up from his bunk and got ready to relieve his senior. As he did so,, the two men discussed the situation.

Philips had just finished transmitting a large batch of messaged to the shore station at Cape Race, Newfoundland. He did not know why the ship had stopped but speculated that it might mean a trip back to the builder's yard at Belfast.

Eventually, Bride was fully dressed and took over the Watch from Phillips. The latter retired to the sleeping cabin and began to prepare for bed.

The Wireless Operating room had two clocks, one kept ship time and the other kept Eastern Standard New York Time, *it* read 10-15 pm. At that moment, Captain Smith arrived and without ceremony placed the scrap of paper in front of young Bride and told him "You'd better get assistance".

On hearing these terse words, Phillips immediately returned to the room and read what was written on the scrap of paper.

"Do you wish me to send this now sir? Is it a distress signal?"

"It certainly is, and yes, send it at once" answered the captain who was already halfway out the door and heading back for the bridge.

After Captain Smith left the bridge, First Officer Murdoch turned to Boxhall.

"Well - you heard him. You had better go away and call the other officers, Mr Boxhall."

Boxhall looked at the clock - it read 11-55 pm; this puzzled him

"Why, sir? didn't Quartermaster Olliver called them at one bell?"

"Olliver hasn't had time to draw his breath. He's been down to get the Carpenter and been to the engine room. Now he's away down to tell the Bosun to call all hands. When he gets back; Moody wants him to bring the boat muster lists."

Boxhall's heart missed a beat -"Boat muster lists? You mean we're going to launch the boats?"

"No.' chuckled Murdoch. It's just a precaution while we get things sorted out. We're stopped, but *Old Man* has brought her head back on course and we're ready to carry on once we get things sorted out. Once both Watches arrive, they will uncover the boats and get them ready as a matter of precaution. If we *do* need them then they'll be ready for action.' He laughed again. "I'm afraid you'll have to do your own dirty work my boy and call your own relief. It must be nearly time for them to go on Watch anyway. Oh by the way! You'd better call Mr. Lightoller as well. Can't let him miss all the fun."

Joe Boxhall stepped over the sill of the port side door to the officer's accommodation and onto the boat deck. The sound of steam vapour venting from the huge funnel above his head shattered his hearing but did nothing to alter his thoughts. He had just called the other three deck officers - Lightoller, Pitman and Lowe - and given the three of them the news about the ice berg. He had not been surprised to find Pitman awake. After all it was almost time for the 3rd Officer to be going back on bridge duty. However, since Lightoller had gone off duty more than 2 hours earlier, he was surprised to find *him* awake. Then again the ship's engines had stopped and that in itself was, to a seaman, like an alarm bell.

Fifth Officer Lowe on the other hand had been dead-to-the-world.

The news had brought Lightoller and Pitman completely, utterly and rudely wide awake. Any remaining idea of sleep had immediately vanished.

Boxhall thought about Lowe again. He hadn't seen him since he had called him - *Lowe? Damn-it! I forgot to check on Lowe. Too late now! I'd better head back to the bridge.* He salved his conscience by thinking there was no doubt the others would remember to call the Fifth Officer. Lowe

He was about to return to his place of duty in the chart room on the ship's navigating bridge, when he remembered that Willie Murdoch had told him that orders had been given to call all deck hands and to prepare the life boats but not to load or launch them. That had been five minutes earlier and there was still no sign of the deck crew, so he decided he may as well start things off

Instead of heading directly back to the bridge, he made a detour via the boat deck; letting go the slip knots and bow and stern lacings on some of the life boat covers as he went.

Boxhall's mind was in a turmoil. Here he was, only 28 years of age and Fourth Officer of the biggest and grandest ship afloat. Now it looked like the ruddy thing might be sinking under his feet. His stomach churned and he could taste the regurgitated tea and biscuit he had so recently enjoyed together with that sneaked pipe of tobacco. Added to all that, the double journey of inspection in less than 20 minutes and what he had found out, had left him breathless and worried.

He did not for a moment, imagine that this great ship would actually sink. Then an uneasy thought broke into his already agitated thought process. He was, after all, the Navigating Officer of the Watch - *perhaps the 'Old man' will want a distress position. Better get back to the bridge.* He broke-off what he was doing and headed back.

When he arrived on the bridge, Boxhall immediately noticed how bright it was.

The single, overhead electric light in the normally dark bridge had been switched on and the place was full of people. Towering above them he spied the ship's Chief Officer Henry Wilde; he was deep conversation with the bearded figure of Captain Smith. Boxhall went over and cautiously interrupted.

"Excuse me sir."

Smith turned. "Yes Mr Boxhall?'

'I've called all the officers sir. I was wondering; do you wish me to calculate a position for the ship?"

"I've already done so Mr. Boxhall - and sent it to the Wireless Office for transmission to all ships".

This answer puzzled Boxhall. He was the Navigating Officer of the Watch and as such had all the necessary information for working such a position.The Second Officer's fixed position, the exact time of obtaining it and the resulting co-ordinates, were in his work book which he kept in the chartroom. All he needed was a time for stopping and a course and speed since the Second Officer had obtained that fixed position earlier. Then he had another thought.

"Forgive me for asking sir, but on what start position did you base your calculations?"

"Actually I used the 8pm Dead Reckoning position written in the Scrap Log, Mr. Boxhall. Why?"

For a brief moment, Boxhall experienced extreme embarrassment.

"Yes sir. I'm afraid there is." He went on to explain.

"When I finished working the evening sights, I noticed that the 8pm DR had been written-down incorrectly. In fact, the position in the Deck Log is in error by 20 miles. I'm sorry about that sir". He was about to elaborate on the error when Smith interrupted.

"Never mind Mr. Boxhall; just go and set things right then take the details to the Wireless Operator. Tell him I want our corrected position sent out right away".

Boxhall quickly returned to the chartroom and retrieved his work book from the bookcase where he always kept it. He turned the page containing the position obtained by star sights earlier that evening and copied the position obtained and time of taking it onto a clean page of his book. The GMT of the evening position obtained by Lightoller was recorded as 10-36 pm which was equal to a ship time of 7-38 pm.

Having noted these particulars of the last known position, he then consulted the Deck Log.

Like Captain Smith before him, Boxhall noted that the time of hitting the iceberg was recorded as 11-40 pm and the time of stopping was recorded as 11-46 pm. He converted that to 3-31am GMT. The difference between these two GMTs gave him a run time of 4 hours 55 minutes.

After finding the run time between the last known position and the place where they hit the iceberg, he needed a speed.

The calculated speed from Noon that day to the fixed position in the early evening was under 22 knots. However considering the flat calm weather conditions since early evening, Boxhall decided to use a speed of 22 knots. By multiply his chosen speed by his run time he obtained a distance run since Lightoller's sights of 108 miles. Earlier, he had calculated that the ship was making good a course of 266True so he now had all the necessary ingredients to calculate a new distress position.

In a few short minutes he had I what he needed, and quickly noted it down on a piece of scrap paper. It read:

'Lat 41°46 minutes North - Long. 50°14 minutesWest'.

Boxhall was about to take the amended position to the wireless room when there was a report of a light ahead of the ship. He quickly found his binoculars, and went out onto the port side. When he got his binoculars focussed, he made-out a single white light low on the horizon and almost ahead.

He returned to the captain and reported the sighting. Thereafter he took the amended distress position to the wireless room, where he found Chief Wireless Operator Phillips with head-phones over his ears, crouched over his Morse key.

The roar of escaping steam from the boilers via the funnels made it impossible to have any form of conversation, so Boxhall simply placed the amended distress position in front of Phillips and by sign language told him it was to be sent immediately.

On returning to the bridge, Boxhall found Captain Smith looking through his binoculars at the light that had been reported earlier. Boxhall found his own binoculars and, once again, focussed them in the same direction.

The light had now metamorphosed into two distinct white lights, one over the other and slightly apart. The lower of the two was to the left. This told the two men that they were seeing the masthead lights of a steam ship which was heading their way and, if it had been visible, would be showing a red side light. It was a steamship which, if it did not stop, would pas down *Titanic's* port side.

Boxhall felt a slight elation - it was coming their way. He turned to the captain. "It looks to me sir that she is coming toward us and will pass down our port side."

"Yes Mr Boxhall, it certainly does. How far off do you think she is?"

Boxhall had another look. "I'd say she's about ten or twelve miles, Sir - perhaps a little less. Should I fire some signals to make sure she knows we need help?"

"Good idea, get the signals ready and send aft for the detonators." replied the captain. At that moment and as if by clairvoyance, the phone in the wheelhouse sounded. Boxhall answered the instrument.

"Hello! Is that the bridge? Do you know that there is a lifeboat off the starboard side?" The caller had a south west England accent.

Boxhall asked "is that you Pitman?" - Third Officer Pitman was a Devonshire man.

"No sir, this is Quartermaster Rowe on the poop."

Boxhall was taken aback. "A lifeboat you say? No, I did not know that. I'll check with the captain. Meantime, go to the explosives magazine locker and bring the two boxes of detonators for the distress rockets. Are you alone?"

"No sir" replied Rowe. "My relief, Quartermaster Bright is here with me."

"Right then!" exclaimed Boxhall, bring them, and him, with you," After putting the phone down, QM Rowe looked at his watch; it read 12-25am. He had earlier set it back by 24 minutes so that when the proper time came he would read the Patent Log. He would also be sure that when QM Bright, his relief, arrived; the latter would be on time.

As it turned out, due to the intervention of the iceberg, Bright had not been called at the proper time therefore he arrived on duty 20 minutes late.

Rowe found the key to the explosives locker which like on most passenger ships, was located at the stern area for safety. They each took a box of signal from it- locked it again, then headed for the bridge.

As Smith and Boxhall watched the approaching vessel, the captain spoke:

"I had word from the wireless room that a German vessel named *Frankfurt* has picked up my signals and we are now waiting for her position. According to Sparks, her signal was strong, so she may be near to us."

CHAPTER 12

THE *"BIRKENHEAD" WAY*

When Boxhall reported the news of the launching of a lifeboat to Captain Smith. He had expected Smith to be surprised, but he was not.

"Yes, Mr Boxhall, I know about that. I didn't order it but is seems that our Chairman took it upon himself to act independently and urged Mr. Murdoch to load and lower boat No.7 as a matter of urgency. He tried the same thing with the Third Officer at No.5, but Mr Pitman came to me for permission before acting. In fact No 7 has now also gone and I have given the general order to embark the women and children and to commence getting all the boats away. I have also sent a message to the Wireless Room to let all ships know we are doing so." Boxhall looked at the clock - it showed 12-35 pm.

At that moment Quartermaster's Rowe and Bright were nearing the bridge, they had noted that boats No.7 and No.5 were gone, leaving a dark, empty space where they once had rested on their chocks. No.3 was in the process of being filled with passengers. They continued onto the bridge deck where they delivered the detonators to Fourth Officer Boxhall.

Titanic had been supplied with standard distress rockets. However, like most modern passenger vessels, she also carried 36 Socket Signals. These were simply modified shells which were loaded into a short, almost vertical launching tube or Socket, much like a short gun barrel which was located on a side rail. At the forward end of the emergency cutters and just behind the bridge cabs.

To launch them a projectile was located in the socket and thereafter, a lanyard-operated friction detonator was located in a narrow tube located centrally down through the projectile. Then by pulling violently on the lanyard and rapidly activating the friction detonator, the propulsion charge was ignited Thus the projectile was launched about 600 feet into the sky where it exploded with an ear-splitting bang, and at the same moment, ejecting a shower of white magnesium stars which descended slowly seaward.

As soon as the detonators were delivered, the Quartermasters and Boxhall prepared to fire them to draw the attention of the approaching vessel.

Boxhall asked the two Quartermaster if they knew Morse code and how to operate the ship's signal light. QM Rowe who had been in the Royal Navy answered that he could. Thereafter, they took turns in alternately firing off these socket signal and signalling the approaching vessel to tell her crew that they were sinking and needed urgent help. Sadly, these calls for help were ignored.

While all this was going on, the lifeboats were being loaded with passengers.

On the port side, the operation was being supervised by Second Officer Lightoller aided by Sixth Officer Moody.

First Officer Murdoch was in charge on the starboard side and had initially been aided by Third Officer Pitman and Fifth Officer Lowe. However Pitman had been ordered away in charge of lifeboat No.5.

The Captain and Chief Officer were overseeing the operations on both sides of the boat deck.

Following the practice originating from the *Birkenhead* sinking sixty years earlier, and in compliance with the Chairman's wishes, Captain Smith had ordered that the remaining boats were to be filled with women and children before men were allowed on board.

However, students of the disaster will be aware that there was considerable outrage at this because, not only were the boats filled in this manner, - they were lowered without the full complement they were designed to carry. The argument then, s it is to this today, was that they should have been loaded to full capacity of all ages and sexes at the embarkation point, and by doing this, many more lives would have been saved. That is a fallacy and here is why.

Although the davits carrying the boats and the rope blocks were of the latest design, the remaining weak point was the manila ropes (falls) from which the heavy boats were suspended and the method by which these falls were slackened -off when the boats were lowered to the sea.

The end of each fall was led through the blocks and back down onto the deck where it was wound around cross-shaped bollard secured to the boat deck.

To lower the boat, the sailors at each end had to slacken the rope around the bollard in a controlled coordinated manner called 'surging'. If, during this action, a rope became jammed, it would receive a sudden shock load, causing the rope to break and allowing one end of the boat to fall and spill its contents. The value of that shock load depended on how many people were loaded into the lifeboat at the beginning of the operation. Thus, the intention of initially under-load the boats was to avoid the problems of shock loads; to lower the boats safely then fill them to capacity from the gangway doors near to sea level after they had been launched.

Now back to the boat deck.

While the under-loading of the boats was a problem, there was an even greater one. Those still on board were divided in thoughts and intent. Wives refused to leave husband, some even believed the media-driven myth that a ship like *Titanic* was unsinkable.

Meanwhile, *Titanic* was sinking inexorably by the head and gradually tilting over on her left (port) side, which in turn, increased the problems of the boat launching operation on the starboard side. To aggravate the situation - as the lower decks filled with water, more and more people - some carrying their worldly goods - headed upward to dry decks.

CHAPTER 13

MEANWHILE DOWN BELOW

Down in the engine and boiler rooms, it had been a different story.

Before impact with the iceberg all had been going well, and the 8pm to Midnight Watch were looking forward to a rest - particularly the Firemen and Trimmers who had strength-sapping work in overheated workplaces.

Titanic had six boiler rooms numbering from aft to forward. That fateful night, the normal routine of those working in the Boiler Rooms was shattered suddenly by a STOP FIRING order from the main engine room.

On seeing this on the Firing Indicator, the Leading Fireman in each Boiler Room shouted the order to stop shovelling coal into the furnaces and shut off the life-giving air to them. However, before the order could be completed, those in the foremost Boiler Room - No.6 - felt a bump and heard a tearing grinding noise approaching them from forward on the starboard side. Within seconds, the seams of the ship's side shell plating, about two feet above the boiler room deck plate, sprung open and sea water at high pressure began to inundate the space. At the same very same time, the Water Tight Doors at each end of the compartment began to descend and render the space watertight; leaving the men had less than 30 seconds to get through them. Only two made in boile Room 6 made it through them before the doors closed. Others managed to climb up the escape ladders and out of the compartment.

In a very short time, Boiler Room Six was flooded to a depth of 8 feet and water was entering the forward of of Boiler Room 5. By then, all of *Titanic's* water tight doors in the machinery spaces and boiler rooms were tightly closed. All Engineering Officers were called and very soon thereafter, were at their posts or making ready pumping equipment.

Starved of life-giving steam, the great engines, which had been turning relentlessly at 75 revolutions every minute of every hour that day, finally gave a pathetic hiss of protest and sighed to a halt. Shortly after that, the engines began turning astern for two minutes, stopped - ran ahead for another two minutes before both they and the great ship herself, stopped forever.

When the ship finally came to a halt, the water tight doors were manually raised and the Firemen and Trimmers returned to all the Boiler Rooms except numbers five and six which were flooded. There, they killed the boiler furnaces and raked them out. Thereafter, they were ordered up onto the main deck while the engineering officers remained at their posts working under the direction of the Chief Engineer.

* * *

At first, only those who were in close proximity to the areas contacted by the iceberg and those who for one reason or another were awake, knew that something had happened. However, after three days becoming accustomed to the beating heart of the ship, the sudden stillness when it stopped had many more awake and aware of something being wrong.

Within minutes of the engines stopping for the last time, the alley-ways and companionways connecting the nine decks of the great ship were thronged with bewildered men women and children - some carrying their entire worldly possession in a tied cloth bundles on their backs. These crowds were augmented by off duty crew members, particularly Firemen and Stewards. The former had been rudely evicted from their warm bunks by the encroaching sea. All were looking for guidance and reassurance.

The crew members were trained for something like this and had often attended Fire and Boat Drills. However, for many of the passengers, particularly the Third Class ones, this was their first time on board a ship.

Many were emigrating to a new life, and this was where *Titanic's* stewards and catering staff - from the oldest to the first tripper - demonstrated their outstanding courage and value.

Assistant Cook/Scullion, 17 year old John Collins from Belfast, had been sound asleep when the ship hit the iceberg. The impact had him wide awake and he looked at his clock at the side of his bunk - it read 11-20 pm. It was not an expensive item and did not keep good time so he knew that it was five minutes fast and the true time was 11-15 pm.

As a day worker, Collins had set hic clock back the full planned clock change of 47 minutes so that it would be correct the next morning, when he went to work in the First Class Galley.

Less than twenty minutes after hitting the icebergs, young John and every steward and member of the Catering staff was busy, gathering supplies for the boats and comforting and assuring those who had been before and still were, in their charge. All passengers were urged to don lifejackets and make their way upward toward assembly points on the upper decks, including the well decks fore and aft, as well as Decks A., B., and C. and the Boat Deck. The constant problem to be avoided was the blockage of companion-ways leading up to those decks.

A fact that is sometimes ignored is that within 20 minutes of *Titanic* stopping, her captain, officers and men were at their stations and working flat our to try and save those in their care. I might add - all without the benefit of modern 'walkie-talkies.

CHAPTER 14

LISTENING-IN

The first vessel to answer *Titanic's* call for help was the German vessel *Frankfurt*, but her Operator was not the first to hear it. There were two claimant's for that honour.

One was a young wireless enthusiast named Artie Moore who lived almost two thousand miles away in the Welsh hamlet of Pontllanfraith. The other, was young James Meryk, an Apprentice Operator at the Marconi wireless station, on Cape Race, Newfoundland.

Both of these lads heard the first transmitted distress position - the one calculated by Captain Smith.

James (Jimmy) Meryk was at the Marconi Newfoundland station with the Duty Operator, and for some unknown reason, the Operator had left the desk - leaving young Jimmy on his own.

Suddenly! The lad heard the equally spaced group of Morse letters: CQD CQD CQD. Jimmy knew this was code for *"Calling all ships - this is a distress"*. These were followed by *Titanic's* unique, three letter call sign MGY-MGY-MGY, and ended with the coordinates of the distress position worked by Captain Smith.

Almost at the same time, far away in Wales, Artie Moore heard exactly the same message.

Artie wrote it down and took it to the local police station - young Jimmy ran out to find the duty Operator.

By the time Jimmy found the Operator and they returned to the wireless shack, *Titanic* was transmitting the amended distress signal calculated by *Titanic's* 4ᵗʰ Officer Boxhall.

Across the ocean - the Welsh Constabulary thought Artie was hearing things- *messages in the air Boy-oh? Really?*

Back in *Titanic's* wireless room, Phillips was waiting for a reply from the *Frankfurt;.* He had also had a call from the Operator on the Canadian Pacific *vessel Mount Temple,* but because of the noise of the escaping steam, was unable to converse with him so did not know for certain, if the man had received the distress call . Meanwhile, he sent young Bride to inform the captain of *Frankfurt's* first response to the call for help, and the problems with the steam. The time was 3-18 am GMT on Monday, April 15.

Bride made his way toward the bridge. He did not find Captain Smith there, but was told that the Captain was on the boat deck.

When he eventually found Captain Smith, he told him about the *Frankfurt,* and about the difficulty in hearing due to the noise of escaping steam, then returned to the Wireless Room.

It was 3-20 am GMT and the two young wireless men were still having a difficult time in hearing anything due to the ear-splitting roar of venting steam from the giant funnels above their heads.

A few minutes after Bride returned, 4ᵗʰ Officer Boxhall had arrived in the Wireless Room beside Chief Operator Phillips. Conversation was out of the question, so Boxhall placed a note on the desk in front of Phillips and pointed to it.

By finger gestures and mime he conveyed to the Chief Operator that this new message contained a distress position, and was to be sent immediately; also, that it was in place of the one delivered earlier by the captain. Then, Boxhall returned to the bridge. It was 3-24 am GMT.

At 3-25 am GMT Phillips began sending the revised distress position: Latitude 41°-46'North - Longitude 50°-14' West.

The next vessel to find out about *Titanic's* predicament was the Canadian Pacific vessel *Mount Temple.* However, her Operator did not respond to Phillips.

Just before 3-50am GMT,April15, the operator on the Cunard vessel *Carpathia* called *Titanic* and advised him that Cape Cod had messages for him. Obviously, the man had missed *Titanic's* earlier cries for help.

As soon as the *Carpathia* Operator had finished transmitting, Phillips advised him of the situation, and gave him the revised distress position. Philips could then take comfort from the knowledge that at least two ships had heard his cries for help.

Suddenly, he remembered that it had been some time since he had updated the captain, so he sent his junior in search of the man once again - this time, to tell him that not one, but two vessels knew they needed help.

Bride found Captain Smith and 4th Officer Boxhall on the bridge . Both men were staring out to sea in the direction of what looked like a ship's lights. The steam had been exhausted from the ship's boilers. Now- except for the hub-bub sounds of people-movement accompanied by anxious murmuring - all was silent.

"Excuse me sir." began Bride. "Mister Phillips sent me to update you on the latest replies to our distress signals."

Captain Smith was immediately alert. "Yes lad - what do you have for me?"

Bride answered in a rush. "We have had replies from two ships, sir - a German ship named *Frankfurt,* which you know about, and the Cunard liner *Carpathia.*"

"So are they coming?" Asked smith.

"I don't know sir." confessed Bride - adding: "I understand that they will reply with their present positions and Mr Phillips is waiting for these now."

Captain Smith turned to Boxhall and pointed to the approaching vessel they had been watching "Try and contact that fellow, Mr. Boxhall. I'm going to the Wireless Room and find out what's happening."

"Will I send for the detonators for the distress signals, sir." Asked Boxhall.

"Yes, but don't let any off before I get back."

When Bride and the captain arrived back at the wireless room, they found Phillips had once again been in contact with the *Carpathia* and now had her position and the news that she had turned toward them and would be with them in four hours.

Captain Smith only stayed in the Wireless Room long enough to verify *Carpathia's* position, then he returned to the bridge.

After the captain left the bridge for the Wireless Room, there was a call from the stern Docking Bridge. Since his junior, 6ᵗʰ Officer Moody, was on the boat deck preparing the lifeboats, Boxhall answered it.

The voice on the other end had an unmistakeable English west country accent so Boxhall assumed it was 3ʳᵈ Officer Pitman.

"Hello - is that you Pitman?" he asked.

"The voice replied "No sir - Quartermaster Rowe here sir. Do you know we have a lifeboat off our starboard side sir?"

Boxhall was taken aback. "A lifeboat you say? No, I did not know that. Thank you Quartermaster." He continued;" Are you on your own?"

No sir, I have Quartermaster Perkis with me."

"Right then, Rowe. Go to the magazine locker and bring the detonators for the distress signals up here. You will find two boxes of them - one of a dozen and another containing two dozen. Make sure you lock the magazine when you are finished.

Boxhall was puzzled, he had not been informed about that boat. This was because, unknown to him, Captain Smith had been placed in an awkward situation by the Company Chairman Ismay.

Ismay, who had been travelling as a passenger, had appeared on the boat deck during the preparation of the lifeboats and had urged the officers beside Lifeboats 7 and 5 to load them with passengers and lower away.

Although Boat No.7 had been launched, the officer at boat No.5 - 3ʳᵈ Officer Pitman - decided that he needed the captain's order to do this, so went to the bridge to find Captain Smith.

He found Smith with Boxhall on the port bridge wing, and explained his problem.

Due to the awkwardness of the situation, Smith had had no alternative but to agree the Chairman's plan and gave Pitman the all clear to proceed with it.

Consequently, as Smith and Boxhall were preparing to contact the approaching vessel, a boat had already been loaded with passengers and lowered into the sea. It now lay off *Titanic's* starboard side, its white painted hull visible in the reflected light from the ship's accommodation. Ismay had triggered the evacuation, and the work to load and launch the lifeboats was now underway.

On arrival, back on the bridge after his second visit to the Wireless Room, the captain found that the detonators for the socket signals had arrived.

The approaching ship was getting nearer, so Boxhall suggested that they should start firing the socket signals to attract her and that as she got even nearer, he could call her up using the Morse signalling lamps.

Titanic had two powerful signalling lamps; they were mounted on short masts - one each side, on top of the bridge wing cabs .

Smith thought for a moment. "Very well, Mr. Boxhall, in fact start signalling and firing now. If you get an answer, tell them to come quickly as we are sinking." adding " I am told we have but an hour or hour and a half left to live."

Boxhall was already prepared to start firing the socket signals. He had decided to use the firing point on the starboard side and use the port side signal lamp. Thus, they could signal and fire at the same time and one would not interfere with the other. QM Rowe would assist. They would alternate duties - firing and signalling in turn. Meantime, the loading and sending away of the lifeboats continued.

The sea remained flat and motionless - the wind had completely vanished and *Titanic* was now settling noticeably by the bow. Earlier, she had taken on a starboard list, but gradually as the invading sea found its way deeper into her innards, and the engineers had started the pumps, she had slowly returned to the upright. Now, she was most decidedly leaning over to port. However, most of this was due to the distribution of weight high on the boat deck due to the number of people accumulating there.

Lifeboats 7 and 5 had been filled an launched and First Officer Murdoch and Third Officer Lowe were almost ready to send away lifeboat No.3. From there, they would move to the next boat ahead of it, which was Emergency Cutter No.1.

At the same time, as lifeboat No.3 was being made ready to go, Boxhall was about to fire his first distress signal from a launching tube secured to the inside of the bulwark close to the bow of No.1. "Stand back everyone". he yelled at the top of his voice. He had already placed the projectile in the launch tube and located the long, pencil-like detonator with the striker lanyard attached to it, down into the igniter tube and was standing back a few feet with the lanyard at the ready. There were not too many people in the immediate vicinity and First Officer Murdoch and Fifth Officer Lowe had almost finished the No.3 preparations for embarking. They stopped work at Boxhall's cry, and everyone moved back a safe distance.

On seeing all was in order, Boxhall pulled violently on the firing lanyard. There was an ear-splitting *Crack!* as the charge at the base of the projectile ignited. This was instantly followed by a *Whooosh!* as the star shell (for that is what it really was) shot upward, leaving a very faint trail of sparks behind it. It was nothing like the conventional rockets which many of them had seen before.

However, all was not over. When the projectile reached its maximum trajectory it exploded with a mind-boggling *BANG!* Which left everyone on deck with ringing ear drums. The bang was the prelude to the grand finale consisting of a shower of brilliant white magnesium stars which gracefully and in deathly silence, drifted slowly back toward the sea. At that moment, the lives of every living soul on *Titanic's* decks as wells as those of Third Officer Pitman and the survivors in boats No.5 and No.7, were suspended in time. All eyes stared upward, up-turned faces illuminated by this announcement of dire emergency. That which had, until then, been a fairly quiet, orderly affair, suddenly took on a sense of urgency. Third Officer Lowe looked at his watch which kept GMT - It read seven minutes past 4 am on the morning of April, 15, 1912. At the same time, the watch of Quarter Master Rowe, read 12-45 am and the time at New York was 11-07 pm.

Boxhall replaced the firing lanyard in the wheelhouse and went over to the port side to have a look at the approaching vessel. He could now clearly see all her lights, including her red sidelight without the aid of his binoculars and reckoned she was no more than five or six miles away. He resumed signalling her with the Morse light. QM Rowe and Captain Smith were standing beside him with binoculars looking for the first sign of an acknowledgement - it never came.

It was time to fire another signal, so QM Rowe, - who was ex Royal Navy, was also a skilled signaller - took over the Morse key and Boxhall prepared to fire another signal.

Back in the wireless room, Phillips had been in contact *Titanic's* sister-ship the RMS Olympic.. At 4 -35 am GMT He received a personal message from her captain to Captain Smith and immediately dispatched Bride to deliver it.

The Captain opened it - It read:

"*Commander,, 4.24 a. m. G.M.T. 40.52 N., 61.18 W. Are you steering southerly to meet us? Haddock.*"

Smith made a quick calculation and estimated that *Olympic* was still over 500 miles away. Then he and Bride returned to the Wireless Room where he dictated a reply. "Mr Philips, Please tell Captain Haddock that we are putting the passengers off in small boats."

Phillips scribbled the message on his pad and commenced calling *Olympic..*

Within minutes he had a reply and immediately sent the captain's message.

Olympic replied " *What weather do you have?*

Captain Smith said " tell him it's calm and clear."

Olympic's captain replied with a personal message for captain Smith - asking if he was steering southward to meet *Olympic*.

Smith decided to let the man know the extent of his situation and replied: that they were sinking fast by the head.

This worked, because *Olympic* replied with the news that they were firing-up all boilers and going as fast as they could.

Without waiting for more, Captain Smith hurried back to the boat deck.

The New York Time was 11-50 pm - in London, dawn was near and the time was 4-50 am on the morning of April 15, 1912.

CHAPTER 15

TIME RUNS - OUT

Slowly but surely the *Titanic* continued to sink deeper by the bow and increasingly heel over onto her port side As she did so, her stern was rising out of the water. Lifeboats were now being loaded and sent away at short intervals. Some of them, like Pitman's No.5 remained close to the ship. Others had been told to row toward the vessel seen on the port bow.

As the ship sank deeper and closer to the sea, caution was cast to the wind and the number of those allowed into the boats was increased. Orders had been given to open the ship's gangway doors to allow embarkation of more people into the boats already launched.

Boxhall and Rowe had continued alternately firing signals and vainly trying to get a response from the nearby vessel using the Morse light.

Earlier, Captain Smith had been told by the Chief Engineers that water was progressively entering the boiler rooms. Consequently the Wireless Operators had been told to advise all ships of this development.

The ship seen earlier was now very close.

Suddenly, Boxhall noticed that the red side light of the nearby vessel was being shut out - beginning to disappear; indicating that she was turning away from them to starboard, reversing her course. Within minutes, all her lights except a single bright white stern light could be seen and she seemed to have come to a halt. By this time, all of the full size lifeboats, except Nos. 10 and 4 and Emergency Cutter 2 on the port side had been loaded and sent away. Some of them were slowly heading in the direction of the nearby white light. However, the boats were heavy and undermanned. Properly manned by young fit sailors, they would have made a good speed of a little over four knots. As it was, most made little over half or less than half that speed. Some, including No.5 commanded by Third Officer Pitman had decided to stay together and close to the ship.

Apart from three port side boats, all that remained to be filled and sent off were the Englehardt composite or collapsible boats. *Titanic* was supplied with four of these. They consisting of a standard wood planked lower hull and retractable canvas sides which had to be raised and secured before the boats were launched. Two were located, one each side of funnel No.1- on top of the bridge housing and the other two were located on the boat deck - one each side inboard of the Emergency Cutters. They could not be launched before the Cutters since the davits of the latter were used in the process of launching.

On the port side of the boat deck, they were loading lifeboat No.4. First Officer Murdoch had loaded and sent away lifeboat No.10 on the port side and had move back to the bridge where he and Sixth Officer Moody, with the help of others, were preparing the collapsible boats.

Boxhall and QM Rowe were still, vainly trying to draw the attention of the nearby vessel. The boat deck was empty of passengers. Most of them had retreated upward and aft as the ship sank down and away from them, by the head.

Captain Smith went to enclosed bridge and found Boxhall with his container of distress signals. The Captain had found that when they had almost completed loading Emergency Cutter 2 with women and children; there were but three men in the boat with them - not enough to handle her in the water.

"That'll do Mr, Boxhall. Stop doing what you are doing and get over to the port side cutter and go with them in that boat."

Boxhall protested. "But we still haven't managed to contact that ship sir, and we have plenty of signals left in the box."

"Never mind that" dismissed Smith. "It is obvious the blighter is asleep or ignoring us. Tell QM Rowe to stop what he is doing and get over and help them with the collapsibles on the other side."

"Very well sir. I'll go and tell him." conceded Boxahall." He immediately walked off thought the enclosed bridge to find QM Rowe. He found him on the starboard side and in the process of firing another socket signal.

"We are wasting our time, Rowe. Stop firing and signalling and give Mr Murdoch a hand with the Collapsibles. The Old Man has ordered me to go in number two."

Rowe was about to pull the detonator lanyard, he did so and *Titanic's* final pyrotechnic call for help shot skyward. As it did so, Boxhall made his way back to Cutter No.2.

As Boxhall passed through the now empty wheelhouse on his way back to the port side, he noticed a box on the deck beside the Flag Locker and recognised it as the box containing The White Star Line private signals. These were green-coloured pyrotechnic flares used to communicate between passing ships of the White Star fleet at night. Boxhall grabbed the box. He thought *I'll take these in the boat with me; they might just come in handy to keep everyone together and to attract the attention of rescuers.* Afterward, he continued toward the port side, being careful not to trip over a large wooden box containing the remaining unused socket signals which lay on the deck where Rowe had left it. *Titanic* had been supplied with two such boxes, one containing 12 projectiles and the other, 24 of them. - only seven had been used.

When he arrived back at Cutter No. 2, Boxhall found it already loaded and ready to lower. He recognised a sailor about to get into the boat and handed him the box of Company Signals. "Here, Lucas - chuck these in the boat and then follow them." Boxhall then clambered into the boat behind Lucas and made his way to the stern where he shipped the rudder. They were now fully loaded and ready to lower away.

The boat deck was now getting closer to the water; consequently, in a very short period of time, Cutter No.2 was afloat. The boat was released from her lowering blocks, and moving off from the ship's side. Within a few minutes, she was a hundred feet away from the sinking ship, which Boxhall deemed that to be a safe distance and ordered those rowing to rest on their oars. He looked toward the west - the white light seen from the deck was still there and stationary.

It occurred to him that if he could see it from where he was now, and it was, as he thought, the steamship's white stern light, then the other vessel could not be more than five or six miles away. *Why was he ignoring them?* His thoughts were invaded by the sound of someone shouting through a megaphone from the deck of the *Titanic:*

> *"Ahoy there, the Cutter, Make your way round to the starboard side gangway and heave-to for further orders."*

Boxhall immediately complied. However, he did so with less than enthusiasm. To get to the starboard side, the shortest way was around *Titanic's* stern which was now high out of the water. This meant rowing under her three giant propellers.

Meantime, Captain Smith had headed for the wireless Room.

He knew that the life of his great ship was coming to an end and that the end itself would be soon.

In the Wireless Room, Smith found both Operators still at their posts. The cabin lights were flickering and Phillips and Bride were wearing lifejackets but finding it almost impossible to remain at the desk due to the now, heavy port list and a deck which was also, steeply falling away toward the bow.

"Right lads! You've done enough, finish up and get yourselves to the boats - it's every man for himself now." With these few words he left and returned to the bridge.

* * *

Eventually, and to the relief of all on board, Cutter 2 was located about 200 feet of *Titanic's* starboard side. Once again, the rowers rested on their oars. To their dismay, they could clearly see by the line of disappearing porthole lights, that the great ship was now hurrying toward her final resting place.

There was an immediate concern in all minds for the possibility of suction pulling them with her.

Boxhall looked astern - there was no sign of the offending iceberg. He then noticed a bright star, high above the horizon to the northeast. Quickly, he and the other rowers brought the bow of the cutter around to point toward the star. Thereafter, they rowed with all strength toward it. Finally, when Boxhall reckoned they were about a quarter of a mile north east of the sinking ship, he stopped the boat and they lay on their oars and watched.

CHAPTER 16

FINALLY

Back on board *Titanic,* it was now obvious that the great ship did not have much life left in her. Her plating, fixtures and fittings were now groaning and complaining at the unplanned-for stresses being imposed upon them. The ship's hull from just forward of the main Engine Room right to the stern was suspended high in the unaccustomed element of the air. The parts of the hull where water met air; and on the uppermost deck, between funnels three and four; were being bent well beyond their strength capabilities - something had to give and soon.

The forward end of the boat deck was now relatively quiet, only a few passengers and crew remained there; everyone else was migrating upward, away from the threatening water and toward the airborne stern.

At the forward end of the boat deck, desperate men fought against the inevitable as they attempted to free the last two collapsible boats which were on top of the bridge housing.

On the starboard side, the Chief, First and Fifth Officer, assisted by crew members were attempting to free collapsible "A" on top of the Captain's quarter. On the port side, Second Officer, Lightoller, Lamp Trimmer Hemming and Junior Wireless Operator Bride, struggled with collapsible "B".

On both sides, they were being assisted by two or three seamen and a couple of male passengers.

Earlier, Junior Wireless Officer Bride and Senior Wireless Officer Phillips had climbed onto the top of the quarters, Phillips opted to retreat toward the stern but young Bride went to assist Lightoller.

By this time, the bow and fore deck were completely submerged and the sea was rapidly rising to swallow the bridge front. Soon it would reach the boat deck and make its way toward the stern. What had been urgent, suddenly became frantic.

The normal operation was to re-use the Emergency Cutter davits on each side to launch the collapsible boats. To do this, the collapsible boats, which were located on top of the bridge housing, on each side of Funnel N.1 had to first be freed from their locations then lowered carefully to the boat deck. However, the rapidly worsening situation concentrated minds - there was no time to be careful. The remaining lashings securing the port side collapsible 'B' were cut free and the boat was unceremoniously chucked down onto the boat deck, landing upside down close to the original location of Boxhall's Cutter No.2. Wireless Operator Bride climbed down to continue the preparation of the boat. Meanwhile, Lightoller and Hemmings had made their way around the funnel base to assist Murdoch and Moody in releasing starboard side collapsible 'A'.

On the starboard side, they rigged a couple of lifeboat oars to form make-shift ramps from the top of the housing to the boat deck, down which they were about to slide the collapsible. After getting the boat down, the next step was to move it to a position under the recently vacated lifeboat - lowering gear - the falls- originally used by Cutter No.1. However, this was no simple task. *Titanic* was now heavily listed to port which meant they would have to haul the heavy collapsible up-hill…up the sloping deck toward the ship's side then lift it over the bulwark and lower it down the sloping ship's side. To do this, they first overhauled the falls thought the blocks, thus lengthening them until they were able to reach and attach them to each end of the collapsible boat. They had just got them attached and were taking the weight of the boat on the falls, when it was realised that because of the port list, they would be unable to launch in the conventional way. Therefore, the idea was to load the boat where she was, release the falls and then she would float off fully loaded when the boat deck eventually went under.

They had no sooner done this than, without warning, the sea rose up over and around the bridge front, immediately flooding the boat deck and washing everyone who had recently boarded the Collapsible out of it and into the sea - everyone that is, except Steward Brown. The collapsible was still attached to the falls when it floated free; fortunately, Brown had a knife and managed to saw his way through the aft fall rope, thus releasing the stern of the boat. Unfortunately there was no one to release the bow fall rope; consequently the boat was being dragged under with Brown still in it. He jumped free and found himself in a mini whirlpool generated by the submerging boat and surrounded by desperate individuals clawing and grasping at each other.

On the port side Wireless Operator Bride was also washed off his feet and carried over the port side with upturned Collapsible into the sea. However, just before it did so, Bride saw Captain Smith dive over the ship's side.

Moments earlier, Lamp Trimmer Hemming, sensing that end was near, had looked over the starboard side but did not see anything so, like Wireless Operator Phillips earlier, decided to make his way aft, upward and along the port side.

Meanwhile, Bride found himself under the collapsible which had turned over. In claustophobic panic, he dived, down and out from under the upturned boat. There was no sign of the ship, all was dark. Fearing that he might be sucked down by the sinking ship, Bride struck out desperately, swimming as hard as he was able. Despite the cumbersome life jacket he had donned in the Wireless Room before leaving, he made progress out from the upturned Collapsible - only stopping when he felt he was far enough away from any danger of being sucked under.

Those who had remained on top of the housing on the starboard side attempting to launch the last Collapsible were caught unawares by the sudden inundation. Second Officer Lightoller found himself in the water and swimming toward the Crow's Nest. Suddenly, *Titanic* took another dive. This time, Lightoller was swept backward and up against the forward end of the funnel - over the open fiddley vent leading down to number six Boiler Room. As the invading sea poured down the opening, he was sucked down with it. He thought he was doomed. However, the invading water displaced the air left below. It formed a large bubble which exited the fiddley vent, taking Lightoller with it. The same freeing air, also freed Colonel Archibald Gracie, a first class passenger who had been in the vicinity, lending a hand to those who were working on the last boats. Both men found themselves in the water with the remainder of the ship suspended above them. At that moment, what was left of *Titanic* seemed to pause; as if pondering its next action. Suddenly, the over stressed parts of the ship failed. That part of the great ship which was out of the water was preparing to return to it. At the same time, the forward part which was mostly underwater, lurched to port and started to hinge downward. The forward funnel guys failed and funnel No.1 fell into the sea, mercifully ending the lives of the drowning people under it and displacing a mountainous wash of water which swept the upturned Collapsible, as well as Lightoller and those in its path, away from site of the sinking ship. At that moment, those in lifeboats heard a number of sharp reports, much like explosions. Some thought it was the boilers exploding.

Others thought that the boilers had defied gravity long enough and had broken away from their mountings in the boiler room.

However, those who had decided to get away from the advancing water and move upward toward the stern were very much aware of what had happened. Like a greenstick fracture, the strength members of *Titanic* had finally given up trying to defy gravity and maintain her longitudinal shape. Suddenly, they had failed on both sides, at the main deck level, below and between funnels three and four. The accommodation and decks above the first failure point at "C" Deck, parted vertically. The hull fracture - for that is what it was - propagated downward slowly, almost like a tantalisingly slow zipper until, finally the after part of the ship that had so recently been suspended high in the air, returned to the sea - settled snugly back onto it and became upright.

As this was happening, those who had sought refuge at the ship's stern witnessed funnel number four seeming to tilt toward them until it and they, were standing almost upright. By this time, the after well deck was clogged with a mass of desperate people of all ages and sexes who had not been able to board the lifeboats. Most were passengers wearing lifejackets, but many were crew members - among them, the valiant engineers who, to a man, had remained at their posts until it was no longer physically possible and had been ordered up out of the Engine Rooms and spaces which were now watery coffins.

When the ship lurched to port, those on the aft well deck were bundled in a seething, struggling mass to the low side of the deck, drifting like black snow against the port side bulwark which only delayed the inevitable.

Those who had climbed the companionways from the aft well deck up onto the Poop Deck, could see that the ship was breaking apart. At that moment, the lights were still burning and many at the stern were able to see that the forward part of the ship was now almost vertical and ready to make its final journey to the ocean floor. The only sounds to be heard were a strange moaning interspersed with little cries from those already in the water, mixed with a myriad splashes, as those who did not want to wait for the end, left the part that was still upright and afloat.

Suddenly! - the forward part lurched farther over to port - the lights briefly flickered -grew dull and then went out. At the same time another two explosive sounds were heard. Those who could see ahead, saw the forward part of the ship begin to descend into the sea - slowly at first then gaining momentum - moving downward as though with a purpose. In just over a minute, the ocean closed, door-like, over the waiting tomb of that part of the great ship with hardly a sound. For a few minutes more, it seemed to those who had sought refuge on the stern section that it would not follow the bow. Their hopes of such a miracle were quickly dashed. Like a child hanging on to its mother's skirts, the stern section tilted forward and down. The rudder and propellers clawed their way sky-ward until the flag staff which so recently had flown the blue ensign, now pointed to the New World, dry-land and safety. The surrounding water became turbulent with the splashed of the hundreds of people - men, women and children who were now jumping into the ocean to escape the assumed suction which must surely drag them down when the stern followed the bow as had always been the intention since the birth of the great ship. The air was full of the wails and cries of terrified, doomed people.

For a few minutes the stern section, like the bow section, hung vertically in the air, then the door of the watery tomb opened once again and the stern slid slowly at first, but at an ever increasing rate downward. In less than a minute it was gone and the ocean closed over the last remnants of what once was RMS Titanic - the biggest ship man had ever built. However, the sounds of despair did not die with the ship. These were now the only sounds to be heard, seemingly louder now on that otherwise still, calm, clear, dreadful star-lit morning.

CHAPTER 17

AS LUCK WOULD HAVE IT

As the drama unfolded, those who had been fortunate enough to secure a place on one of the lifeboats had been watching from nearby. Most of the boats were stopped less than a mile to the northward and around to the southwest of where *Titanic* lay dying. Initially, some had rowed toward the distant white light which was still visible in the west but eventually they too had stopped and had rested on their oars to watch.

When all the lights went out, many assumed that moment to be the moment when the ship had sunk. Among those who did so, was Third Officer Pitman who claimed that he consulted his watch and it showed a time of 2-20 am.

However, others in nearby lifeboats were close enough to see the silhouette of the ship against the background of the stars and they witnessed the moment when finally, the stern section disappeared. Among them was Stewardess Mrs Annie Robinson. She claimed that she consulted her watch and it showed a time of 1-40am.

Being a Day Worker on board the ship, Robinson had set her personal time piece back the required 47 minutes before she retired the previous evening. Consequently the unaltered time of final sinking was 2-27 am. This tells us that the stern section was probably visible for seven minutes after the forward section disappeared.

When *Titanic* hit the ice berg, she had a total of fourteen conventional Lifeboats, two Emergency Cutters and four Collapsible boats A, B, C and

D. When she eventually sank, she left all of her conventional lifeboats, both her cutters and three of her Collapsible boats - B, C and D - on the surface. All of these contributed to saving lives. Collapsible C went down with her parent.

One of the last persons to leave the ship was Coal Trimmer Patrick Dillon.

Previous to joining *Titanic,* Dillon had been an Able Seaman working on deck. This was his first trip as a member of the Engine Room crew known as "The Black Gang". As you will learn later, Dillon was extremely observant.

In much in the same way as did the hero in James Cameron's film, "TITANIC", Dillon also went down with the stern section. However, unlike Cameron's ill-fated hero; Dillon kicked and clawed his way back to the surface.

On reaching the surface, Dillon looked around and found he was surrounded by a seething, countless mass of desperate human beings, He decided to swim out from it. Eventually he saw the gleaming white side of a lifeboat, and made his way to it. It turned out to be Lifeboat No.4 commanded by Quartermaster Walter Perkis.

Dillon was pulled aboard, but his ordeal had taken its toll of him and he lost consciousness. However, he survived to tell the tale.

Dillon wasn't the only one to make it to that lifeboat, several more did so. These included Lamp Trimmer Hemmings, Engine Room Greasers Scott and White, Catering staff members Prentice, Cunningham, Seibert and Able seaman, Lyons. Unfortunately, the last two died shortly after being pulled from the sea.

Steward Ed Brown also had a lucky escape. When he was washed from the last collapsible, the one which went down with the ship, he found himself in a mini whirlpool. He was wearing a lifejacket so remained on the surface. However, Brown could not swim.

As noted earlier, fifty four year old First Class Passenger, Historian, Colonel Archibald Gracie had - like Second Officer Lightoller - been sucked down by the sinking ship. He used all his strength to swim to the surface and found himself among a crowed of dead and dying people. Desperately, he paddled his way to a large wooden structure which was among the wreckage and climbed onto it. He was not long there when he dimly made out what seemed to be an upturned boat with people standing on it. Leaving his first choice of safety, he struck out in that direction and found that it was, in fact, the upturned Collapsible boat D which had earlier been swept overboard with Wireless Operator Bride.

Soon he discovered that as well as Bride; Second Officer Lightoller and a dozen more had already found refuge on top of that same upturned boat.

Lightoller, Gracie and one of the others, a young passenger named Thayer all had a similar luck. When funnel number one had fallen, the wash of it had swept the three of them clear of the wreckage and close to the upturned Collapsible D.

After Gracie arrived, more survivors found the same upturned boat. Eventually no less than forty souls stood side by side on top of it. So many, that it submerged to where most of them had cold North Atlantic water up to their knees. Unfortunately that upturned boat also became the last resting place for a few of those who managed to swim to it. Among those who succumbed to the deadly cold was *Titanic's* heroic senior Wireless Operator, Jack Phillips.

CHAPTER 18

FOR THOSE IN PERIL

The stories of heroism and calm acceptance that night are legend - and there are far too many to mention in this short dissertation. However, the Officer of *Titanic* lived up to the reputation of the men who have served in the British Merchant Navy and deserve a mention here.

Unfortunately, too many armchair experts completely disregard this in their anxiety to condemn. To them I say: *When judging the actions of individuals, I suggest you all keep in mind the well known caution - "Judge not that ye be not be judged".*

Third Officer Pitman

Third Officer Pitman was in charge of Lifeboat 7. It was the second one to be sent away.

Pitman, like so many crew members and passengers during the first hour of that morning of April 15, 1912, did not believe for a moment that this monster of the ocean was going to sink. He and they, thought that the boats had been sent away with the most vulnerable passengers until the problem had been sorted, and that as soon as that happened, they would all return to the warmth and safety of the ship. This comforting belief was to be shattered in no uncertain way.

Shortly after Lifeboat 7 left the ship's side, there was a flash and a loud report from the bridge. A few seconds later, there was an ear-shattering explosion high overhead. Suddenly, in an instant, the stark reality of their dire situation was illuminated in a shower of bright white stars. Pitman instantly recognised it as the first distress signal - a signal that told him he would not be returning to the ship - they were calling for help! His training kicked-in. He knew that a potential rescuer would better be able to see a large collection of white boats on a wide expanse of ocean, rather than a single white speck. With that in mind, he decided to gather as many loaded lifeboats as possible as they soon were launched and clear of the ship's side and herd them together. Lifeboat 5 had been the first boat launched.

The distress signal stars had shown it to be nearby, so Pitman moved his Lifeboat 7 close to it and passed them a rope. Now lifeboats 7 and 5 were tied together not more than a few hundred yards from where the ship had sunk.

Fifth Officer Low.

Meanwhile, Fifth Office Lowe in lifeboat 14 had had a more productive time. His lifeboat 14 was one of four located at the after end of the port side boat deck. He loaded his boat with the maximum number allowable then warded off any more who would jump aboard the fully loaded boat by firing his pistol downward between the boat and the ship's side.

As soon as he was able to get his boat away from the ship's side Lowe towed undermanned lifeboat12 out to a safe distance of about 140 metres from the side of the sinking ship. Thereafter he rounded-up four loaded lifeboats and had them tie-up together with lifeboat 12 in a line, bow to stern - ordering those in charge of the lifeboats to step (raise) the masts and remain together. He next distributed all the survivors he had in his lifeboat among these four boats but retained six males to man his own Lifeboat 14. Thus, with an empty lifeboat except for five rowers and a lookout, he left the four loaded lifeboats and headed back among the dead and dying people in the water in an attempt to save as many as he could.

As soon as Lifeboat 14 arrived at the site of the sinking, it became impossible to row; there was no clear water between the lifeless bodies which covered the entire sea surface. There was little of what could reasonably called wreckage - certainly not what might be expected following the demise such a huge vessel.

Earlier, the air had been filled with the cries and moans of poor, desperate souls. Now there was complete silence except for the lapping of the water against the boat.

The first living person they found was an enormously over-weight man. They managed to haul him on board the boat, but despite every effort, he was too far gone and soon died. Shortly after that, they heard cries for help from the middle of the sea of dead and dying. They came from what looked like a praying man kneeling on a broken staircase. Normally they would have been beside him in minutes, but because of the close-packed people in lifejackets covering the sea surface, they had to pull themselves at a snails' rate through them, checking each body as they went.

Fortunately, they found two more living survivors and hauled them onto the lifeboat.

Eventually, after what seemed like an eternity, they were within oar's length of the 'praying' survivor on the staircase. They stretched out an oar to him; he held on to the end, and they hauled him back to the dry safety of the lifeboat over the heads of his former shipboard companions.

After a little time, the horrific truth had to be faced up to - they were not going to find any more survivors.

Lowe finally gave up the search and decided to head back to where he had left the three lifeboats and the loaded collapsible tied together. There was now an appreciable breeze blowing from the north, so he hoisted the boat's lugsail and sailed back to his little flotilla. As they cleared the wreckage area, they saw the lights of a steam ship away to the south east.

Arriving back at his little flotilla, Lowe became fearful that the steamer, which was now in plain sight, might not see them in the early dawn light and consequently, steam past and away. He knew that under sail, he could head the vessel off and warn them of the presence of all the survivors in boats. However, he was reluctant to leave the loaded, undermanned collapsible with his flotilla; therefore, he decided to take the collapsible boat in tow and headed southward.

The breeze was now brisk enough and boat 14 was making a good four or five knots. However, Lowe's harvesting of survivors was not finished.

On his way toward the approaching vessel, Lowe spotted Collapsible B. It was loaded with survivors and looked to be in dire straits so he altered course and headed toward it. As he got closer, he could see in the greying light that it was low in the water and sinking. He had only his crew and the four survivors from the wreck site on board, so he stopped alongside the sinking boat and took everyone off it. Then, with his own Lifeboat 14 now full once more, and with Collapsible in tow, he resumed sailing toward the approaching vessel.

Fourth Officer Boxhall.

Half a mile to the northeast of where *Titanic* had finally disappeared, Fourth Officer Boxhall, in Emergency Cutter 2, could see the dim lights carried by some, but not all of the ship's lifeboats. To attract as many of them as possible to his position he had started letting off his green, hand-held signals, this was shortly after *Titanic's* lights had gone out and he had presumed she had sunk. His hope was that those in the other lifeboats would see his signals and converge on them, and use them as a rallying point. After all, the bigger the target - the more likely it would be seen by potential rescuers.

He knew that other lifeboats boats had rowed toward the white light seen earlier on the port bow as the ship was sinking and that several of them were already well to the westward of the sinking position. In fact, the survivors were scattered over an area of about nine square miles.

From the very beginning, when Cutter 2 left the side of *Titanic,* Boxhall had helped with the rowing, he and the three men in the boat had each taken an oar and Boxhall had engaged the help of a lady passenger to operate the boat's tiller in accordance with his instructions. It cannot have escaped the attention of the reader, that although he was in charge of the boat, Boxhall had decided to share the rowing of the heavy boat with the male survivors.

After they had reached a position of safety, Boxhall exchanged places with the lady at the tiller, and positioned himself standing at the highest point in the stern of the boat. It was from there and from a hand extended skyward that he had started firing his green signals at regular intervals. Readers should keep in mind the importance of this act.

Initially, they could not see any sign of ice, but they were constantly aware of its presence. In the silence period between the hissing of the hand held pyrotechnic signals, those in the boat could hear the sound of the sea washing against ice…it was not too far away.

Almost an hour and a quarter after *Titanic* had gone down, Boxhall and the others heard the sound of a distant gun being fired. The sound came from behind them. When they looked in that direction, they saw above the horizon, what looked like a shower of stars falling seaward. It could be but one thing…a ship's rocket - perhaps they had seen his green flare?

The lower of these was slightly left of the higher one. This indicated to him that she was on a course that would take her to the northward of his location. He had a moment of panic. *Perhaps her lookouts had not seen his green signals? -Perhaps she would steam past them, oblivious of their presence?* He turned the boat round and pointed it to a spot to the left of steaming lights and ordered his rowers to row. Then he ignited another green signal - holding it as high as his outstretched arm would allow while praying that those on the other vessel would see it.

Boxhall's prayers were answered. Suddenly, the two white masthead lights beginning to line up vertically, one over the other. This told him that the vessel was now heading straight for his position. This was confirmed when he very clearly saw her red and green coloured side lights below and on each side of her vertically-aligned white steaming lights. She could have been no more than half an hour away. He headed directly for her.

Almost at the same time, the survivors in the other boats spotted the same potential rescuer. Those which were sufficiently manned with rowers, turned to row in the direction of their saviour. The sky was brightening in the east with the promise of yet another fine day. However, the northerly breeze was gaining strength, as though lending credence to the old sailing ship belief that "The wind rises with the sun."

It was a cold wind and one that made the sea conditions challenging for an experienced oarsman, let alone boats under-manned by a mixture of semi-skilled and rank, amateurs.

The joy and relief among all those cold, miserable anxious people can only be imagined.

The approaching rescue ship, - for without a doubt, that is what it was - got nearer and nearer until Boxhall and those with him in the boat began to wonder if she would run them down. Suddenly, he saw an iceberg between him and the approaching vessel. Her captain must have seen it at the same moment, because she turned sharply to their left and showed them her green sidelight.

Moments later, Boxhall saw that her white steaming lights were beginning to line-up vertically once again - she was turning back toward them. She steadied back on course, still showing her green sidelight. She was not heading straight for them now, but would pass to the southward - to leeward - of their location. However, she would pass very close to them. Boxhall thought; *if she doesn't stop and go astern soon, she will pass us and her wash will swamp us.*

He need not have worried; those on the approaching ship had seen them and had stopped their engines. Even then, she was still making too much speed and would have to go Full Astern on her engines.

As though reading Boxhall's mind, the rescue vessel slowed down rapidly. The thump-thump-thump of cavetating propellers running full astern could plainly be heard. Within a few minutes, her captain had brought his ship to a standstill with his bridge no more than a hundred feet to the south of Boxhall and his people. In front of them were the brightly lit decks of a passenger steamer, a haven of warmth, safety and compassion.

PART 3

CHAPTER 19

SS CALIFORNIAN -- 8 AM APRIL 14

PIC 6
SS Californian
National Archives

The SS Californian was owned by the Leyland Line and went into service in 1903. Her as-built service speed was 12 knots. She was what was known as a Passenger/Cargo vessel. This was because although her principal role was the carriage of cargo for profit, she also had accommodation for 57 fare-paying passengers. Her captain for the voyage was Stanley Lord.

Californian left the port of London on the 5th of April, 1912. She did not have fare-paying passengers aboard on that voyage but was fully loaded with cargo for the port of Boston, USA.

It was a fine morning; the wind was moderate and from the North West; there was a slight swell and a moderate sea running. *Californian* was ten days out from London, and had almost completer her transit of the long curving Southern Track from the south of England. Soon she would arrive at *The Corner* and would be pointed West, in the direction of her destination. We join her Captain Stanley Lord and his Chief Officer, George Stewart, on the port side bridge wing. The latter had just been relieved by the ship's 3rd Officer Charles Groves.

Captain Lord opened the conversation.

"Morning George! What kind of day have we got then?"

"No too bad now sir. I think the weather's clearing from the northwest. The barometer is high and still rising. I got a Pole Star latitude earlier, but there was too much cloud, so I didn't get a fix…but I've worked-up an approximate position and time for the turn."

"Aye, right-enough, George. I had a look at your 8 am dead reckoning position. So you think we'll be at *The Corner* by twenty to ten? What speed are you using?"

"11 knots, sir." Stewart replied.

Lord thought for a moment. "I doubt if we'll be making the full 11 knots George. I'd be totally surprised if we're not getting a bit of Gulf Steam pushing us backward. However, I may be wrong. So, as you say, twenty to ten it is." He added: "We'll get a longitude after breakfast but we'll find out for sure at Noon."

Stewart answered. "Yes, sir, that's right. If we keep up this speed we should be at the turning point about that time. However, it's clearing-up nicely and you should get a good longitude before you are due to turn."

Lord's reply had a tinge of doubt. "Do you think so, George? By the time we get things set up for a longitude, and calculate a result, we will have already turned, because I'm going to turn her onto the next course at twenty to ten as you have reckoned; we can adjust the course afterwards, if we have to." Lord added "The sky's clearing nicely and I'm sure we'll find out for sure at Noon sights."

The captain then went over to the other wing of the bridge and had a quick word with the Third officer. Thereafter, he and Stewart went below for a hot breakfast.

After breakfast, Lord joined his Second Officer Herbert Stone. 3rd Officer, Groves and the ship's only Deck Officer Apprentice James Gibson, on the port side of the bridge for the ritual of Morning Sights, which was standard practice aboard all British Merchant Navy vessels. From these, they would get an accurate longitude which would enable them to determine if the ship was east or west of where she was supposed to be. However, they would have to wait until Noon.

At that time, they would obtain a latitude which would determine exactly where they were, and they could adjust the ship's clock for accuracy.

By 9-30 am, the morning sights had been taken and each man found a corner of the bridge and began the long task of calculating the results. Meanwhile, despite nagging doubts concerning the speed, Lord, as indicated, decided to go with George Stewart's earlier estimated time for turning. Consequently, at exactly twenty to ten he ordered the Quartermaster to alter course to the right and pointed his ship due west. Shortly after that, the results of the morning sights were known.

It turned out that as Lord had anticipated the *Californian* was still too far to the east of where she was supposed to turn but her latitude was still unknown. The question now was - *was she north or south of where she should be?*

During the course of completed his sight calculations, 2nd Office Stone had established the error of the ship's Standard Compass. Consequently, shortly after the initial alteration of course, the ship's head was altered slightly to compensate for the new compass error.

At Noon, in time honoured ritual, the ship's officers including her Captain, gathered on the bridge once again. With their sextants, they calculated the ship's Noon position and found her to be five miles north of her intended track, and further east of where they thought she should be. Lord had been right about The Gulf Steam. He had turned his ship too soon...before she had reached the position of *The Corner!*

The Captain decided that he wanted to be on his originally planned track, so he gave orders for the course to be altered a degrees southward; thus gradually bringing *Californian* to where he wanted her to be - on the latitude line of 42° North. Once there, he would resume his planned course of due West, and follow that latitude line towards his destination.

Throughout the day, the wind backed into the north and slowly dropped away. At 4pm, Lord went onto the bridge to witness the change of Watch. George Stewart was in the act of relieving Second Officer Stone.

"A fine day indeed gentlemen! Let's hope it keeps clear for tonight"

"Certainly has been sir." Agreed Stewart.

Lord continued. "I was thinking this wind must have set her a bit south since we turned *The Corner*. But since it's been easing all the time, I think we'll wait until you obtain your evening star sights Mr. Stewart before we make any alterations to the course."

Stone made a suggestion.

"The sun is still high enough for a sight sir. Perhaps I could have a go at getting a longitude?"

"You do that Mr. Stone. Let me have your answers as soon as possible. We don't want you to spend any more time up here than you have to; do we now?" With that Captain Lord left the bridge.

By 5 pm, Stone had taken a sextant observation of the sun and worked-out the ship's longitude. He took his findings to Lord who examined the work carefully.

"Sixty miles since Noon lad? I don't think so. Something's wrong here. By your reckoning, the old Californian is making almost 12 knots on reduced coal consumption. I'm sure the Owners would love this to be true but I think you should have another go. Nip up and take another sight before the sun gets too low".

Stone flushed with embarrassment, *Bloody-hell I must have made an arithmetic error or young Gibson read the chronometer wrong.*

Closing the captain's door behind him, Stone headed rapidly for the bridge where he got out his sextant and took another sun sight - this time, with George Stewart checking the time. Within twenty minutes, he had worked out a new longitude and took it back to Lord's cabin.

"Sixty four miles since Noon? Now that sounds more like it. Still, the old girl is making over 11 knots. We can't complain. If Mr. Stewart gets a Pole Star latitude, we'll have a pretty good idea of where we are. Thank you Mr. Stone. Now you can get below and have a bit of a rest."

After Stone had left, Lord went back onto the bridge to have a word with his Chief Officer.

"Hello again George - I've just had young Stone's latest effort. Seems we are making close to 11.5 knots and that's us saving on coal! At this speed, we'll soon be up to the position of these three bergs mentioned in that ice warning we got from the *Parisian*. Better keep a sharp lookout!"

Earlier, Evans had received a message from the Leyland Liner *Parisian* advising of three icebergs in position 41 degree, 55 minutes North, 49 degrees, 14 minutes West. She was about 50 miles ahead of *Californian* and heading westward on the same track.

The air temperature began to fall as the sun tumbled toward the western horizon. Just after 6 o'clock and after everyone had finished the evening meal, three very large, icebergs were seen about 4 points on the port bow. They had found the ones in *Parisian's warning*.

There was still plenty of light causinf the floating mountains of ice to stand out starkly white against the background of the blue-grey surface of the smooth sea, while their west- facing sides were tinged orange by the setting sun.

Half the ship's company went on deck to see what was, for many of the younger members, their very first real-live iceberg. They would soon learn that these three would by no means be the last ones they would see!

At 6-30pm, the bergs were abeam and about 5 miles to the south of *Californian*.

Lord was able to work out a fairly good estimated position for his ship relative to the bergs and therefore for the bergs themselves. He noted the ship's estimated position, then went to the wireless room and ordered *Sparks* to transmit a warning message to the SS Antillian, another Leyland Line ship which was within wireless range:

> "MSG: To Captain, 'Antillian,' 6.30 p.m. apparent time, ship; latitude, 2.03' North; longitude, 49. 09' West.
>
> Three large bergs five miles to southward of us.
>
> Regards...Lord."

Privately, Lord thought...*thank God for wireless! Because of it, other ships within range and fitted with wireless will also be able to receive this warning.* His thoughts were vindicated.

Shortly after *Sparks* had sent the ice warning message, he received a call from the RMS Titanic. She was outward bound on her maiden voyage to New York.

Titanic's wireless operator called him to exchange positions and compare ship times. He also confirmed that he had heard Lord's ice warning to *Antillian*.

At 7-20 pm George Stewart made ready his trusty sextant. He lifted it carefully out its polished mahogany box then selected the long star telescope and screwed it into position on the instrument. The conditions were perfect for a sextant observation of *the Chief Officer' friend*, Polaris - the Pole Star.

Out on the starboard bridge wing, Stewart squinted through the sextant telescope at the horizon to the northward. It appeared as a dark, razor-sharp line upon which he was able to firmly place the small but perfectly reflected image of the Pole Star. Of all the celestial observations taken by a ship's navigator, that of the Pole Star was the simplest and easiest to resolve.

Consequently, a few minutes later, he had the calculation result.

Californian was firmly on the latitude line of 42 degrees 05 minutes North. It confirmed that the ship's latitude had not changed since Noon that day, which meant that the northerly wind had not had any effect on *Californian*. In fact, it seemed that there was a current setting the ship to the north and westward.

CHAPTER 20

A NEAR-MISS

Despite all its shortcomings, most captains in 1912 recognized the usefulness of wireless as a navigation-warning tool. Consequently, while in the Grand Banks area of the North Atlantic, during the spring and early summer, ships fitted with wireless would broadcast warnings of ice-sightings. Not only were such broadcasts useful in warning of ice, they could be used to warn ships about other floating dangers...abandoned vessels, floating wreckage and much more. As a matter of fact; by International agreement, wireless operators were obliged to warn their captains on hearing mention of such dangers.

Lord had never experienced sea-ice in the North Atlantic but he was no stranger to it. Having spent several years sailing in the Southern Hemisphere, he had seen it off Cape Horn, at the southernmost tip of South America. This had been before he got his first command so at that time, the worry had rested on other shoulders. However, this time, if anything went wrong, the blame would be entirely his.

Despite the fine weather, he had spent most of the time since dawn that day on the bridge of his ship. By early evening, he was getting weary but the thought of encountering ice banished any thoughts of rest from his mind.

He knew, and had been taught, that ice at sea might be found in many forms and shapes. The biggest pieces were the bergs. Some were huge, block-like monsters like those of the Antarctic Ocean which in some cases, extended beyond the horizon for over fifty miles. Others, like those of the

Arctic and North Atlantic were also big, but most had craggy mountainous peaks. Lord also knew that the ice bergs had off-spring - smaller versions of themselves.

Under normal circumstances, because of their size, icebergs were fairly easy to see, therefore there was usually plenty of time to avoid them. Even low-profile Growlers and pack- ice could be relied on to give a bit of warning by the presence of waves breaking over them and producing the tell-tale presence of phosphorescence as a bonus however these were not normal circumstances! There would not be a friendly moon to help with visibility and the sea had fallen flat calm so there would not be any wind-generated movement of the sea-surface. Even the ubiquitous North Atlantic swell had gone, so there would be no significant swell which, on breaking against floating ice, would give away its position to the watchful seafarer. Consequently, at dusk, as well as the usual look out in the Crows Nest, Lord had ordered extra vigilance in the shape of an additional lookout on the ship's bow.

Just after 8 pm when almost fully dark, he joined Third Officer Groves on the bridge keeping a lookout from the starboard side, while Groves watched out from the port side. Lord's caution paid off!

Shortly after 10 pm., after 4 bells had been sounded, Californian *was* quietly steaming across the now flat, oily-looking surface of the North Atlantic. The night was cold, sharp and clear. Without the aid of binoculars or a telescope, stars could be seen right down to the horizon it. In fact, without the stars, it was almost impossible to see where the sky ended and the sea began. It was a most peculiar night.

The only sound heard by those on duty on the darkened bridge or by the Lookout in the crow's nest was the muted thump – thump of ship's triple expansion engine buried deep within her cavernous innards. These were accompanied by the swish-thump of her self-generated bow wave as she cut her way through the cold April sea. Under normal circumstances, Lord would have been down in his warm, private quarters, perhaps reading or maybe even writing letters.

On at least two occasions, during the Watch, the lookout from his position high in the crows nest, had rung the warning bell to alert the officer on watch... mistaking a star low on the horizon for a ship's white mast head light.

At seventeen minutes past ten...before any of the other watchful eyes spotted it, Lord became aware a vast, thin, area of low-lying ghostly grey mist on the horizon, directly in the path of his ship. Until that moment, there had been not the slightest vestige of a mist. Instinct told him this was different -something a bit more substantial...an immediate danger to his ship! As always, his training kicked in. "Hard -a-port" he yelled

In 1912 this helm order had the opposite meaning to its present day meaning. It was a remnant from the days when the rudder was turned by a tiller arm. Thus when the tiller arm was turned to port- to the left, the rudder turned the bow to the right - to starboard.

The Quarter Master, who was almost half-asleep, nearly jumped out of his skin but reacted instantly. He spun the wheel expertly to the right. In less than five seconds, he had the steering wheel turned over as far as it would go to the right. "Hard-a-port she is sir!" he yelled. The ship's head responded immediately; swinging at ever-increasing speed to the right. He watched the dimly lit compass in font of him. The compass card was swinging; attempting to keep up with the bow and faithfully record the ever-changing direction in which the ship was pointing.

Captain Lord did not take time to acknowledge the Quartermaster's report because the mist had now taken on the very solid outline of floating ice. He was already at the engine telegraph and first rung-down STOP, immediately followed by the order - FULL ASTERN At the same time he shouted to the Quartermaster "Midship the helm".

The order was immediately obeyed and the steering wheel returned to a neutral position. "Helm's amid-ship sir". The ship's bow was now swinging rapidly to the right, away from the danger.

The engine order had two effects; it slowed the ship down rapidly and caused the stern to turn in the opposite direction from the bow. Thus, even without the help of the rudder, the ship's bow continued turning to the right; away from the immediate danger. This was a little trick Lord had learned when in training but had hoped never to have to use for real. His attention to study paid off! However, despite his quick action, the ship's bow entered the lighter elements of the floating ice.

During all this time, the ship vibrated with indignant outrage at having its smooth forward passage so rudely interrupted. Doors rattled, rigging clattered against masts and crockery shook in its racks down in the saloon. Lord had resumed his position on the starboard side of the bridge wing and was watching the sea in the vicinity of the ship's stern. He could see that there was no heavy ice anywhere near there that might cause damage to the ship's rudder or propeller. As he watched, the churning turbulence caused by the spinning propeller formed an ever-increasing white crescent of foam. As soon as the near edge of the crescent started to move toward him, The Captain knew the way was off his ship. She was stopped dead in the water. "Stop her!" he yelled.

Groves, who by this time was standing by the engine telegraph, immediately complied and rung the telegraph to stop the ship's engine. The engineers below responded and the noise of thumping engines and vibration died almost immediately. The silence could almost be felt!

Lord took a walk aft, along the boat deck on both sides and had a quick look at the sea in the immediately vicinity of his ship. She was almost surrounded by loose, light, ice. There was just enough starlight for him to see heavier stuff to the south and westward. It was about half a mile ahead and in the direction *Californian had* so previously been travelling. He could not see how far it stretched across his path, nor could he immediately see a way though it. They would not be going any further in the meantime. He returned to his bridge and joined the helmsman at his post behind the wheel and the steering compass.

"How's she heading now Quarter Master?"

"North East, sir." was the curt reply.

Lord mentally applied the compass error and then told Groves to enter both the compass and true headings into the scrap log. This consisted of a notebook not unlike a school jotter. However, it was not kept as a record. Each morning its contents were neatly copied in ink copied into the ship's Official Log Book, by Chief Officer Stewart, and thereafter the pages were truly "scrapped".

However, it was an improvement on earlier times when such information was noted on a blackboard in chalk and wiped at the end of each Watch.

After filling-in the Scrap Log, Groves returned to the upper bridge and rejoined his captain. The Watch would be maintained up there during the time the ship was stopped.

"Right!" concluded Lord. "You can stand down the lookout in the bows Mr. Groves, but keep the man in the Crows Nest to watch how the ice is behaving". Then, turning to the helmsman…"Very well, Quartermaster, that will do the wheel for the moment. Stand by in case you are needed."

Lord resumed briefing his Third Officer.

"I'll head down below now and work out our DR (approximate position) then have a word with the Chief Engineer. I don't know how long we're going to be lying here but I think it best we keep the engine and the Watch on standby." Indicating the solid ice edge in the distance he continued. "Keep a weather eye on that lot and for any bigger bergs like the ones we saw earlier that might come our way. Oh! and be sure to let me know if you see approaching lights". Inwardly he knew that if the ice moved, so would Californian *so* there was little or no danger there. "If anyone needs me, I'll be handy in the chart room or my day room. I may be lying down but will be fully dressed."

"Very good sir." acknowledged Groves.

Lord turned to leave the upper bridge…it was close to 10-35pm. He glanced over the starboard bow, to the eastward, in the direction from which they had come. For brief moment, he thought he saw a single white light right on the horizon and pointed it out to his young Third Officer. "In fact, there's a light coming along now."

Groves lifted his small, stubby night glasses and after a moment's search in the direction indicated, replied. "I think it's just a star low on the horizon, sir."

"You may well be right." agreed Lord. With that, he heaved a sigh of relief then turned and left the upper bridge. Little did he know then, that his relief would be short-lived. The meeting with that pack ice would haunt him for the rest of his life. He would know scant relief or peace of mind until his death some 48 years later.

CHAPTER 21

STOPPED FOR THE NIGHT

On leaving the bridge, the captain made his way down to the chart room where he had a look in the Scrap Log. He remembered that his Chief Officer had worked a pole Star Latitude just before 8 pm so he knew that the 8pm DR. end-of -Watch position noted in the log would be the nearest accurate one from which to calculate the present, stopped position. Consequently, he concluded that *Californian* was stopped at latitude 42degrees 05 minutes North, longitude 50 degrees, 07 minutes West.

Having established where his ship was, he then went aft to meet with his Chief Engineer and keep him in the picture.

He found Chief Mahon draped over the starboard rail outside his cabin, puffing away at a pipe full of foul smelling Thick-Black tobacco.

This was an odious mixture of leaf tobacco soaked in rum which was left to harden before being cut into little black curls and loaded into his pipe. It was a pleasure to be enjoyed by a hermit!

"Evening Chief! - All well down below?"

"It is now captain" the other replied in his thick Liverpool Irish accent.

"Gave our lads a bit of fright it did... that emergency movement of yours. I've never seen that Fourth Engineer of mine move so fast, I just happened to be down there when the telegraph woke them all up. Still, credit where credit's due, he did us proud and that's the truth!"

He certainly did Chief! Please give him my complements."

"So what's the problem, captain?" asked the Chief.

"That's it right there" Lord answered; pointing toward the heaviest concentration of ice, which could just be seen, about half a mile beyond the stern of the ship.

Thereafter, the two men leaned sociably, elbow to elbow over to the starboard rail, chatting about this and that. Lord was inwardly thankful that there was no wind and that the Chief's foul-smelling tobacco smoke was rising vertically. "I am of a mind to stay here until it starts to get light, Chief. I reckon that will be around four o'clock in the morning. However, I would be obliged if you will maintain steam pressure; just in case we have to move quickly."

"A wise decision I think captain. Better to be safe than sorry!" agreed the Chief.

They continued their conversation - among other things, discussing the implication of the uncalled for stop. The time was getting on for 10-45pm.

Suddenly, Lord was aware that his ship was not alone on this part of the ocean. Looking back to the eastward, in the direction they had come, he saw that he had not been mistaken earlier about seeing a distant light. There was indeed one there. While they had been talking, it had become more evident. There was no doubt that it belonged to an approaching ship travelling in the direction of the USA. He drew the Chief's attention to it.

"Here's a ship coming along Chief. I wonder who she is. Let's go and see if *Wireless* knows. She might have a wireless. If so, I'll get him to warn her of this ice."

The affectionate nickname given to Wireless Operators by other crew members on British ships back then was either *Sparks* or *Wireless* In this case the *Wireless* on *Californian* had been christened with the grand-sounding name of Cyril Furmstone Evans.

Captain and Chief Engineer made their way back up toward the wireless room. However, before they got there, they met Evans coming from the opposite direction.

"Good evening sir! I was actually on my way to see you. Do we have a problem?"

"Not with the ship, *Wireless*. In fact, I was on my way to see you for two reasons. The first is to tell you we have stopped because of all this floating ice, and the second is to get you to send a message, warning any ships that might be in area of this ice danger. Do you have any ships around?'

"The only ship I have heard tonight sir, is the new White Star liner, *Titanic,* and by the strength of her wireless signals, she's not too far away".

Lord pointed out the approaching ship's lights on the starboard side.

"Well this one coming along certainly cannot be *Titanic* -not nearly enough lights on her. I've seen *Olympic, Titanic's* sister ship. You just can't make a mistake about these big ships at night. They're all ablaze with lights...like Blackpool's Artificial Sunshine and all the way down to the waterline. No, I think this one coming along is more like ourselves; a humble *carrier of the sea and since you have not heard anyone but Titanic* we must assume she has no wireless, In any case, you had better let *Titanic* know our situation."

"I'll do that right away sir. Do I need our position?"

"I don't think that matters; *Titanic* will be almost 20 miles to the south of us, heading for New York."

Evans went back to his wireless room - lifted his earphones and listened. Immediately, he heard *Titanic,* communicating with the wireless station at Cape Race in Newfoundland.

Since he was much nearer to the great liner, he could block-out Newfoundland and interpose between the two stations. In the jargon of wireless operators this was called *jamming.* He decided to do this and sent the following:

MSG..... From: MWL, (Californian).To: MGY (Titanic)- 11-55pm time ship "Say old man, we are stopped -and -surrounded- by -pack ice.

The operator on *Titanic* was obviously unhappy that his communication with Cape Race had been so rudely interrupted. As soon as Sparks stopped transmitting, he responded with:

'shut-up...keep out'.

This was not meant as a rudeness. It was a phrase well known by operators, and simply meant *'stop interrupting me, I am busy.'*

Evans noted the time – it was 10-55 pm by the ship's clock.

The fact that there was no evidence that the *Titanic* operator had actually received the vital ice warning niggled at the young man's conscience. He decided to wait until *Titanic's* operator had finished with Cape Race and then call him again.

Half an hour later, *Titanic's* operator was still in communication with Cape Race. Evans was fed-up waiting; tiredness won the battle and he decided to go to bed. He was dog-tired and had been on duty more or less since 7 o'clock that morning. It was now 11-25 pm.

After leaving the wireless room, Lord had gone outside onto the saloon deck and watched the approaching vessel for a while. Eventually he was able to clearly see her green navigation light and reckoned she was no more than 5 or 6 miles away.

At 11-30pm she appeared to stop. However, the cold soon got to him and he went into the chart room and shut the louvered door. No doubt Groves would contact the other ship or come down and advise him of her arrival nearby. He could hear the sound of the Third Officer's footfalls overhead as he kept watch on the exposed upper bridge which was at the front end of the mid-ship accommodation. It was the highest part of the mid-ship superstructure and extended right across the ship from side to side above the wheelhouse.

The area was protected by wood bulwarks topped by portable canvas weather screens designed to give some protection from the wind. However it had no roof so when it rained, those up there got wet!

The deck area was clear except for an upper steering position and the Standard Compass Binnacle which stood like a sentinel at its centre.

CHAPTER 22

ALONG CAME ANOTHER STRANGER?

After Captain Lord had left the upper bridge, Groves, in time honoured fashion, had begun pacing back and forth across the upper bridge. As he walked, he hunched down inside the high collar of his bridge coat. The air was almost at freezing temperature due to the nearby ice. His breath was visible in a white cloud in front of his face. *Bloody freezing!* He thought. *God, this is boring!* Then his mind turned to the injustice and humiliation he felt when Captain Lord had demoted him from Second Officer to Third Officer at the beginning of the present voyage.

Herbert Stone, who was the current Second Officer had a First Mate Certificate which was a superior qualification the Second Mate's Certificate held by Groves, so in the time-honoured protocol, when Stone arrived on the scene, Groves had to step down to the rank below his current Certificate.

Before that particular ceiling had fallen in on his dreams, he had been making plans as to what he would do with the extra wages the promotion brought. His main idea was to buy some wireless equipment when he got back home. Like many young men of the day, he was very interested in wireless telegraphy. However, the equipment was pricey and way beyond the wages of a lowly Third Officer. Now, because of that miserable, stiff necked, arrogant bastard, Lord, he would have to put his dreams on hold until he passed his First Mate's Certificate. He thought *thank goodness for old Sparks – at least he'll let me muck around with his company gear until I can get some of my own.*

It should be noted, that the foregoing assessment of the feelings of Groves is not backed by evidence, but is made, based on past experience of similar situations.

Since they were normally of a similar ages, it was usual for the Third Officer and the Wireless Officer on a ship to be off-duty and go-ashore friends. Often, the Senior Apprentice of the ship was included in this clique. In fact, at 24, Groves was only four years older than Cyril Evans and James Gibson, the ship's one and only Navigation Apprentice, but that age difference simply enhanced his influence over the younger men.

At about 11-10pm, Groves thought he saw a white light way down on the horizon, a little to the west of due South. It looked to him to be about 10 or 12 miles away. At the time, *Californian* was pointing toward the Northeast and the light was in the direction of half way between *Californian's* starboard beam and her stern. This meant that those on the ship in question would only be able to see *Californian's* stern light, because her masthead lights and green side light would be invisible to them.

Groves raised his night glasses but could not be absolutely sure of what he was seeing. However, ten minutes later he confirmed it was indeed a ship showing two white masthead lights, the lower of which was to the left of the upper one. This told him she as a steam ship and was approaching *Californian* at an angle of about 45 degrees. He could not see her coloured sidelights. However, the fact that the lower of the two lights was to the left told him that if he had been able to do so, he would have seen a red sidelight and this newcomer would pass just ahead of Californian.

Remembering Lord's orders, Groves went down below to inform the captain of the situation. It was close to 11-30pm.

Groves knocked the louvered wheelhouse door and was immediately rewarded by an answer from within.

'Yes?'

'We have company, sir! There's vessel coming up on our starboard quarter; approaching us from the south-south-west."

"Thank you Mr. Groves, do you have any idea who or what she might be?'"

"Not really sir, she does seem to have rather a lot of lights and may well be a passenger ship but she is approaching at an angle so I can't be sure."

"How far of is she now?"

"I'd say about 8 miles but she was nearer 10 or 12 miles off when I first was aware of her."

"Very well! Call her up on the signal lamp and see what you can find out. Tell her about this ice. I'll be up in a minute or two."

Groves returned to the upper bridge and in a matter of seconds had got the Morse Lamp signalling key out from its box and plugged its wire lead into a nearby socket. He immediately began to tap-out the universal call-up signal in Morse code: AA - AA - AA - AA...

The signal lamp supplied to Californian was a particularly powerful one. On a clear night, it could be seen all round the horizon for well over 10 miles. It also had the undesired effect of floodlighting the bridge every time that it flashed; ruining the night vision of everyone there, as well as the lookout in the crow's nest.

For the next ten minutes, Groves kept flashing away at the other vessel. Alternatively calling the other ship then raising his night glasses to see if she was answering his signal. For a moment he was sure he could see a responding flicker of light from the bridge of the unknown vessel but this proved to be a false alarm. He concluded it must have been smoke from the other ship's funnel, momentarily obscuring a white masthead light thus creating the illusion of a flashing signal light.

At 11-40pm, ten minutes after he had reported her presence to the captain, the other ship seemed to stop and put out her lights. Despite this, Groves continued to try and contact her. Obviously she had been stopped by the ice.

He had just finished yet another round of call-up signals when he became aware of a presence by his side in the dark. Captain Lord had joined him.

"Any reply Mr Groves?"

"Nothing yet sir."

Lord raised his night glasses and almost immediately observed the same flickering light.

"Well she's replying to you now."

Groves had a look and immediately saw that it was the same flickering light he had seen earlier. 'I saw that myself sir but it is not Morse code... probably just a bad light; might even be an oil lantern, or funnel smoke passing her masthead light."

The Captain kept his glasses to his eyes.

"Doesn't look much like a passenger ship to me. More like ourselves; a lowly hard working cargo ship."

"But he did show a lot more light than that sir." Groves protested. "They must have switched most of them off when they stopped." Adding, "I reckon he's about five or six miles away now sir."

Lord thought to himself *if I saw her ten miles away and half an hour later she's still 5 or six miles away then she's a bloody slow passenger ship indeed!*

"Keep trying to contact him, anyway, Mr. Groves. Meantime, since we don't know when we will be getting away from here, and we are close to Longitude 50 degrees West, I have decided to set our clocks back to the Local mean Time which at Midnight will be 3-20 am GMT. That means we set the clocks back another ten minutes. You will get an extra five minutes on Watch, and Mr. Stone can have the other extra five minutes on *his* Watch after he gets here."

With that, Lord left the upper bridge and went below.

As soon as he had left the bridge, Groves looked at his Watch, it read 11-50 pm He set it back the full ten minutes until it read 11-40 pm. At the moment he did so, the Quartermaster standing by on the deck below sounded One Bell. This was the signal to tell all those who were awake, that the Watches would be changing in fifteen minutes - the time when Second Officer would be taking over the Watch.

Just before the change of Watches, Captain Lord was standing by the wheel house door on the starboard side of the bridge, looking across at the nearby ship through his binoculars. He could clearly see the other vessel's single white masthead light, her red port sidelight and two or three accommodation lights to the right of it. *Probably port holes and* accommodation *doors* he thought. He was sure she was no more than four miles away because he could also see her lights reflecting on the glassy surface of the sea. He considered what this young Third Officer had said about the other ship switching off her lights when she came to a halt and thought sarcastically *what rubbish! Oh yes! Her captain wanted to save electricity and coal so he had the stewards go round his ship telling passengers to switch off their cabin lights!*

His own limited experience of passengers on ships was that although public room lights were sometimes switched off late at night, those in cabins below main deck level soon learned that no one could peek in their port holes so they seldom bothered to switch off the light before leaving the cabin or moving from a state room to a bedroom. It did not occur to him at that time, that the ship he and Groves had been looking at carried two white masthead lights, but the one he was looking at had but one.

The captain's mind was thus occupied when a dark, shadowy figure materialised beside him. *Gracious! he thought - Is it that time already?*

"Ah Mr. Stone is that you I see?"

"Yes sir." replied the Second Officer, while stepping into the dim light coming from nearby chart room porthole. "I see we've met-up with that Ice they've been telling us about, sir."

"Exactly!" replied Lord. He then brought his officer up to date with the current situation. Pointing to the stranger just abaft the starboard beam he continued. "That fellow is about 4 or 5 miles away. He arrived there about half past eleven or shortly thereafter and has stopped, just like us. Mr Groves has tried to contact him by signal light but so far he has not had a reply. Keep a weather eye out for him. Let me know if he moves or drifts closer. Perhaps he might even find a way through that lot," he speculated... indicating the barrier of ice to the west, "and we can follow his track. Personally, I don't think we will move before daylight," he continued, "As you saw in the Night Order Book. I am to be called at daylight. Right now, I'm going to try and get some sleep. As I told Mr. Groves, I'll be on the Chart room settee if you need me. Have a good Watch. Good night." He finished the conversation by closing the wheelhouse door.

After his Captain had gone, Stone climbed the bulkhead ladder and joined Groves on the upper bridge.

"Good morning old boy. Sorry I'm a little late, got way-laid by the Old Man on the way up here'. As he finished speaking, it crossed his mind that the age old title of *Old Man* for a ship's captain did not seem to suite the man he was referring to. After all, there was only eleven years difference in ages between him and Lord.

Groves acknowledged the greeting andpointed out the nearby ship - gave a brief report, then added: "Not too late, old boy, the clocks have been put back ten minutes so you're just a mere five minutes overslept." The last was tinged with a modicum of sarcasm. He continued with his end-of-Watch report.

"Anyway, I still have not been able to contact her. I think everyone has switched off the lights and gone to sleep. She was bearing South by West when I first saw her and stopped bearing South-South-East. I haven't been watching her too closely. I really don't think she has moved any more since she stopped. Our bow is swinging slowly round to the right all the time. She'll soon be ahead of us if she doesn't move before then."

"I've been told to keep an eye on her." responded Stone; while at the same time checking the bearing over the standard compass. "She's still in about the same direction. I'll keep taking the bearing from time to time; just to make sure it doesn't change."

"Where's the Apprentice then?" asked Groves.

"Young Gibson is checking on the log and making us a cup of coffee. When he comes up, I'll let him have some signalling practice. Like us, the lads over there are probably in the throes of changing over Watches. Gibson can try and make contact a little later."

"Right then!" exclaimed Groves while rubbing his hands in anticipation. "It's coffee and a warm bunk for me. Enjoy yourself!" With these few remarks, he disappeared below.

On reaching the lower deck, Groves made his way to the Wireless Operator's shack where he found his friend Evans almost asleep in his bunk.

"Lazy bugger!" he greeted sarcastically. "One would think you had had a hard day. What a life you have! All this" he indicated with a wave of his arms, "as well as free food and pay! What do you think you're on? You're Daddy's Yacht?"

The other young man knew this was all said in jest. It was the usual banter he expected so took no offence whatsoever.

"Anyone around?" continued Groves.

Evans replied wearily "Earlier on I exchanged time rushes with the new White Star boat *Titanic* and the Old Man had me send him an ice warning. That was just before 11 o'clock.The cheeky bugger told me to shut up. He was working Cape Race at the time so I don't know if he got my message. I heard him again at 11-25. Then, he was *still* working Cape Race so I decided to turn-in. Other than that, the only other one I know about is the one stopped nearby!"

"Do you mind if I have a listen" asked Groves...indicating the ear phones Sparks normally wore like an extension to his head.

"Not at all old boy! Be my guest!"

Groves donned the phones and listened avidly. Apart from a constant hiss, there was nothing else to be heard. He continued listening for a few more minutes then removed the earphones. "Nothing doing. All is quiet! That ship stopped nearby must have turned in too, or she doesn't have the luxury of wireless. No point in me staying any longer and wasting good deck-head study time". His expression referred to lying on a bunk staring at the ceiling which on a ship was known as the deck-head.

"Remove yourself," urged Sparks, "and allow one of the ship's proper workers some well earned rest."

"Right then!" laughed his friend and did as he was bid.

A few feet above them on the upper bridge, Second Officer Stone kept watch while at the same time trying to contact the nearby vessel by signal light. His efforts continually failed to extract a response. Gibson would soon bring hot coffee.

CHAPTER 23

CONFUSING SIGNALS

About fifteen minutes after midnight, Apprentice Gibson brought two steaming cups of sweet coffee and joined Second Officer Stone on the upper bridge.

Grasping his hot mug in both hands, the twenty-year-old asked "Anything around sir?"

Stone pointed out the nearby ship. "Only that fellow over there. When you've had your coffee, see if you can get him to answer the signal light. The gear is already rigged and ready for use. Mr. Groves and I have both tried to get him but have had no luck! It's your turn to get some practice."

"Any idea what kind of ship she is sir?"

"Going by his lights, I'd say she's perhaps a small tramp with two, perhaps three masts."

Gibson changed the subject.

"We have a problem with the log gear sir. We must have lost the rotator and a chunk of log-line when we made the emergency stop for the ice".

"Yes I know about that. It's a damn pest! The captain has already told me about it. Never mind; after you have a go at signalling and finished your coffee, you can go below and get some new gear ready for putting out once we are underway again." adding…"After you call the Chief Officer at one bell - you can make it ready for streaming the minute we are underway again and clear of the ice."

As with the *Titanic*, the log gear he was referring to be a long rope, which was trailed behind the ship when she was underway. The outboard end had a spinning device (rotator) attached to it. The inboard end terminated at a clock-like unit on the ship's rail. This recorded how far the ship had travelled.

Normally, if the ship stopped the rope and rotator would be brought on board to be re-deployed when she started moving again. However, when Gibson had gone to pull the rope inboard, he found that about 75 percent of it, together with the spinning device was missing. It had probably been caught up in the reversing propeller when the ship went astern.

Instead of waiting until he had finished his coffee before signalling, Gibson decided to combine the tasks. However, having tried without success to contact the other ship, Gibson finally finished his coffee then returned below to carry out his search for replacement log gear. The time was twenty-five past midnight.

After Gibson had gone, Stone continued to try and contact the other ship

The upper bridge was equipped with a speaking tube twhich led down to the chart room and wheelhouse. These were copper pipes about 40 mm in diameter which had a brass trumpet shaped mouthpiece at each end. A whistle was plugged into each trumpet aperture.

By removing the whistle and blowing into the tube at one end, the whistle at the other end would sound; telling anyone nearby that conversation was required.

At about twenty-five minutes to one, the whistle on the tube from the Chart room sounded shrilly. Stone answered immediately - it was the captain.

"Yes sir?"

Lord's tired voice echoed up the tube.

"Anything new to report Mr. Stone?"

"No sir. I've been watching the other ship and taking regular bearings of her. Gibson and I have been trying to make contact with our signalling light but we have had no luck so far. At one point, Gibson thought she was replying but as before, it was just her masthead light flickering. I think it may just be smoke from her funnel swirling around the light, sir."

"Thank you Mr. Stone. I'll be here if you need me." Lord replaced the whistle and went back to his settee.

At quarter to one - ten minutes after his conversation with the captain -Stone glimpsed a flash in the sky in the direction of the nearby vessel. By the time he focused his binoculars it was gone. He thought *probably a shooting star.* On such a night there had been and would still be, plenty of them.

Three or four minutes later, he was again looking with his glasses in the direction of the nearby ship when he saw what looked like a rocket burst just above her deck. In fact, it was not much higher than her masthead light. The burst looked to be little white stars. However, He did not see a flash of the detonation nor a rocket trail on the ship's deck. Nor did he hear any sound. In fact, it was so low relative to the other ship's masthead light that it looked as if it had come from far beyond her. He had never seen anything like it and was therefore ignorant of what he was seeing so he went over to the voice pipe and blew down it to the captain's room.

Within a very short space of time, Lord answered.

"What is it Mr. Stone?"- His part irritation and part-apprehensive tone indicated his regret at having been awakened so abruptly.

"Sorry to disturb you sir, but you did say I was to let you know of any changes in the circumstances."

"So what's happening?"

"That nearby ship seems to have just fired a rocket. I thought he had fired one earlier but it was just a flash in the sky and nothing after it. This time I definitely saw a rocket. It burst and threw out stars but I didn't hear any sound or a bang."

Lord was fully awake. "A rocket you say? What colours were in these stars?"

"None that I can see sir, they all seem to be white but they're quite a way off. In fact, they seem to be well beyond that other ship."

"How do you figure that?"

'Well, they only seem to be as high as her steaming light sir.'

"Might they be Company signals?"

"I don't know sir" Stone's answer carried doubt. "They don't look like any I've ever seen before."

"Very well Mr. Stone. Try calling him up again and see if you can find out what's going on. Wireless did not hear anything from him earlier so he probably does not have the apparatus. If you get an answer, send young Gibson down and tell me what they say."

"Will do! Sir."

The time was getting on for 1am.

After replacing the whistle in the end of the speaking tube, Stone resumed trying to contact the nearby vessel. The moment he started to do so, he saw another rocket. This was followed by two more. He also had the feeling that during that time, the other vessel had started to move.

From the moment *Californian* had stopped, he and Groves had been taking continuous compass bearings of her, on the universally accepted principal that if the compass direction between two stationary vessels did not change then neither of these vessels was moving to the left or right of the original direction between them.

However, in this instance, the principal was additionally tested, because from the time since she had stopped, *Californian's* bow had been swinging very slowly, at about a degree a minute toward the right - thus the bearing of the other vessel relative to *Californian's* bow was continuously changing, i.e., the angle between her starboard bow and the nearby vessel was decreasing - a situation which gave the impression that the other vessel was moving from right to left - to the eastward.

However, when Stone took a compass bearing of the nearby vessel just after the first, positive, rocket sighting, he noticed that the bearing in compass degrees - not relative to the direction of *Californian's* bow - had changed. Instead of the original bearing of SSE - 146 degrees, the reading was now 144 degrees. The nearby vessel was truly starting to move ever-so-slightly to the left - toward the eastward. As she did so, Stone saw another rocket in the same direction as the others.

Minutes later, Gibson was standing at his side so he brought the Apprentice up to date with the situation - telling him about the flash and four rockets he had seen and about the conversation with the captain and ending with: "Right then! We'll take turns signalling and watching with the glasses and see if we can find out what those fellows are up to."

For the next fifteen or so minutes the two young men signalled continuously and watched for the slightest response from the other ship. They got none. However, during that time, her bearing continued to change and they saw another three rocket bursts.

Gibson was sure he saw a detonation flash on the other ship's deck as the first of the three were fired; it was in the direction of about 2 points - twenty two and a half degrees on *Californian's* starboard bow. From the very beginning, the nearby vessel had been on *Californian's* starboard side - she still was.

About five minutes later, another rocket was seen - this time, the nearby vessel was only a point - eleven and a quarter degrees on the starboard bow of the *Californian*. Gibson thought the nearby vessel's lights looked peculiar - *funny*, as he put it. The red side light appeared to be higher than before. Making it seem that the nearby vessel had a heavy starboard list. He thought the other vessel looked a bit peculiar and told Stone. "Look at her now sir. Her lights look funny. Looks as if she has one high side and one low side."

Stone raised his binoculars and watched for a while. 'I think you're seeing the reflection of her lights on the water Gibson. Tends to distort things a bit'.

A few minutes later Stone observed that the nearby ship seemed to be turning away from them. He could tell this by the set of her navigation lights. Her White masthead light had all but disappeared and her red side light had vanished. It looked as if the other vessel was turning away toward the south. He immediately went to the compass and took yet another bearing. He discovered that the bearing of the other vessel had indeed appreciably changed to the left.

Shortly after, they saw another rocket - the last of seven. It was seen about a point - 11 and a quarter degrees - on *Californian's* port bow.

As the two of them watched, the bearing of the other vessel continued to change at an ever-increasing rate - in the opposite direction - toward the west. This told them that the other ship had most definitely started to move. She was underway and picking up speed and moving from left to right - drawing away from them, and most decidedly in a south westerly direction To Stone, her course seemed a bit erratic.

While their erstwhile neighbour was leaving them, they speculated as to the reason for the rocket signals.

None of the two of them had ever seen such signals before, but they agreed that the signals were certainly not being sent up without a reason.

Anyway, the other vessel was now almost out of sight. She had obviously pushed her way through any pack ice that might have been there, and was slowly becoming a fading memory in their minds.

Lord had specifically requested to be informed by Gibson if and when, contact was made with the other ship. This had not transpired. It occurred to Stone that the *old man* would not be too pleased to be awakened just to be told that the other ship had steamed away. After all - that's what ships did all the time.

Just after 2 pm, Stone had another niggle from his conscience. *Perhaps he should just let the old man know about the disappearing vessel anyway?* Consequently, he ordered Gibson to go down and knock on the chart room door and give Lord an update of the situation.

Arriving at the louvered door of the chart-room, Gibson knocked on it gingerly. He got no reply. He knocked again, this time with a little more weight to his knuckles. He was sure that this second knock had brought a response from the man inside.

He carefully turned the door handle, opened the door and stood in the entrance.

"Sorry to disturb you sir" he apologised quietly. "Mr Stone told me to tell you that that other vessel has now disappeared toward the southwest. She fired-off a total of eight signals. We have swung round and are now heading West South West."

From the direction of the chart-room settee came a mumbling reply which to Gibson sounded like "what time is it"?

Gibson replied quietly "Five past two sir!"

There was silence for almost a minute then the Captain continued in a voice thick with sleep.

"Were there any coloured signals amongst the ones you saw?"

"No sir" replied Gibson. "All of them were white."

"OK lad! -Thank you". Then, in a dismissive tone...

"Shut the door when you go".

Gibson returned to the upper bridge.

He found Stone crouched over the standard compass and taking a bearing of something though his binoculars. He could not see what Stone was looking at but obviously it was very far away.

In fact, Stone could still just make out the white stern light of the vanishing vessel and had continued to observe it after Gibson had left to report to the captain.

Finally, at around 2-20m pm, Stone straightened and announce that he could no longer see any sign of the mystery vessel. Apart from the light ice that now surrounded them, there was not another object or light in sight - they now had that bit of ocean entirely themselves.

Since the nearby vessel had not replied to their signals and the captain had been kept up-to- date, Stone saw no rush to wake him again. However, 20 minutes later, his conscience bothered him yet again. He went over to the voice pipe and blew down it. Les that a minute later, he was rewarded by the sleep-drugged, impatient voice of Captain Lord asking "What now?"

Stone once again confirmed the disappearance of the vessel under observation. Once again, Lord acknowledged receipt of the news.

Thereafter, the midnight to 4am Watch continued without further event until about 3-30am. At that time, Gibson thought he saw a flash of light on the port beam...away down on the southern horizon. He immediately told the Stone about it.

"Are you sure?" asked Stone.

"Absolutely! In fact, there's another one, almost in the same place."

Sure enough, Stone saw this second flash - this time through binoculars.

He observed that it was right on the sharp line of the horizon, and in such a position that if it had been any farther away they should not have seen it at all. In fact, it was so low that it could easily have been missed if Gibson had not drawn his attention to it.

Stone checked the compass. *Californian* was heading about WSW. These recent flashes on the horizon were in the same general direction as was the nearby ship before she has sailed off toward the south-westward. He decided to call the captain and up-date him yet again.

As he was on the voice tube updating Captain Lord, One bell was sounded - there was 15 minutes left until the end of the Watch at 4 am. He therefore sent Gibson aft to make sure the Patent Log was ready fro streaming and to call the Chief Officer George Stewart. Meantime, he, Stone, got ready to hand over the Watch. He did not see any more flashes.

CHAPTER 24

CALIFORNIAN TO THE RESCUE

Just before 4am, George Stewart arrived on the bridge. He greeted his subordinate in the tone of someone who had enjoyed a good night's sleep.

"Good morning Mr Stone."

To Stone, who by this time was thinking very much about his warm bunk, his relief sounded far too much awake for his liking. Never the less he was very glad to see the man.

"Good morning sir! I trust you slept well?"

"Always do! Like a baby in fact. Comes from having an untroubled mind". Stewart continued…"I see we have stopped for ice. - Young Gibson told me about it when he called me at one bell". Then he pointed to the grey mass of ice ahead of them."I suppose the captain will be waiting for sunrise before attempting to go through that lot."

There was a greyness in the early morning sky which had the effect of improving visibility. Dawn was a not-too-far-off, promise - Stewart continued talking to Stone.

"I take it you had an uneventful Watch?"

"I wouldn't say that" answered Stone. He then explained in detail about the white rockets he had seen earlier.

"Do you think they were distress rockets?" asked Stewart

"No! They did not go very high…barely the height of the other ship's masthead light. Apart from that, I did not hear the bang these things are supposed to make nor did they leave a trail in the sky."

Stewart was curious. "She was firing off white rockets and steaming away? What on earth would she do that for?"

"I was puzzled about that my self, Sir. There seems no explanation I can think of. In any case, she's gone now."

While the Second Officer had been talking, his superior was scanning the horizon with his binoculars. As he swept the horizon to the south, the lights of another ship came into view. She was showing two white masthead lights and her green side light, meaning she was heading in the same direction as *Californian*. There was a great deal of ice between the two ships but the other ship seemed to be stopped. He pointed her out to the Stone.

"There's your mystery ship! Seems to me to be OK now."

Stone looked where Stewart was pointing. The other ship was a little abaft port beam and almost due South.

"It's the first time I've seen that one. She wasn't there twenty minutes ago. There weren't any ships in that direction at half past three this morning. If she had been, there, we'd have seen her when we were watching those last three flashes on the southern horizon. No, I'm pretty sure she's not the ship I saw last night. Besides, that one has two white masthead lights; the one last night had only a single masthead light."

Stewart inwardly considered the possibilities, and then dismissed them from his mind. The two men completed the handover formalities then Stone went below.

Thirty minutes after Stone and Gibson left for their well earned rest, it was light enough to see the ice barrier confronting the ship. It stretched from right ahead, to the north-northwest and abaft the beam to the south-southeast, in both directions and as far as the eye could see. *Californian* *had* swung round a full 180 degrees and was back heading in the direction she had been travelling in before she stopped the previous evening. Ahead, less than half a mile away, the ice formed a low, solid barrier, rising to a few feet above the surface.

Several large begs were locked within the arms of the pack ice to the southward of *Californian*.

Stewart heard a polite cough behind him - Captain Lord had arrived on the bridge.

"Good morning George, it promises to be a fine day. What do you think of this little lot?"

Pointing to the ice, he continued. "What's your idea on the situation? Do you think I should try and push my way through the heavier stuff? Or do you think we should head along this eastern side until we find the end of it and go around it?"

Stewart thought about it for a moment then gave his opinion.

"It looks a bit thick ahead of us sir, but you can see that it is not too wide - can't be more than a couple of miles at most. Perhaps if we wait until the sun is up, I can join the lookout in the Crow's Nest and get a better idea if there are any thin bits we can push our way through?"

Lord thought about that suggestion. While he was doing so, Stewart decided to broach the subject of the rockets seen during the Midnight to 4 am Watch, and to find out if Lord knew about them.

"The Second Officer was telling me he saw rockets during his Watch, sir."

The captain confirmed that he *had* been informed "Yes, George. He was telling me about it just before you came on Watch. Is there anyone else around?" Stewart drew his attention to the vessel stopped to the southward adding: "Given that rockets were seen down there, do you think we should go down and see if they are all right?"

Lord raised his binoculars and studied the vessel for a moment or two. "He seems to be Ok now George. However, go and call young *Sparks* and get him to give a general call to see if there is anyone in trouble. In the meantime, I'll get underway it is almost full daylight now and we can see our way ahead without any problems."

As the Chief Officer left the bridge, heading for the wireless room, he heard the shrill sound of the engine telegraphs. Before he arrived at his destination, the tell-tale thump-thump sounds of *Californian's* triple expansion steam engine told everyone that it was awaking from its temporary rest.

The time was close to 5-15 am.

When *Californian* was built, she did not have cabin space dedicated to the use of wireless - very few vessels had that luxury at the time. Consequently, when she eventually modernised to include wireless in her equipment, existing accommodation had to be rearranged for that purpose. This resulted in a reduction in the spacious Captain's accommodation.

Arriving at the wireless accommodation, Stewart unceremoniously knocked and opened the sleeping cabin door. Evans immediately sat bolt upright in his bunk - eyes like saucers as he recognised his unexpected visitor. "Good morning sir, is there something wrong?"

"Not that I know of *Sparks*, grinned Stewart. That's why I am calling you. There has been a ship sending up rockets during the night and there is one stopped to the south of us. The *Old Man* wants you to fire up that contraption of yours and find out if there is indeed something wrong with her or anyone else, for that matter."

Evans immediately jumped off his bunk, donned trousers and slippers and made his way to the Operator's Desk. He fired up his equipment and began sending the general call signal to all ships followed by *Californian's* unique three letter identification signal... CQ-CQ-CQ...MGY. The call sign of all ships equipped with Marconi wireless equipment began with the letter 'M'. Translated, it meant 'All ships-CALLING ALL SHIPS - *Californian* calling.'

In less than five minutes, a reply was received from the Canadian Pacific vessel RMS Mount Temple - call sign MLQ. Followed almost immediately thereafter by the German vessel SS Frankfurt - DTF. Both Operators advised Evans that the *Titanic* had struck ice and was sinking. *Mount Temple* also gave *Titanic's* position as being 42 degrees, forty six minutes North - 50 degrees, fourteen minutes West. The time was then getting on for 5-40 am.

Sparks wrote the coordinates on a piece of scrap paper and gave it to Chief Officer Stewart who immediately made his way back to the bridge and made a verbal report to Captain Lord while at the same time, handing him the note containing *Titanic's* coordinates.

When Stewart arrived on the bridge. Lord stopped his engines, and; after insuring it was safe to do so, he and Stewart made there way to the Chart Room where Lord calculated the course and distance from where he reckoned *Californian* was at that moment, to the *Titanic* distress position. The results showed that the distress position given was south, sixteen degrees West and 17 miles away from where *Californian* was then stopped.

While Stewart had been at the Wireless Room, the captain had taken his ship southward along the eastern side of the heavier ice barrier in an attempt to find a way through to the west. It had occurred to him that since the ship seen earlier by Stone had managed to get through, there had to be such way to the south.

Lord was about to start his engines and proceed in that direction when his thoughts went into confused overdrive.

> *During the night, Second Officer Stone and Apprentice Gibson had seen their rockets, low on the horizon in a south-easterly direction. However, this position given for where Titanic was sinking was in the direction of almost South-south west - an entirely different direction altogether. Something did not fit.* He plotted the two positions again. *Either Stone, or Grove and Gibson had got their compass directions wrong or the distress position being transmitted was wrong.*

It also occurred to Lord that the messages containing these position were of a general nature and not specific to him. He needed corroboration of the distress position being transmitted.

After pointing this out to his Chief Officer, the two of them quickly made their way back to the Wireless Room.

Back in the Wireless Room, Captain Lord instructed Evans to call another Leyland Line vessel, the SS Virginian - MGN, which he knew was in the area. *Virginian* responded almost immediately. Her captain replied that he too had received the same distress position coordinates and that he had been told that *Titanic* was sinking and that they were loading the lifeboats.

That was the confirmation that Lord needed. After confirming his intentions to the *Virginian*, he and Stewart returned to the upper bridge and Lord took over the Watch. Thereafter, he started his engines and proceeded ahead - *Californian* was underway again, and this time, on what everyone on board her believed was a rescue mission. But first they had to cross the ice barrier.

CHAPTER 25

HAS ANYONE SEEN *TITANIC?*

It was 6 am - the sun was now above the horizon, visibility was perfect. Captain Lord was on the bridge with his first Officer George Stewart and the two men were looking for a way through the ice barrier on their quest to rescue the survivors from the sinking *Titanic*. The course to steer from where they were to the last known position of the sinking ship was South 16 West and the engines were on Dead Slow Ahead and Lord was determined to try and maintain that course, The daylight had shown that the ice barrier was little more than a couple of miles wide.

Almost imperceptibly at first, *Californian* eased her way forward; soon, she was pushing her bow into the thick stuff. Lord expected resistance, but was surprised to see the edge of the ice tilt upward on either bow, and slide sideways on top of the pack. It looked to him, no thicker than five or six feet - a couple of metres. As he watched with satisfaction, he was aware of someone at his elbow, turning; he found his Wireless Operator with a piece of paper in his hand.

"Yes *Wireless* - what can I do for you?"

"I have just been in touch with a Russian ship sir, the SS Birma, sir. He tells me he is heading toward *Titanic* as well, and wants to know where we are. He says he has about twenty miles to go."

Lord made a quick mental assessment.

"Tell him we will have about fifteen miles to go when we get clear of this lot, which I hope will be very shortly."

"Will do sir". With these few words, Evans returned to his cubby hole and his earphones.

About five minutes after Sparks left the bridge, Lord noticed a decided pick-up in ship speed and the western edge of the ice barrier was about a ship's length ahead. He had been crossing it diagonally and it had taken almost half an hour. A few minutes later *Californian* broke clear of the heavy stuff. Lord rang FULL AHEAD on the engine then phoned the engine room.

"Give her all she's got Chief, that's us clear of the ice." Almost immediately he heard the tempo of the engine rising sharply - soon the bow was flinging slabs of ice left and right - out of the way. The time was 6-30 am. Lord turned to his Chief Officer. "Right George! It's time to call all hands."

At 6-40 am, barely an hour and a half after he had turned in, Second Officer Stone was awakened by the Chief Officer and given the news about *Titanic*. Following this, George Stewart called Third Officer Groves and Apprentice Gibson.

By 6-45 am, the ship was a-buzz with the news. All hands had been called and were now making their separate ways to the Galley and mess rooms for a quick cup of something hot before mustering at their stations. The deck crew would head for the boat deck and prepare the boats under the supervision of the Chief and Second Officers while the Third Officer and Apprentice would be required on the bridge.

Just before 7 am, Groves and Gibson arrived on the bridge. As they did so the Lookout in the Crow's Nest sounded two bells which indicated a sighting on the port bow. Captain Lord lifted his binoculars and saw two ships about three points on the bow - one had four masts and the other had only two. They were about seven or eight miles away and a little apart. The smaller of the two seemed to be right up against the western edge of the ice barrier. Lord altered course for a point between the two of them. As he did so his mind was in turmoil once again - stirred by a myriad of unanswered questions.

This barrier stretches way far south of the distress position, did Titanic plough her way through it? If so, where the heck has she gone to? My God! Surely she hasn't gone down already? Then other thoughts nagged at the back of his mind. *What if Second Officer Stone did see Titanic's distress signals? If he did, why did they stop firing them between one o' clock and 2 o'clock and then start firing them again an hour later? What if the position we are heading for is on the wrong side of the ice?*

The foregoing would have to remain unanswered for the time being, his ship was fast-approaching the two ships reported earlier.

It was now 7-15 am; young Evans appeared once more at Lord's elbow. "Excuse me sir, I am in contact with the Canadian Pacific passenger ship *Mount Temple*, and by the strength of her signal she too seems to be very close. Her Operator tells me that they are at the last position given by *Titanic*."

Lord had been studying the vessel on his port bow through the binoculars. "Thanks, *Wireless*. My guess is that the fellow on our starboard bow is indeed that very vessel."

A few minutes later, his guess was confirmed. Groves, who had been studying the vessels on the port and starboard bows through his binoculars, confirmed that he could now see the name of the vessel on the starboard bow. It was indeed the *Mount Temple*. She was either stopped or heading slowly northward, and *Californian* would pass about a mile to the eastward of her.

As Groves looked at her, he noticed another vessel way beyond her - to the west, and right on the horizon. He noted that it had a pink funnel and reported the fact to the captain.

Lord had a look - it immediately occurred to him that it might be one of his own Company's ships, and sent the bridge messenger to the Wireless room with a note to the Operator - requesting that he try and find out the ship's identity. Thereafter, he returned his attention to the vessel on the port bow.

It was much smaller and was stopped, hard-up against the barrier. He could not identify her. All he could see was that she had a black funnel with a device on it.

At 7-30 am, Groves was proved correct and *Californian* passed a mile to the eastward of the *Mount Temple*. However, there was still no sign of the *Titanic*.

At about the same time, Evans was in contact with the Cunard Line passenger vessel *Carpathia*. During the exchange, *Carpathia's* Operator revealed that they were engaged in recovering survivors from *Titanic*. Evans immediately passed the news to Captain Lord.

When Lord received the information concerning the activities of the *Carpathia,* he immediately guessed that his doubts regarding the true position of the disaster were correct, and that in all probability, the rockets seen by Stone and Gibson *were* from the sinking *Titanic.* He went down to the chartroom and plotted the likely position and the current estimated position of the *Californian.* If his calculations were correct, then *Carpathia* should be in sight across the ice barrier in the direction of south east. He went back to the upper bridge. Raising his binoculars he scanned the sea to the south east on the far side of the ice. Sure enough, he spied a passenger vessel with a red funnel and four masts about eight or nine miles away. He had found the true disaster sight.

Californian continued down the western side of the ice barrier which at that point stretched north and south as far as the eye could see. Lord was looking for a way through to get to *Carpathia* and render any necessary assistance.

At about 7-45 am, *Carpathia* was abeam to port on the far side of the ice. Through binoculars, they could all now see that she had several lifeboats along her starboard side and that her flags were flying at half mast. However, there still did not seem to be any way to get through the ice to her side.

Just before 8am, Captain Lord was beginning to despair that he would ever find a way through. His ship had passed to the southward of *Carpathia and she* was now a couple of points abaft *Californian's* port beam.

Suddenly, what appeared to be a thin fissure interspersed with little ice floes was spotted. Lord immediately ordered the helm hard-a-starboard and *Californian's* bow swung rapidly to the left and was steadied pointing directly at the *Carpathia.*

Thereafter; Lord proceeded to push his ship through the ice toward the other ship.

Half an hour later, *Californian* passed across *Carpathia's* bows. As she did so, Lord set his engine at Full Astern and ordered the helm hard -a-starboard - in the same way as he had done a mere ten hours earlier.

The result was that *Californian* came to a halt about 200 yards to windward of the other ship's starboard beam.

As he had noted earlier; Lord could see a few empty lifeboats moored by their painters to *Carpathia's* sides. Now, that the distance between the two ships could be measured in metres rather than miles, he could also clearly see, floating in the water around these boats, what looked like wood planks, cushions and wooden deck chairs interspersed with a few life jackets. It immediately struck him that the amount of visible floating wreckage bore no easy connection to the sinking of the biggest ship in the world. He thought; *looks more like an old fishing boat had sunk here.*

Meanwhile, Groves had been studying the nearby vessel through his binoculars. Immediately he saw that she was flying a single code flag. It was dark blue divided horizontally by a broad white stripe - the International Code flag signal letter 'J', which meant *I wish to communicate with you by semaphore.*

Groves reported this to Captain Lord, who immediately wondered why *Carpathia's* captain should wish to use such a method of communication when he knew *Californian* was equipped with wireless.

Never the less, Lord ordered the answering pennant and the signal flag 'J' to be hoisted to indicate compliance.

Carpathia's first question to *Californian* was to ask if they had rescued any survivors. To which, the answer was an emphatic 'No'.

Then *Carapthia* advised *Californian* that *Titanic* had hit an ice berg at midnight and had sunk at 3 am. Also that she had recovered a total of 19 of *Titanic's* lifeboats and that one was missing. He also advised that he had rescued 700 passengers and was returning to either Halifax or New York with them.

Captain Lord then asked if he could assist by searching for any further survivors down wind to the east and southward. *Carpathia's* Captain Rostron concurred.

At 9 am, *Carpathia* commenced to steam away from the location and headed southward to circumnavigate the ice barrier before making for her chosen port. Her departure point was marked by a few pathetic remains that marked the grave of *Titanic* - an upturned Collapsible lifeboat, some deck chairs, a few cushions and a mass of floating cork.

After *Carpathia* had departed, Captain Lord put his engine on Full Ahead once again. His height of eye in the upper bridge was about 55 feet and the height of eye in the Crows Nest was near to 70 feet, consequently he planned to survey a circular area of ocean, down wind to the southward corresponding to his maximum range of visibility which, in this case would be ten nautical miles. The sea was still relatively calm therefore an object carried southward by the wind since about 3-30am might just be visible through binoculars at maximum range.

By 10-40 am, *Californian* had completed her search and returned to the spot where she had left two hours earlier - *Titanic's* grave-markers.

Despite the number of straining eyes in use, they had not sighted any more survivors or wreckage.

In fact there wasn't any sign whatsoever of the recent disaster. Consequently, Captain Lord decided to call off the search and resume the voyage to Boston. However, first of all, he had to find his way back through the ice barrier.

The southern extent of his search area had brought him to the end of the ice barrier, consequently, he decided to first sail southward then turn westward and negotiate the ice barrier at the first weak part he found

At 11-20 pm, *Californian* was turned due West and began pushing her way through the ice barrier. At 12 Noon, they were able to obtain an accurate position which placed *Californian* at Latitude 41 degree, 33 minutes north, Longitude 50 degrees, 9 minutes West.

About ten minutes later, the saw the German vessel SS Frankfurt passing astern of them. She had come from the North West - from the direction of the incorrect distress position. The last they saw of her was when she showed them her stern and steamed through the ice barrier, back in the direction they had recently come from.

After leaving the scene of the disaster, *Californian's* crew were consumed by gossip concerning recent happenings. The mess room consensus was that their captain had seen the distress signals sent up by the sinking *Titanic*, and had ignored them. The main source of this dreadful accusation was an engine room greaser by the name of Ernest Gill who claimed he too had seen the distress signals when he couldn't sleep and had gone up on deck for a smoke. Unfortunately, as is on all ships, the gossip ran from stem to stern, gaining indignation on the way. Our American cousins term this phenomenon "Scuttle-butt".

It did not take long for the stories to reach the ears of the captain. He knew full-well that a formal Wreck Commissioner's Inquiry would be convened into the disaster and that since *Californian* had been involved in the search for survivors, he and members of his crew would be called as witnesses. Consequently, on the morning of April 18th, three days later and the day before they were due in Boston, Captain Lord summoned Second Officer Stone and Apprentice Gibson to his cabin.

"Right gentlemen, I have no doubt that the recent events will result in a formal Wreck Commissioners Inquiry when we get back home and since *Californian* was involved, you can bet your sea-boots that some of us will be called to attend as witnesses. With this in mind, I have jotted down a few notes to assist my memory. I want both of you to sit down quietly somewhere and write me a report. I know a lot of unusual things have happened during the last few days, but I want each of you to try and remember the events that took place during your Watch on deck that morning - from the time you went on Watch at Midnight on the fourteenth until four in the morning at the end of the Middle Watch, when Mr Stewart took over. I don't want you to collaborate over this, just write it down as you remember it then sign and date it." (See Appendix for transcripts)

The remainder of the voyage to Boston was uneventful. They were once again delayed for a few hours due to fog, but that was to be expected in that part of the ocean in spring.

Finally, in the early hours of April 19, *Californian* arrived at the Boston Pilot station. Within a short space of time, she was safely alongside her berth within the port. However, although that part of the voyage had ended, Captain Lord's nightmare was about to begin.

CHAPTER 26

BOSTON - THE NIGHTMARE BEGINS

Once *Californian* had been securely tied alongside her berth, the cargo derricks were topped, the hatch covers removed and the process of discharging the cargo began.

At 8 am, Captain Lord's Steward announced that the Company shore Manager and Port Officials were aboard and waiting for him. He quickly washed, shaved and donned a newly laundered white shirt, and within a very short time, had joined the visitors in the unoccupied Passenger's Saloon.

After the formalities and the visitors had gone, the captain sat down to breakfast with his officers. There was a strange quietness around the table - not the usual first day in port chatter and excitement stirred by the promise of shore leave. In fact, every meal time had been like this since the ship left the disaster area and resumed the voyage. Lord could not put his finger on it, but all would become clear to him in a very short space of time.

The ship's Agent had brought the morning papers with him and Lord decided to read them with his after-breakfast coffee. The word *TITANIC* jumped out of all the front pages. He learned that the US Senate had decided that a formal Inquiry into the disaster was to be held on this side of the Atlantic, and that the first hearings of that Inquiry were being held in New York that very day.

This puzzled Lord. *Titanic* had been a British registered and owned vessel on the high seas at the time of the disaster. The American connection had been a financial one. So how was it legal to have a formal Inquiry into an accident to a foreign vessel in International waters? Why was this being allowed by the British Board of Trade - the organisation under who's Rules, *Titanic* was sailing at the time she was lost?

The next morning, Saturday, 20th April, Captain Lord awoke feeling fresh and invigorated. He washed, dressed and made his way to the saloon for breakfast. After breakfast he commenced reading the morning papers. These were full of the first day's Inquiry into the *Titanic* disaster. Immediately, the name *Californian* stood out.

On Day One of the US Inquiry, the Chairman of the White Star Line, the captain of the RMS Carpathia, the Chairman of the Marconi Company, two officers and a steward of the *Titanic* had been interviewed. When being questioned, Captain Rostron of the *Carpathia* mentioned seeing three vessels on the morning of the disaster, one of which was the Leyland Liner SS Californian.

As soon as he saw this, Lord knew there was a chance he would be summoned as a witness. Hardly had the thought passed though his mind, before his steward advised him that there was a group of newspaper reporters at the gangway wishing to interview him.

Lord had earlier discussed such a possibility with his Shore Manager and his superior had cautioned him to be careful concerning the amount of information he should give out. Consequently, with this in mind, Lord gave permission for the press to board.

Captain Lord played with his questioners - answering their questions in a negative way and when asked information concerning ship's position, declared jokingly that these were "State Secrets". However, unbeknown to him, two other members of his crew were not keeping any secrets, State or otherwise.

Assistant Donkeyman-Greaser Ernest Gill had been approached by journalist of the *Boston American* newspaper with a promise of $500 for his story. Since that amount was more than an entire year's pay, Gill jumped at the chance. The story he related was damning to Lord and his Officers.

Gill was not alone in his condemnations.

The ship's Carpenter named McGregor had a sister living in the town of Clinton which was about 30 miles east of Boston. On arrival at Boston, McGregor had been granted a few days shore leave to go and visit his family. While there, he had been talking about the *Titanic* disaster and the part played by his ship in the rescue attempts. He also passed on ship scuttlebutt which among other things suggested that Captain Lord and his Officers had seen *Titanic's* distress signals and had totally ignored them, suggesting they had been complacent in the needless loss of life.

His Bother-in-law, in a sense of outrage, went with the story to the local Clinton Newspaper, *The Clinton Daily Item.*

The Editor of the Clinton Daily - true to his craft, saw $ signs in neon and had the story syndicated. Thus the story of Captain Lord's alleged ignominy spread before him like a contagion, gaining scab-like add-ons as it went.

Two days later, on the late afternoon of Thursday, April 25, the Gangway Quartermaster reported the arrival of a US Marshall requiring to see the captain. The Marshall had with him a subpoena issued by the US Senate Inquiry Chairman, requiring the attendance of Captain Lord at a Senate Inquiry meeting to be held at the US Capital of Washington DC the following day, April 26, 1912.

However, Lord could not simply up-sticks and leave his command, he had to get a clearance from his Shore Manager, consequently he and the Marshal went ashore to find a public telephone and call the man in question.

They soon found one and permission for Lord to leave his ship in charge of his Chief Officer was obtained. Thereafter, Lord made his way to the railroad station and boarded the night train for Washington DC. Two other members of *Californian's* crew boarded the same train, heading for the same destination - Cyril Furmstone Evans aka "Wireless" and Assistant Donkeyman-Greaser Ernest Gill.

PART 4

CHAPTER 27

THE SS MOUNT TEMPLE-MIDNIGHT APRIL 14

PIC 7
SS Mount Temple
National Archives.

While this tale is essentially about three captains, there was, as we have seen, yet another positively identified vessel whose captain answered *Titanic's* cry for help, that morning and since the evidence of her Captain and Wireless Operator as crucial to the outcome of the Inquiries, This is her story.

The *Mount Temple* was an Immigrant ship built in 1901, and had a service speed of 12 knots. At the time of the disaster she was owned by the Canadian Pacific Company. Her captain for the voyage was James Moore...a Liverpool man and veteran of 32 years.

The ship had left the Belgian port of Antwerp on April 3, and was bound for the port of St, John New Brunswick in Canada.

Besides cargo for that port, she also carried emigrants to the New World.

Late in the evening of April 14, 1912, her wireless operator heard *Titanic's* distress signal and consequently, she was turned her toward the distress position.

Since evidence from her Captain and Wireless Operator figure prominently in this tale, I ask you to join me aboard her at around midnight on April 14, 1912.

James Durrant, *Mount Temple's* sole Marconi Wireless Operator sat at his desk. He had his earphones clamped to his head and was vaguely listening to the hiss and crackle of atmospherics. He was contemplating packing up and going to bed. Suddenly! the hisses took shape in the form of the Morse letters CQD - the International call for help - he immediately knew that a ship was in trouble.

This was followed by the ship recognition letters MGY *(Titanic),* and the word "ice". He looked at his wall clock which kept Eastern Standard - New York time - it read 10-17 pm. He could hardly believe his ears.

As he listened, he heard the call sign of a German vessel who's Operator had apparently heard the same call and was trying to contact *Titanic.*

Switching to 'transmit', Durrant immediately replied to the stricken vessel. However, although *Titanic's* Operator could hear Durrant calling, he, told the latter that his signals could not be read. Never the less, the *Titanic* Operator gave Durrant a distress position.

Durrant had been writing the information as it was being transmitted. When the transmission ended, he saw that he had written:

> *"Titanic sends C. Q. D. Requires assistance. Position 41° 44'*
> *north, longitude 50° 24' west Come at once. Iceberg."*

He remained unconvinced as to the accuracy of what he just heard, so to cover his rear, he added a note to the bottom of the message: "Can't hear me." Then, with this information, Durrant headed for *Mount Temple's* bridge where he handed it to the Second Officer who was Officer of The Watch. The latter, passed it to the Captain's Steward with the order to deliver it into the captain's hands - to make sure he was awake and read it.

The Steward arrived at the captain's cabin and firmly knocked on the door. He immediately received a loud reply from within. Captain James Moore had finished reading, switched off the bunk light and was drifting off to sleep. The assault on hid door brought him fully alert. "Enter" he yelled, while at the same time, switching on his bed-head light and looked at his clock. It showed the time of 12-30 pm.

The door opened to reveal the Captain's Steward, known among the ship's Complement as the *Old Man's Tiger*.

"Yes steward? Moore, demanded…adding: "I hope this is worth it."

Inwardly, the steward, who did not know the contents of the folded note, hoped the same, and simply replied: "This message came from *Sparks*, sir". Then the man stood back as Moore opened and read the note.

Without making any comment, Moore threw back the bedcovers and sat up on his bed. He then reached for the bridge communication tube and blew on it. It was answered by the bridge Messenger. "Get me the Second Officer".

As he waited, Moore donned his dressing gown, mentally estimated an approximate position for his ship and quickly did a mental calculation. This gave him an idea where *Mount Temple* was, relative to the distress position being sent-out. As he finished, the 2nd Officer answered.

"I presume you have seen this message about the *Titanic* Mister?" Come down and meet me in my chart room and we'll check this position."

The Second Officer confirmed that he was aware of *Titanic's* predicament, and was not surprised when Moore added: "and before you do so, if all is clear, bring her head round to North East, Mister, I'll get dressed and join you immediately.

When he returned to the wireless room, after delivering the first message to the bridge, Wireless Officer Durrant tuned-in once more.

Titanic was still transmitting her distress call. However this time, her transmission was much clearer and he noted that the distress position had been changed and that it now read Latitude 41 degrees, 46 minutes North, longitude 50 degrees, fourteen minutes West. He immediately wrote down the amended position and headed once more for the bridge.

When Durrant arrived on the bridge he was redirected to the captain's chart room. There he found Moore and his Second Officer. On receipt of the update, Moore plotted the new, amended position.

Originally, Moore had calculated that *Titanic* was 39 miles away in the direction of northeast, but this new position was south of, and 7.5 miles east of, the first one so he adjusted his ship's course to east-north-east.

Shortly after he had adjusted the course of the *Mount Temple*, Captain Moore saw the lights of another vessel on his port bow. From the way its direction was changing, he knew it was heading across his bow- from left to right, and would pass safely ahead of his ship. It seemed to be moving toward the south and eastward.

About 2 ½ hours after she turned toward the sinking *Titanic, Mount Temple* began to meet light ice. Suddenly! - a green light was seen a little on the starboard bow - to the right of the direction in which *Mount Temple* was heading.

Captain Moore adjusted his direction a little more to the left, his idea being to make sure the vessels passed at a safe distance. However, rather than this happening, the other vessel seemed to be getting closer, so Moore ordered a hard left rudder and rang full astern on his engines, thus stopping the *Mount Temple* and swing her bow to the left. As soon as this happened the green light vanished.

After that, the engines were put on slow ahead. However, fifteen minutes later, the ice was so closely packed that Captain Moore stopped his engines and thereafter crept forward at slow speed.

At 4 pm, *Mount Temple* met an impenetrable barrier of pack ice and Captain Moore decided to stay where he was until full day light - already the sky was brightening in the east.

Just after 4-30 am, Moore was able to get a clear picture of his surroundings.

He discovered that his ship was bow-on to a vast barrier of pack ice which stretched north and south as far as the eye could see.

To his south, he could see a smallish cargo ship with two masts and a single funnel; she too was against the ice barrier.

There was no sign of the *Titanic* or any other vessel remotely resembling her. He scanned the ocean in the direction from which he had come. The sea in that direction was also empty and desolate. He thought: *Where the hell is the Titanic? Had she gone down? No! Not here, she hadn't. There as no sign of wreckage or lifeboats or any other indication that the biggest ship in the world had been anywhere near this spot. So where was she?*

Moore decided that it was highly unlikely that *Titanic* had even got as far as his present position and would most certainly not have been able to easily get through the ice barrier in front of him. Consequently, he conclude that she must still be somewhere to the eastward. He therefore rang standby on his engines and shortly after, backed *Mount Temple* out of the pack ice and headed southward along the western edge of the ice barrier to try and find a way through to the other side. The ship time was 5-06 am on the morning of April 15 at New York.

As *Mount Temple* headed southward, she passed the smaller vessel which Moore had earlier seen stopped there. Shortly after she did so, the smaller vessel's captain followed her as Captain Moore sought a way through the barrier to the eastward.

Less than an hour after he had started heading south, Moore's lookouts reported more ice right ahead. Raising his binoculars, Moore could see that once again, it was stretching across his horizon and trending toward the south west. He decided to turn back north and try and find another way through to the eastern side of the barrier.

Just as he turned north again, Moore spotted a large, four-masted vessel about 8 or 9 miles away on the far side of the ice barrier, she seemed to be stopped. The sun was now above the horizon, bathing the sea in bright dazzling light. The weather was holding up and the sky was still cloudless.

A few minutes later, *Mount Temple's* Second Officer, reported that he had obtained a good observation of the rising sun and had ascertained that *Mount Temple* was running northward on the longitude of 50-09'West.

As *Mount Temple* headed northward, the Lookout rang his warning bell three times, indicating that he had sighted something ahead. Captain Moore raised his binoculars and scanned the horizon in the direction indicated. Sure enough, he could see a column of thick black smoke, and under it a medium sized four master with a single funnel and she was heading strait for *the Mount Temple* with a fine white bone across her bow. This told he that the approaching vessel was making full speed and soon they would meet.

Meantime, *Mount Temple's* wireless man Durrant, had had his ears blasted by a call from a vessel which, by the strength of her signal, was very close. It was the SS Californian and her operator wanted to know the position of the ship ahead of his ship. Durrant was not surprised, because he had been in contact with the *Californian* earlier and had advised her operator about the *Titanic*. He had also overheard *Californian* in conversation with the Russian vessel *Birma* and another vessel name *Parisian*. He looked at the wall clock which kept Eastern Standard - New York time, it read 5-20 am - they had been running two hours since they backed out of the ice. It was now shortly after 7 am on the ship's clock.

Shortly after, that the *Californian* passed a mile away to east of the *Mount Temple* which by this time had stopped. Captain Moore was able to read her name on her starboard bow as the other ship charged southward.

Half an hour after she passed the *Mount Temple*, Captain Moore saw *Californian* suddenly turn hard left and go through the ice in the direction of the four master he had seen earlier.

CHAPTER 28

CAPTAIN MOORE'S TALE

The story of the *Mount Temple* and her involvement in the *Titanic* disaster is a strange one, and is full of inconsistencies - even accusations of outright falsehoods.

In his evidence, the captain of the *Mount Temple* stated that he had received the early warnings of ice on his intended course -the 42nd parallel of longitude. And down as far as 42°-25'North Consequently, as a matter of caution; instead of heading west along that latitude after he reached *The Corner*, he decided to head farther south and west to the 50th meridian of longitude, thus giving the ice a wide berth. He stated that he crossed that longitude in either 41°-15' North or 41°-20'North, depending on what version you believe, and thereafter headed toward his destination in Canada.

When asked where his ship was at half past Midnight, when he received *Titanic's* distress signal, he first said she was at longitude 51-44'West and then amended that to longitude 51-14 West. In fact, a plot of his movements shows that *Mount Temple* was closer to 50°-54'West and much nearer to the distress position than he claimed.

To be kind to the man, It could be suggested that he was mixing-up the 'minute' parts of the distress positions co-ordinates - Boxhall's was 50-14'West and Smith's being 41-44'North. History can be his judge.

However, it cannot be ignored that one of Cxaptain Moore's passengers - a Canadian named Dr. Quitzrau -signed an affidavit declaring under oath that

> *"About 3 o'clock New York time, 2 o'clock ship's time, the was sighted by some of the officers and crew; that as soon as the was seen all lights on the Mount Temple were put out and the engines stopped and the boat lay dead for about two hours; that as soon as day broke the engines were started and they circled the position, the officers insisting that this be done, although the captain had given orders that the boat proceed on its journey*

In addition; the Third Officer of the *Mount Temple* noted protest concerning the same thing.

Although it is not possible to verify the foregoing, there is, as they say -' no smoke without fire'.

Captain Moore also told his questioners that he had a total of 49 miles to run from his 12-30 am position to the distress position. However this is totally absurd. Because the reader will remember that Moore said he ran his ship at Full Speed until around 3 -25 am., when he had to stop his engines and run them at Full Astern to avoid another vessel.

It follows that since *Mount Temple* was an eleven (11) knot ship, she could not have covered much more than 33 miles before he had to drastically slow down.

Moore tells us that thereafter, he crept forward slowly until he had to stop when he reached the ice barrier. In other words - *Mount Temple* moved ahead at a very slow speed until she could go no farther because of the ice barrier

To re-cap: *Mount Temple* was an 11 knot ship which ran in a constant direction for a total of 4 hours. For the first three hours, she ran at full speed, and virtually crawled ahead for the final hour. Consequently, it is likely that she covered no more than 38 miles on her rescue run, despite the claims of her captain.

Since the evidence tells us where she was at both 6 am and where she stopped at 7-30 am that morning of April 15, 1912, we are able to re-construct her movements from around 8-30 pm on April 14, when she crossed the 50th Meridian and headed for her destination until she was passed by the *Californian* at 7-30 am the following morning.

In the US Captain Moore said he crossed the 50th at 50-15'N, whereas in the UK he said he crossed it at 50-20'North.

The broken line shows the track claimed by her captain, whereas the solid lines are the track indicated by the evidence.

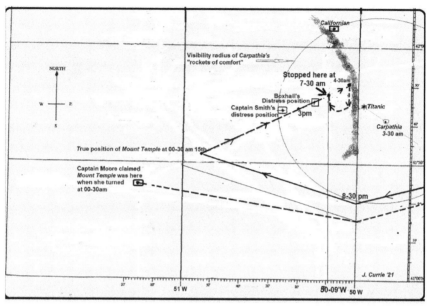

J. Currie

PART 5

CHAPTER 29

THE RESCUE

Having drawn the picture of events during April 14 and the morning of April 15- and before I start dissecting the evidence from each ship, I will take you back to that moment when Captain Rostron first became aware of the extent of the disaster.

After breaking the news to Captain Rostron, *Titanic's* Fourth Officer Boxhall and the survivors in Emergency Cutter No.2 were taken into *Carpathia's* passenger accommodation where they received comfort and attention. Meantime, the lifeboats carrying the remaining survivors were converging on their rescuers. Those to the northward and westward of *Carpathia* were helped by the wind. For those who had pursued the mystery light seen as *Titanic* was sinking, it was a hindrance which prolonged their moment of relief and it would be a considerable time before *Carpathia* would be able to rescue them all. The second boat to arrive at *Carpathia* was lifeboat number 14 commanded by *Titanic's* fifth Officer Lowe. Earlier, Rostron had seen her under sail, towing another boat. Once again, the process of transferring survivors was carried out with efficiency and compassion by *Carpathia's* crew.

For the next three hours, lifeboats arrived alongside *Carpathia* and the survivors in them were carefully taken on board and dispersed throughout the ship. She began to fill with the survivors. Passengers whose journey to the Mediterranean had been delayed were not resentful. In fact, many gave up part of their accommodation to *Titanic's* survivors.

As each boat disgorged its human load of misery, a head count was taken and added to a growing list. Very soon, it became obvious that a human tragedy of enormous proportions was rapidly unfolding.

The sun finally rose above the horizon at just after 5-20 am and flooded the now choppy sea surface with warming light. *Titanic's* lifeboats continued to converge on *Carpathia*.

As they had been doing so, Captain Rostron had manoeuvred his ship in the direction of the most hampered.

Carpathia's accommodation was quickly filling with thankful, sad, bewildered individuals, most of whom were females and children. However, a substantial number of them were men which included passengers, deck and engine crew.

While the recovery of survivors was underway, Captain Rostron sent one of his young officers aloft to survey the area.

To the North West, west, and south east, the young man could see a vast ice field. About four miles to the west of the ship it consisted of what seemed to be a low-lying ice barrier which extended from the North West to the southward, at its north end he could see several small icebergs trapped by it. To the south eastward, in the direction from which they had come, many, much larger, icebergs were seen. These he already knew about - they were the ones *Carpathia* had been dodging them on the way to the disaster site. However, the nearest berg was about 500 yards (463m) away to the south eastward of where she now lay. This one was the berg which Captain Rostron had swerved to avoid just before he stopped to pick the survivors in Cutter No.2. It was not an Arctic giant, but big enough to have done a great deal of damage. I

In the clear water to the westward and south ward - between *Carpathia* and the ice, - he could also see a number loaded lifeboats making their way toward his location. Most of them were now no more than a couple of miles away.

He could also see clear water beyond the ice barrier and noted two steam ships on its western side and to the northward. They appeared to be stopped. One had four masts and the other was smaller and had two masts. It too seemed to be stopped near to the ice barrier.

The following is a plot developed from the foregoing:

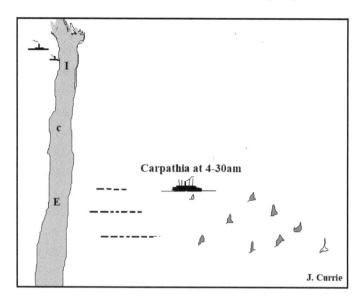

As he surveyed the scene, it occurred to him how fortunate it was for the survivors that although there was now a cold, brisk northerly breeze; the sky was clear and bright, visibility was perfect and the usual North Atlantic swell was almost tamed, but the small waves were increasing in size and a few white caps were staring to show.

Around 7-45 am, most of the boats had arrived alongside *Carpathia*. Her captain had manoeuvred his ship closer to the last of the approaching lifeboats. At that time, thick black smoke was seen on the far side of the ice barrier. This proved to be yet another steam ship - a four-masted vessel heading southward along the barrier's western side. Captain Rostron watched her progress southward.

At 8 pm as the last of lifeboat was being recovered, Rostron saw the southward moving ship he had been watching earlier, suddenly turn directly for *Carpathia* and commence transiting the ice barrier; he reckoned she was about six miles away. Soon she cleared the eastern side of the barrier and continued heading strait for *Carpathia*. As she got nearer, it could be seen that she had a pink funnel with a black top. This told him she belonged to the Leyland Line, but she was still too far away for him to make out her name. As this was happening, the *Carpathia's* deck crew were completing the task of recovering *Titanic's* empty lifeboats and landing them on deck then securing them in place. The full size boats were loaded on *Carpathia's* boat deck using her own lifeboat davits. The remainder were loaded on the foredeck using the ship's cargo derricks. The sea where they had recently been was littered with discarded personal items and bottom boards which had fallen from the last of the lifeboats as they were unceremoniously lifted out of the water by bow or stern and loaded on board *Carpathia's* foredeck.

Of *Titanic's* original complement of fourteen lifeboats, two Emergency Cutters and four Collapsible boats, Rostron had recovered thirteen lifeboats, two collapsible boats and Emergency Cutters 1 and 2.

Upturned Collapsible B was left where they found it.

Earlier, survivors had been rescued from a damaged lifeboat. This too had been left where it lay.

However, survivors and lifeboats were not all that was recovered from the sea that morning. Three unfortunates, who did not survive, were also surreptitiously brought aboard and hidden from the view of the living. Rostron planned to bury these unfortunates at sea, but would wait until well clear of the ice area before doing so.

Meanwhile, the Leyland Line vessel seen earlier was getting nearer by the minute. Rostron decided not to use the wireless to communicate with the approaching vessel, but would wait until she was close enough to use the hand held semaphore flags. To this end, he sent for one of his young Officers and ordered him to hoist the "J" flag and the Answering Pennant.

The first meant "I wish to communicate by semaphore" and the second would be used during any ensuing conversation with the semaphore flags. He also had an officer stand by on the upper bridge with a par of semaphore flags.

Soon the approaching ship began to slow down as she got nearer. Rostron saw a tell-tale semi circle of foam around her stern which told him that the other ship's engines were running astern and that the ship would soon be stopped in the water near to *Carpathia*. Before she came to a halt, Rostron could clearly see the name *Californian* etched in white on her black-painted starboard bow. *His* Wireless Operator had told him earlier that he had heard *Californian's* Operator transmitting, so he already knew that she was around. He also noticed that the *Californian* had made ready her lifeboats and was also flying the "J" flag and the Answering pennant, thus indicating that she was ready to communicate, He also saw that she had what looked likje a coal basket with a lookout posted in it, hoisted at her mainmast.

Finally, *Californian* came to rest; the time was 8-30 am.

Almost immediately, Rostron saw a signaller on *Californian's* upper bridge giving the call up signal. His own man on *his* upper bridge replied and the conversation between the two ship captains commenced.

First of all, Captain Rostron wanted to know if Captain Lord had picked up any survivors. The answer to that question was no.

Then Rostron advised Lord that he had recovered.700 survivors from *Titanic* and most of *Titanic's* boats and landed them on *Carpathia's* decks, and that when all were secure, it was his intention to return to either Halifax, Nova Scotia or New York where he would land the passengers and the salvaged lifeboats. He also advised that one of *Titanic's* boats was unaccounted for.

On receipt of Rostron's last message, Lord scanned the area of sea around *Carpathia* and was surprised to note the lack of debris. In fact, with the exception of the last boat to be recovered, all that remained of the disaster were some deck chairs, planks of wood, bits of cork and a few cushions. He also noted the wind direction. He called to his signaller. "Make to *Carpathia*:

Suggest I search the area to leeward for any remaining survivors and the missing boat."

Rostron's reply was brief: "I agree."

Shortly after the semaphore exchange, at exactly 8-50 am, *Carpathia* got under way and *the Californian* began her sweep search to the south and eastward.

CHAPTER 30

NEW YORK - NEW YORK

Before leaving the disaster site, Captain Rostron had decided to wait until he had gathered enough information before sharing the news of the disaster with the world. However, because of an unofficial wireless message sent by the *Carpathia* Operator to the White Star Line vessel *Baltic,* that was not to be.

Baltic had been heading eastward when her operator heard the distress call, and her captain had immediately turned around in answer to it.

While *Carpathia* was at the scene of the disaster, and unbeknown to his captain; her wireless operator Cottam, sent the following message to his counterpart on *Baltic:*

> *"The Titanic has gone down with all hands, as far as we know, with the exception of 20 boatloads, which we have picked up. Number not accurately fixed yet. We can not see any more boats about at all."*

The *Baltic* Operator immediately took this to his captain who replied directly to the captain of *Carpathia:*

> *"Can I be of any assistance to you as regards taking some of the passengers from you? Will be in the position about 4.30. Let me know if you alter your position. Commander".*

Rostron had no choice but to break wireless silence and reply to Captain Ranson. Consequently, the following curt reply was transmitted:

> *"From the captain of the Carpathia to the captain of the Baltic. Am proceeding for Halifax or New York, full speed You had better proceed to Liverpool. Have about 800 passengers aboard. Rostron."*

As far as the records show, next to Captain Lord of the *Californian*, Captain Ranson of the *Baltic* was the second captain to know the extent of disaster and that *Titanic* had in fact, sunk with a great loss of life.

Before leaving the scene of the disaster, Rostron had a clergyman passenger on board *Cartpathia* hold a brief Christian Service of thanksgiving for the survivors.

One of the surviving passengers from the *Titanic* was Bruce J. Ismay, the Chairman of the Mercantile Marine Company who was the ultimate owners of the White Star Line. He had left *Titanic* on the very last intact boat to leave the side of the sinking ship. The man was lodged in the cabin of one of *Carpathia's* doctors and in state of extreme shock and under sedation. Never-the -less, before making up his mind as to which port to head for, Rostron decided to consult Ismay. Between them, they decided that New York would be the best destination to land the survivors. They also agreed to divert *Titanic's* sister ship *Olympic* away from the course they would have to take. The principal being that the sight of *Titanic's* twin sister might evoke unasked-for responses in the already traumatised minds of the survivors on *Carpathia*. Consequently the appropriate message was passed to Captain Haddock of the *Olympic*.

However, the first Official message giving details of the disaster and listing the survivors was not relayed to the world until late in the afternoon of April 15 and more than 12 hours after *Titanic* had gone to her grave.

Captain Rostron decided to head *Carpathia* south until she cleared the end of the ice field before turning west. However, she was but an hour into her journey when the ship's doctor reported the death of one of *Titanic's* surviving crew members. Now Rostron had four to bury at sea. Shortly after that, the ice had almost disappeared from sight to the northward and Rostron turned *Carpathia*, westward - toward New York.

At Noon that day of April 15, the ship's position was determined by sextant altitude of the sun. She was close lat. 41° 18.1 North, Long 50° 24.5 West. (See Appendix).Four hours later, Rostron rang STOP on his engines and *Carpathia* glided to a halt. Before then, the four deceased had been sewn into weighted white, duck canvas shrouds - the last stitch being traditionally passed through the septum between the nostrils of each victim. Thereafter, each prepared body had been placed on a hatch board resting on the ship's side rail, ready for the final journey.

The Clergyman stood with head bowed in front of the four, an open bible between his s hands. A large crowd of bare headed seamen consisting of survivors from *Titanic* and crew of the *Carpathia* lined the deck behind him and a single seaman stood ready at the inboard end of each board.

After a brief service, the clergyman stood at the first board and uttered the words:

> *"Forasmuch as it pleased Almighty God, to take unto Himself the soul of our brother departed, we commit his body to the deep, and his soul unto God, in sure and certain hope of the resurrection to eternal life, Through Jesus Christ our Lord."*

As he finished, the seaman at the inboard end of the board lifted it upward and the shrouded body slid off the outboard end. Thereafter, gravity took it to its watery grave. The same procedure was carried out with the three remaining bodies.

As soon as the burial service was finished, Rostron rang full a head on his engines. At the same time, he sent the following cryptic message to the captain of the *Olympic*:

> *"Captain Olympic - 7.30 G. M. T. 41.15 north longitude 51.45 west. Am steering south 87 west true, returning to New York with Titanic passengers. "ROSTRON."*

Thereafter, the return voyage to New York was uneventful, however the world was now aware of the tragedy and the air waves were full of demands for information.

Many influential Americans had booked passage on *Titanic's* maiden voyage. Of these, some were Millionaires; others were business and political dignitaries. Prominent among them was a Major Archibald Willingham Butt.

Butt was an influential military aide to the incumbent US President Howard Taft and before that, to his predecessor, President Theodore Roosevelt. Consequently, when Taft heard about the disaster, he re assigned two US Navy Scout Cruisers, USS Chester and USS Salem with orders to contact *Carpathia* and obtain as much information as possible concerning the names of survivors and provide escort if necessary.

Titanic's only surviving Wireless Operator, Harold Bride, who had been rescued form the top of the upturned collapsible and who had suffered agonies with immersion foot, was deputised into assisting *Carpathia's* Operator Cottam who was snowed-under with work. With the exception of a few hours sleep or when they dozed-off at the wireless desk, both young men manned *Carpathia's* wireless for the entire trip back to New York.

Captain Rostron had imposed a form of censorship on all outgoing wireless messages. Not one single message of any kind was to be transmitted without his approval. Consequently, the first official report received by the White Star Line, New York was agreed by Ismay and then relayed through the *Olympic*. It was delivered to the White Star Offices at 6-15 pm on April 15 and read:

> *"Carpathia reached Titanic's position at daybreak. Found boats and wreckage only. Titanic had foundered about 2.20 a.m. in 41.46 north, 50.14 west. All her boats accounted for. About 675 souls saved, crew and passengers, latter nearly all women and children. Leyland Line steamship Californian remaining and searching position of disaster. Carpathia returning to New York with survivors; please inform Cunard. HADDOCK."*

It occurred to Captain Rostron that with his boat decks cluttered by *Titanic's* recovered boats, docking operations at New York would be hampered.

Consequently, a message was sent to the White Star Office in that city to arrange for a tug and sailors to meet *Carpatha* at the Quarantine station on the way in and to take charge of the recovered boats which were stowed on the boat decks. The rest would be discharged after *Carpathia* had docked.

During the evening of April 18, three and a half days after she had left the scene of the disaster, and almost a week after she had dropped the New York pilot, *Carpathia* arrived back at the Ambrose Light vessel where the Pilot boarded her to take her and her passengers and crew up channel to New York. Of those on board her - just over 700 poor, sad, traumatised souls would finally get to their ultimate destination, and the remainder were back where they started from.

At the Quarantine Station, the Port Medical Examiner and other officials boarded to complete the standard procedures for such a vessel entering port. At the same time, *Carpathia's* crew with the assistance of some of *Titanic's* surviving sailors unloaded *Titanic's* life boats onto the water where they were taken in tow by a harbour tug and relocated safely within the harbour.

Despite many ingenious attempts by press reporter to board the ship, this would not be allowed until free practique had been granted. This was a formality whereby the Port Medical Officer would, after consultation with the ship's medical staff and Master, sign a Declaration of Health. Since *Carpathia* had recently left port and her Bond seals had been broken, the Customs Officials would also need to get in on the act.

Finally, *Carpathia* was securely docked back at her original departure point. Then, all hell was let loose. It seemed that Reporters from every newspaper in America was looking for a scoop. However, Captain Rostron received two unexpected distinguished visitors inn the forms of Senator William Alden Smith and another ember of the hastily convened Senate Sub Committee.

PART 6

CHAPTER 31

AFTERMATH

I now lay before you, all the rubbish and nonsense that has been written, and continues to be written, about our three Captains and their men.

Up to this point, I have attempted to paint you a verbal picture of the events leading up to, during, and after the disaster, so now, let us "pick over the bones" so to speak.

First of all, let's consider witness evidence.

In doing so, I caution readers not to blindly accept verbatim, survivor stories which appeared in the press at the time. I do so because then, as nowadays, the sources of such reports - whether they be passengers, crew or from a Journalist, had nothing to lose and in most cases, had a great deal to gain by the use of - shall we say - *poetic license?*

On the other hand, we should very carefully examine and dissect witness evidence given by surviving members of the crews of all the vessels involved.

There are two reasons for this:

1. If they were found to be lying under oath, they could lose income and career and possibly freedom in one fell swoop.
2. The most difficult thing to do on a ship where men are confined at close quarters with each other, is for an individual to lie without contradiction.

Many historians and legal experts tend to judge the evidence given by survivors in the same way as they would judge witness evidence given in connection with a land based event. This is a fundamental mistake.

They also mistakenly believe that the crew members of all departments of a merchant vessel would have closed ranks when "The Company", a senior officer, any officer, or a ship mate was accused of a serious or life-threatening misdeed. Nothing could be farther from the truth.

To compound the felony, they also believe that non contract crew members would lie to save their job or that of a shipmate. Again - this is total garbage.

In reality, the greatest problem any ship's crew member had when contemplating lying about an event on board his or her ship was that he or she would seldom be alone when on duty. Consequently, there would not have been a positive guarantee that unknown to him or her, someone else would also have witnessed the same event and be asked to testify.

I would emphasise that during the following process, poor sailor men should not be the only ones under scrutiny. There was also a great deal of officially approved distortion of evidence which I will also point out to you as we go along.

For the less technically inclined I will, accompany my arguments with simple sketches where appropriate.

So let us begin by finding out how the world viewed these three captains. In modern speak -what was the official *word on the street?*

I deliberately use the word "official" since, as we all know, the press, then, as now, based their stories less on fact than on what would sell newspapers.

To discover the deliberations of Officialdom, we have to delve into the records.

There were two Official Inquiries into the disaster. One was held in the United States of America and the other in the United Kingdom.

The first was hastily called without the approval of the then US President William Howard Taft. In fact, when approached about the possibility of such a thing taking place on US soil, the President had voiced the opinion that the US Government had no intention of interfering in the matter.

However, there was strong pressure in The Senate for the US to hold its own Inquiry. This was led by Senator William Alden Smith, the

Republican Senator for Michigan. Why Smith pushed so urgently for this Inquiry is perhaps a "transparent" mystery for others to solve. It is more so a mystery since the man's previous interests had been in railroad safety and he had no direct connection with maritime trade.

Suffice to say, it was an election year.

On the other hand, the Brits had Rules already in place to deal with such an event. Therefore, in accordance with the 1898 Merchant Shipping Act, the British Government ordered a Wreck Commissioner's Inquiry into the disaster.

To head The Inquiry, they appointed a 71 year old retired judge named Lord John Charles Bigham QC who held the lofty title of Baron Mersey of Toxteth - an aristocratic title manufactured for him when he retired. Until the *Titanic* disaster, Bigham had little or no knowledge of marine matters, but he could be depended upon to toe the political line and to have the Shipowner's interests at heart.

So what was the purpose of these Official Inquiries and on what legal grounds were they called?

Ostensibly; the remit of such an Inquiry was to find out what happened and why it happened. Thereafter; from the answers obtained; to develop a strategy that would prevent it happening again - or at least, to lessen the consequences resulting from it, happening again.

Titanic was a British registered vessel, engage in lawful trade in international waters when the disaster took place.

Never the less, by April 17 - less than two full days after the disaster, Senator Smith had raised a Resolution in the Senate that a sub committee of the Committee of Commerce be formed. Its purpose would be to look into the disaster on behalf of the American lives that had been lost.

Subsequently, The US Senate passed the Resolution and the sub committee, consisting of seven Senators, was formed and, surprise-surprise - with Senator William Alden Smith at its head.

The US legal justification was outlined by Senator Isidor Raynor in his post Inquiry speech to the Senate when he declared

> *"It is because Congress has jurisdiction to regulate commerce between the States and foreign countries that the committee had the right to undertake this investigation. It would have*

had no right whatever to summon and examine witnesses unless it had jurisdiction over the subject matter, and the jurisdiction that it has is based upon the fact that by virtue of this examination it is able to recommend to the Senate, under this clause of the Constitution, such improvement in our laws as will enable us to avoid a recurrence of this accident. Therefore the Senate was perfectly right in appointing this committee, and the committee, acting strictly within its jurisdiction"

So, in a nutshell, it seemed that despite the law of a foreign country - if the US Senate had the right to regulate trade with any other country, it had the automatic right to grill that other country's citizens if the actions legal or otherwise of said citizens of said other country, effected that trade outside US jurisdiction. You have to give the man credit for his ability to wield the verbal corkscrew.

Despite the nonsense that has been written over the years on the subject of legality, the truth is that the Owners pf RMS Titanic had no legal obligation to the United States or any other country on the face of the earth.

By he Law of the land, according to the previously mentioned Merchant Shipping act of 1898, the ownership of a British registered vessel had to be divided into 64 shares, each of which had to be wholly owned by persons of the following description

a. Natural-born British subjects.
b. Persons naturalized by or in pursuance of an Act of Parliament of the United Kingdom, or by or in pursuance of an Act or ordinance of the proper legislative authority in a British possession.
c. Persons made denizens by letters of denization.
d. Bodies corporate established under and subject to the laws of some part of His Majesty's dominions.

Denization was an ancient English law which was an act by which a foreigner became a subject of England; but had not the rights either of a natural born subject, or of one who had become naturalized.

As I said: the Brits didn't need to concoct an excuse for having an Inquiry, they already had legislation in place dealing with such an event.

I do not intend to take you word-for-word through the proceeding of these two official Inquiries. I simply intend to provide you with the basics, and in particular, a condensed version of the findings. Thereafter, I will dissect them and comment as found necessary.

However, for those of you who are interested in doing so, the transcripts can be found on the Internet at <u>https://www.titanicinquiry.org</u>.

Both inquiries sought answers to questions concerning happenings during three specific times. These were:

A. Before hitting the iceberg
B. Hitting the iceberg and
C. After hitting the iceberg.

From the answers obtained they would determine:

- Whether the ship was properly equipped, manned and fit for purpose according to law before she hit the iceberg.
- Whether the accident was the result of negligence on the part of the Master or any member of his crew and,
- Last, but not least, if the actions taken by all involved parties after the event were timely and appropriate in accordance with the practice of good seamanship.

The course of events would have very much depended on the answers to the first two questions. If not they were simply derived from knowledge gained after the event. In which case, no blame could be laid at the door or doors of individuals.

At this point, the main purpose of an Official Inquiry into the loss of a vessel at sea should be kept in mind - that it is not convened to apportion blame, but to attempt to discover the truth.

However, if during the course of such an Inquiry, criminal or incompetent action or actions by an individual or individuals is discovered, then subsequent to the Inquiry, such an individual or individual will be called to account in accordance with the law in force at the time.

CHAPTER 32

THE US INQUIRY

The RMS Carpathia docked at New York on Thursday, April 18, 1912 and as earlier mentioned, Senator William Alden Smith and a colleague were there to meet her. They boarded the ship and served subpoenas on the recently traumatised surviving crew members and on several of the surviving passengers. The following morning, Friday, April 19, at 10-30am, less than four and a half days after *Titanic* has sunk, the American Inquiry into the *Titanic* disaster began.

The first venue for the Inquiry was the Waldorf Astoria Hotel. However, by the beginning of the following week it was changed to a committee room in The Russell Senate Office building in Washington DC and continued thereafter, for another 18 days and concluding on Saturday, May 25, 1912.

On the last day, interviews were held on board *Titanic's* sister ship the RMS Olympic at New York. She had returned there from the UK.

Significantly, one of *Titanic's* surviving crew members, leading Fireman George Barratt, had signed on for that return voyage and he too was interviewed by Senate Committee members. The following directly involved individuals were interviewed:

1. Captain Henry Rostron of the *Carpathia* and his Wireless Operator, Harold Cottam
2. Four Officers, 34 Crew and 21 passengers from the *Titanic*

170

3. The Captain, wireless Operator and a Greaser from the *Californian*.
4. The Captain and Wireless Operator of the *Mount Temple*.
5. The Captain and Wireless Operator of the *Olympic*.
6. The Wireless Operator of the *Baltic*.

In addition to the foregoing, shore personnel including the management of the Marconi Company and the white Star Line were also interviewed.

The questioning of individuals was tortuous and times wandered.

On Tuesday, May, 28, 1912, - after it was all over - Senators William Alden Smith and Isidor Raynor addressed the assembled US Senate in full session. Senator Smith's speech was lengthy and full of Shakespearian eloquence worthy of Sir Lawrence Ollivier's Hamlet. It is difficult to separate the *meat* from the body of that flowery oration, however, he basically reported as follows:

US INQUIRY CONCLUSIONS

1. "It was of paramount importance that we [The US Government] should act quickly to avoid jurisdictional confusion and organized opposition at *home or* abroad."
2. "No sufficient tests were made of boilers or bulkheads or gearing or equipment, and no life-saving or signal devices were reviewed.
3. "When the crisis came, a state of absolute unpreparedness stupefied both passengers and crew,"
4. "We shall leave to the honest judgment of England its painstaking chastisement of the British Board of Trade, to whose laxity of regulation and hasty inspection the world is largely indebted for this awful fatality".
5. "Capt. Smith's indifference to danger was one of the direct and contributing causes of this unnecessary tragedy. Overconfidence and neglect to heed the oft-repeated warnings.... when other and less pretentious vessels doubled their lookout or stopped their engines."
6. "Capt. Smith touched no liquor of any kind."
7. "There is evidence tending to show that even the watertight compartments were not successfully closed either above or below."

8. "No general alarm was given,"
9. "No ship's officers formally assembled."
10. "No orderly routine was attempted or organized system of safety begun."
11. The lifeboats were not properly equipped.
12. "The lifeboats were filled so indifferently and lowered so quickly that, according to the uncontradicted evidence, nearly 500 people were needlessly sacrificed to want of orderly discipline in loading the few that were provided."
13. Certain officers and crew members exhibited cowardice by considering their own survival ahead of all others.
14. *Titanic's* two Wireless Operators were unselfish heroes
15. The operator of the *Carpathia* caught the distress signal by accident as he prepared for bed.

   Senator Smith was scathing in his characterisation of the part played by the captain officers and men of the SS Californian.

16. "The steamship *Californian* was within easy reach of this ship for nearly four hours after all the facts were known to Operator Cottam."[of *Carpathia*]
17. "I am of the opinion it [*Californian*] was much nearer than the captain is willing to admit, and I base my judgment upon the scientific investigation of the Hydrographic Office of our Government."
18. [Captain Lord] "admits that the morning after this accident he "was practically surrounded by icebergs, the largest from 100 to 150 feet high and from 700 to 800 feet in width above the water."
19. "The captain of the *Californian* deluded himself with the idea that there was a ship between the Titanic and the Californian, but there was no ship seen there at daybreak."
20. "That ice floe held but two ships - the *Titanic* and the *Californian*. The conduct of the captain of the *Californian* calls for drastic action by the Government of England and by the owners of that vessel, who were the same owners as those of the ill-fated ship."

CHAPTER 33

THE UK INQUIRY

Following the US Inquiry, those survivors who had been held back from returning home to their loved ones by subpoenas, returned to the United Kingdom where each surviving crew member was required to make a written statement to an Official of The Board of Trade. Thereafter, a number of them including Officers, crew members and passengers surviving the disaster were summoned to appear before the Wreck Commissioner and Legal representatives of The Government. In addition, Captains and crew members from the *Carpathia, Californian* and *Mount Temple* were also summoned.

The United Kingdom Wreck Commissioner's Inquiry into the disaster was convened within The Scottish Drill Hall, London on Tuesday, May 2, 1912

During the following 23 days, 97 individuals were interviewed. Excluding indirect, expert witnesses these included.

1. Four Officers 38 crew members and 2 passengers from the *Titanic*
2. Captain Rostron and his Wireless Operator from the *Carpathia.*
3. Captain Lord, three Officers, the wireless Operator, the Apprentice and a Greaser from the *Californian.*
4. Captain Moore and his wireless Operator from the *Mount Temple.*
5. The wireless operator of the *Mesaba.*

Expert witnesses included numerous retired and serving Ship Masters, Government Officials and Shipping Company Officials.

In addition to the aforementioned evidence sources, the lead councils in the UK had transcripts of the evidence given earlier in the USA.

As I pointed out earlier, the UK Government had specific legislation in place to deal with disasters at sea. These were contained within part 6 of The Merchant Shipping Act of 1894.

To ensure that all aspects of the disaster were covered, the UK Government provided the Wreck Commissioner with 26 specific questions. I reproduce these below in condensed form.

1. What was the total number of Crew, and passengers of all ages and sexes on board when *Titanic* left Ireland?
2. Did *Titanic* comply with the requirements of the Merchant Shipping Acts, 1894-1906?
3. What were the specific provision on T*itanic* in the event of collisions and other casualties?
4. Was *Titanic* sufficiently and efficiently Officered and manned - were the watches of the Officers usual and proper - was *Titanic* supplied with proper charts?
5. What was the number of boats of any kind on board -how many could they carry - were the arrangements for manning and launching proper and what were the arrangements for boat drills?
6. What installations for receiving and transmitting messages by wireless telegraphy were on board *Titanic* - how many operators were employed on working such installations - were the installations in good and effective working order, and were the number of operators sufficient to enable messages to be received and transmitted continuously by day and night?
7. Were safe, adequate and proper instructions given to the Master before departure?
8. Did *Titanic* follow the recommended track across the ocean for the time of year and did she stay on it?
9. What ice warnings were received by *Titanic's* Master?
10. What times might she have reached the area of any ice warnings received - what ice warning did she pass-on and did she vary her speed?

11. Were binoculars provided for and used by the look-out men?

12. What other precautions were taken by *Titanic* in anticipation of meeting ice?

13. Was ice seen and reported by anybody on board *Titanic* before the casualty occurred?

14. What was the speed of *Titanic* shortly before and at the moment of the casualty - was such speed excessive under the circumstances?

15. What was the nature of the casualty? In what latitude and longitude did the casualty occur?

16. What steps were taken immediately on the happening of the casualty? How long after the casualty was its seriousness realised by those in charge of the vessel? What steps were then taken? What endeavours were made to save the lives of those on board and to prevent the vessel from sinking?

17. Was proper discipline maintained on board after the casualty occurred?

18. What messages for assistance were sent by *Titanic* after the casualty? What messages were received by her in response?, and from what vessels did she receive answers? What vessels other than the "Titanic" sent or received the messages at or shortly after the casualty in connection with such casualty? What were the vessels that sent or received such messages? Were any vessels prevented from going to the assistance of *Titanic* or her boats owing to messages received from *Titanic* or owing to any erroneous messages being sent or received? In regard to such erroneous messages, from what vessels were they sent and by what vessels were they received and at what times respectively?

19. Was the apparatus for lowering the boats on *Titanic* in good working order?

20. Were the boats put into the water and got away under proper superintendence? Were the boats sent away in seaworthy condition and properly manned and equipped for the saving life?

21. How many were saved including children and how many adults? Did each boat carry its full load and, if not, why not?

22. How many persons on board *Titanic* at the time of the casualty were ultimately rescued? How many lost their lives? Of those rescued

how many have since died? What was the number of passengers, distinguishing between men and women and adults and children of the 1st, 2nd, and 3rd classes respectively who were saved? What was the number of the crew, discriminating their ratings and sex, which were saved? What is the proportion which each of these numbers bears to the corresponding total number on board immediately before the casualty? What reason is there for the disproportion, if any?

23. What happened to the vessel from the happening of the casualty until she foundered?

24. Where and at what time did *Titanic* founder?

25. What was the cause of the loss of *Titanic?*

26. When *Titanic* left Queenstown was she properly constructed and adequately equipped as a passenger steamer and emigrant ship for the Atlantic service?

27. The Court is invited to report upon the Rules and Regulations made under the Merchant Shipping Acts, 1894 -1906, and the administration of those Acts, and of such Rules and to make any recommendations or suggestions that it may think fit, having regard to the circumstances of the casualty with a view to promoting the safety of vessels and persons at sea.

The foregoing were the original questions. It should be noted that there was no mention of the SS Californian in that list.

The UK Inquiry commenced on May 2, 1912 and was concluded on May 25 the same month. On July 30, 1922, the final report was made in writing to The Board of Trade. It concluded as follows

UK INQUIRY CONCLUSIONS.

1. "The total number of persons employed in any capacity on board the "Titanic" was: 885 .and the total number of passengers was 1,316. It listed the passengers by sex and age.

2. "Before she sailed, Titanic complied with the requirements of the relevant parts of the Merchant Shipping Acts, 1894-1906,"

3. The "Titanic" was sufficiently and efficiently officered and manned, and the watches of the officers and crew usual and proper."

4. "Titanic" was supplied with proper charts."

5. "The "Titanic had 2 Emergency boats, 14 standard lifeboats and 4 Englehardt collapsible boats each with a capacity as follows: Emergency: 40, Standard: 65 Collapsibles: 47. Total boat capacity was 1178 persons."

6. "A Boat drill had not been carried out before the disaster and the arrangements for manning and launching the boats in case of an emergency were not proper nor were they efficient."

7. "Titanic was supplied with a Marconi 5 Kilowatt motor generator with two complete sets of apparatus supplied from the ship's dynamos, with an independent storage battery and coil for emergency, was fitted in a house on the boat deck. She had two Operators and the equipment was manned at all times."

8. "No special instructions were given to the Master prior to commencement of the voyage but standard instructions given were safe, proper and adequate, having regard to the time of year and dangers likely to be encountered during the voyage, but having regard to subsequent events they would have been better if a reference had to be adopted in the event of reaching the region of ice."

9. "*Titanic* followed the Outward Southern Track from Queenstown to New York, usually followed in April by large steam vessels. instead of altering her course on approaching the position 42° N., 47° W. she stood on her previous course for some 10 miles further South West, turning to S. 86° W. true at 5.50 p.m."

10. "Titanic" had reason to suppose she would encounter ice, at or before 9-30 pm. A proper lookout was not kept and full speed was maintained.

11. "Binoculars were not provided for and used by the look-out men - the use of them was necessary or usual in such circumstances."

12. "Special orders were given to the men in the crow's-nest to keep a sharp look-out for ice, particularly small ice and growlers and the fore scuttle hatch was closed to keep everything dark before the bridge. However, there is evidence to show that some Masters would have placed a look-out at the stemhead of the ship."

13. "Immediately before the collision, the helm was put hard-a-starboard and the engines were stopped and put full speed astern. Proper measures and actions were promptly taken."

14. "Shortly before and at the moment of the casualty, the speed of the "Titanic" was about 22 knots. This speed is considered excessive under the circumstances."

15. "In latitude 41° 46' N., longitude 50° 14' W., "Titanic" collided with an iceberg at or about 11.45 p.m. on the 14th April last It pierced the starboard side of the vessel in several places below the waterline between the forepeak tank and No. 4 boiler room. The 12 watertight doors in the engine and boiler rooms were closed from the bridge, some of the boiler fires were drawn, and the bilge pumps abaft No. 6 boiler room were started. 15 to 20 minutes later, the situation was considered serious and he boats were ordered to be cleared away. The passengers were roused and orders given to get them on deck, and lifebelts were served out. Some of the watertight doors, other than those in the boiler and engine rooms, were closed. Marconigrams were sent out asking for help. Distress signals (rockets) were fired, and attempts were made to call up by Morse a ship whose lights were seen. Eighteen of the boats were swung out and lowered, and the remaining two floated off the ship and were subsequently utilized as rafts."

16. "Proper discipline was maintained on board after the casualty occurred."

17. "*Titanic* did not receive any erroneous messages."

18. "The apparatus for lowering the boats on the "Titanic" at the time of the casualty was in good working order and the boats were swung out, filled, lowered, or otherwise put into the water and got away under proper superintendence. The boats sent away in seaworthy condition and properly manned, equipped and provisioned and they prove to be efficient and serviceable for the purpose of saving life."

19. "At least 8 boats did not carry their full loads for the following reasons:

    a) Many people did not realise the danger or care to leave the ship at first.

    b)   Some boats were ordered to be lowered with an idea of then coming round to the gangway doors to complete loading.

20. "The officers were not certain of the strength and capacity of the boats in all cases."

21. "Seven hundred and Twelve (712) persons were rescued by "Carpathia" from the boats. One died before arrival at New York."

22. "The disproportion between the numbers of the passengers and crew saved is due to the fact that the crew, for the most part, all attended to their duties to the last, and until all the boats were gone."

23. "*Titanic* foundered at 2.20 a.m. (ship's time) 15th April. in Latitude 41° 46' N., 50° 14' W.''23."

24. "The *Californian* could have reached the *Titanic* if she had made the attempt when she saw the first rocket. She made no attempt."

CHAPTER 34

MARKS OUT OF TEN

As we have seen in the last two chapters, the conclusions were very different on each side of the Atlantic.

The US Inquiry, blamed the UK Board of Trade, lack of crew training and a perceived cavalier attitude of Captain Smith for the disaster,

On the other hand, the UK Inquiry found the ship and her crew almost perfect and avoided directly laying specific blame at the cabin door of Captain Smith.

The UK barely mentioned the role played by the *Carpathia* and her Master, Captain Rostron, whereas Senator Smith waxed lyrical about the man, almost comparing him to the Greek heroes of old.

In his speech to the assembled Senate, Senator Smith trumpeted the praises of Captain Rostron and the crew of the *Carpathia,* culminating in proposals for a gold medal for the Captain and a special medal for each member of his crew.

However, both Inquiries had one thing in common; they decided on a diversion - a Scapegoat if you will- in the shape of the captain of the *Californian.*

As can be seen in previous pages, the Chairman of the US Inquiry - Senator Smith - reserved almost a third of his written report, and a lot of his speech to The Senate in vilifying Captain Lord and his men consigning him to eternal damnation. However, at no time did that self-inflated gas-bag in America - or the British Intelligencia on the other side of the ocean - ever mention the name of the *Mount Temple* or that of her Captain in their Final Reports. This was despite her name being included on the chart provided by the USN Hydrographer, and the fact that her captain spent lengthy times in the witness boxes on both sides of the Atlantic. Consequently their lack of reporting of the evidence given by her captain and wireless operator or any opinion of it on both sides of the Atlantic, although being significant to say the least, leaves the world in doubt..

So were the learned individuals of both formal Inquiries fair and correct in their findings? Were their judgements fair, reasonable and accurate? Did they properly assess the evidence? Did they use it all?

In the following pages, I will attempt to answer each one of these questions in detail. However, before continuing, I think it best that we develop a true picture of the disaster area and the prevailing conditions on April 14/15, 1912. After that I will draw your attention to the differences between these and the picture painted by those charged with finding the truth.

CHAPTER 35

"CURRENT" THINKING?

Using present day logic, many self-proclaimed "Experts" and pseudo Historians, try to understand the thinking processes of individuals at the time of the disaster.

That is, and will continue to be a very big, basic mistake. However they are not alone; shore personnel back in 1912, made the same basic assumptions.

Principal among these were the assumptions that since The Labrador Current brings ice down from the north in Spring; the ice that sank *Titanic* was moving under the influence of the Labrador Current at the time of the disaster, and that if *Titanic's* Lookouts had had binoculars and *Titanic* was travelling at a slower speed, they would have seen the iceberg in time to avoid it.

Basically, to prove or disprove the foregoing, we need answers to the following:

A. How did all that ice get to where *Titanic* and other ships found it during the period April 14/15?

B. How did experts of the day determine the positions and movements of ice in the area of the disaster?

C. What was the accepted practice among highly experience North Atlantic Captains regarding the movement of ice relative to ship speed in the region of the disaster?

D. What was the opinion of highly experienced North Atlantic Captains regarding use of binoculars by Lookouts?
A & B: Ice Movement.

The following was the reference used by the expert advisors to the Official Inquiries on both sides of the Atlantic.

It is an except from the United States Pilot (East Coast), part I. (second edition, 1909, page 34, relative to the ocean passage of large, transatlantic mail steamers, and stated:

> *"To these vessels, one of the chief dangers in crossing the Atlantic lies in the probability of encountering masses of ice, both in the form of bergs and of extensive fields of solid compact ice, released at the breaking up of winter in the Arctic regions, and drifted down by the Labrador Current across their direct route. Ice is more likely to be encountered to in this route between April and August, both months inclusive, than at other times, although icebergs have been seen at all seasons northward of the parallel of 43° N., but not often so far south after August. These icebergs are sometimes over 200 ft. in height and of considerable extent. They have been seen as far south as lat. 39° N., to obtain which position they must have crossed the Gulf Stream impelled by the cold Arctic current under-running the warm waters of the Gulf Stream. That this should happen is not to be wondered at when it is considered that the specific gravity of fresh-water ice, of which these bergs are composed, is about seven-eighths that of sea."*

Back in 1912, the art of oceanography was in its infancy, so there was an excuse for making the foregoing assumptions.

However, modern Oceanography tells us that in fact, icebergs could not have crossed the Gulf Stream or its easterly extension - The North Atlantic Current.

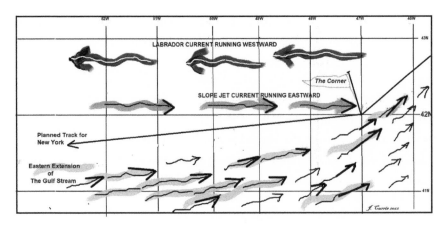

PIC 8

The above is the situation during the months of April, May and June. As you can see, it shows the presence of a very localised current - a mobile liquid wall if you like - running for fifty miles due east directly north of where *Titanic* met her fate.

To dismiss this, it might be claimed that very deep draft, large icebergs could cross the Slope Jet Current, but this was, and is an impossibility (except in severe) northerly gales, and the explanation for this comes from the same source.

> "[The Labrador Current] *is forced to the right by the Coriolis force* [to the westward] *and follows the topography around the coast of southern Greenland and the Labrador Sea, eventually crossing under the Gulf Stream and flowing south along the east coast of the U.S. at depths between about 2,000 to 4,000 meters (1.3–2.5 miles). This water, known as North Atlantic Deep Water (NADW), continues south until it joins the Antarctic Circumpolar Current, from where it supplies much of the salt to the deep waters of the southern hemisphere.*"

The foregoing, completely debunks the assertions by Assessors and Hydrographers at both Inquiries, as well as academics and historians over the years, which, I remind you, was -has been, - and still is, that at the time of *Titanic* sinking, there was a south-setting cold current running across the area which was responsible for the presence of ice bergs and field ice in the path of the *Titanic.*

Apart from scientific fact; simple physics hasn't changed and *it* tells us that cold water is heavier than warm water and sinks below the warm stuff.

The truth is that if there *had* been a cold, south flowing current in the area at the time of the *Titanic* disaster, it would have been thousands of feet below the surface and way below and beyond the reach of even the biggest and deepest draft icebergs in the world.

The foregoing takes care of the page 182 questions A and B but it begs another question:

> *"if, as you say, the Labrador Current didn't bring the ice into the path of Titanic - what did? How the heck did the ice get where it was?*

OK, good question! I'll try and explain it by answering question C. Every experience North Atlantic ship Master knows, and in 1912, knew, that once sea ice and icebergs are formed, they are influenced by two things…currents and wind, therefore, the direction the ice takes depends on the strength of these and the air profile and draft of the ice.

We have seen that the bergs could not have crossed the deep waters of the Gulf Stream. However, unlike icebergs which may be a couple of years away from their birth place - lighter, shallow draft pack ice is formed annually and is usually a few feet or metres thick. Consequently, in spring, it is often driven southward, ahead of strong northerly winds from where it formed in the bays and inlets around Newfoundland during winter.

By coincidence, the records show that there was a period of strong winds from the North East in the weeks before the disaster. The following quotation is from the April 19, 1912 edition of The Philadelphia Inquirer:

> *"All Navigators agree that the condition were unusual, that constant northeasterly gales had driven ice hundreds of miles further south than is usually to be expected at this time of year."*

North Easterly gales drive ice to the south west. So much for the Labrador Current!

As we have seen from modern scientific data, the big Bergs head westerly along the margins of the Grand Bank until they meet the prevailing winds blowing from the south west. Being like giant sailing ships, they are blown north east, into the northerly limits of The Gulf Stream where they then sail and are carried eastward. All Ship Master of old knew, and expected this.

During this time, the ice would melt above and below the surface and they would lose draft and "sail" area. Eventually they would be at the mercy of the current, which drove them to the area of the *Titanic* disaster. Ship master knew this too. They also knew that by far, the strongest winds in the north Atlantic were from the South West And that combined with the Gulf stream, ice invariably moved in a northeasterly direction.

I have employed the genius of modern Oceanography to illustrate the Slope Jet Current This time I will use the same source again, but this time to illustrate the foregoing narrative.

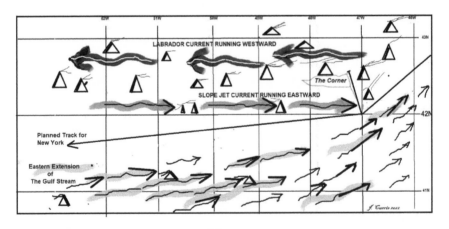

PIC 9

In the above; the white triangles represent the main movement of ice during Springtime.

Now for the questions of speed in the event of a ship entering an ice region and the use of binoculars by Lookouts.

D: Speed and Binoculars.

No less than seven highly experiences Ship Masters gave evidence at the Inquiries - all of them agreed that under normal conditions of sea and swell - night and day, it was not necessary to reduce speed because ice could always be detected in good time to avoid it.

The reason for this confidence was that a berg behaves much like a ship when there is a sea and swell running therefore, when it pitches, rolls and heaves, it displaces water which slaps back in against its side - much like a ship's bow wave.

This in turn causes a white reflective wash which is often enhanced by the presence of phosphorescence.

As for binoculars - all captains agreed that the use of binoculars by Lookouts was the exception rather than the rule. Not one of them condoned their use as an aid to the Lookout.

CHAPTER 36

THE TRUE SHAPE OF DANGER

As we have seen, westward heading vessels including *Titanic,* were following prescribed tracks from Europe to the New World. The track in question was developed by a famous USN Officer named Matthew Fontaine Maury.

Ironically, Maury's idea was to ensure that vessels heading for the North American Continent were well south of the area where sea ice was most likely to be met with during the months of January to September - a time when the previous year's icebergs were most prevalent in the ocean South of Newfoundland.

In addition to these precautions, vessels were encouraged to note and report the positions and nature of any ice they might see or encounter during the voyage.

By 1912, this system was well developed and many such reports were received at the USN Hydrographic Office in Washington.

In the previous chapter we saw how the ice arrived in the vicinity of the disaster. Of more importance - where was it relative to the vessels involved? Of even greater importance - where was it relative to the sinking *Titanic?*

Fortunately, and thanks to the efforts of *Titanic* researcher and author Dr. Paul Lee, we have access to copies of the actual reports received by the USN prior to and after the event - particularly those which describe the locations of the ice in the disaster area during the period April 14/15, 1912. It is these, together with the finding of *Titanic's* wreck site in 1985 by Dr Ballard which open the "can of deceitful worms." which in reality, is the true Titanic story.

During the Official Inquiries, Captain Knapp of the USN Hydrographic Office produced the following plot of the area. In it, we can see the official distress position sent out by the *Titanic* and the plots of the ice reports received.

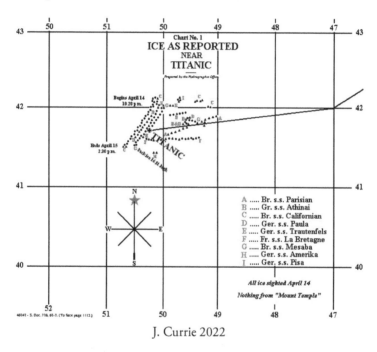

J. Currie 2022

The above was used in conjunction with other evidence to develop the Final Reports on the disaster. In referring to it Senator Smith said:

> "I call attention to the fact that from the chart you can readily see the position of the Californian, and that to the eastward there is no ice, to the southward of her there is no ice, and to the northward there is no ice; this ship was not surrounded by ice."

The foregoing is a complete fabrication. We get an entirely different picture when we include the following information in Captain Knapp's chart:

1. The Ice Reports of vessels C. G and E
2. True position of *Titanic's* wreck
3. The ice evidence of Captain Rostron of the *Carpathia,*
4. The ice evidence of Captain Lord of the *Californian*
5. The ice evidence of Captain Moore of the *Mount Temple.*
6. Ice messages between the RMS Olympic and the SS Parisian,
7. The ice reports of the SS Frankfurt.
8. The ice report of the SS Birma.

To help us do all this, I employ specific extracts from the research work of Dr Lee, entitled

"ICE REPORTS SUBMITTED TO THE US HYDROGRAPHIC OFFICE."

The relevant information used from it can be found in the Annex to this work.

By plotting each relevant report onto the original chart supplied by Captain Knapp to the US Inquiry, I will create a true picture of the area for you; thus illustrating the situation which confronted the *Titanic* that terrible night. So let's see what that true picture *really* was.

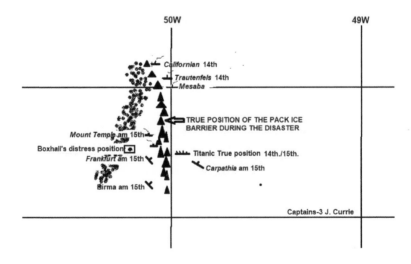

From the foregoing, we can see that the true position of the barrier of ice confronting *Titanic* was 8 to 10 miles east of the position depicted in

Captain Knapps' chart. This being the case, we should all ask ourselves how it was possible on "God's green earth" for two Official Inquiries, supported by the best Marine engineering and nautical minds of the day, to honestly develop such a scenario with the information they had - the same information I have just used?

This was the scenario which they subsequently presented to the world, and the one upon which they based their assessment, of the conduct and professional capabilities of our captains.

Were these characterisations true? On what did they base such opinions?

Before attempting to answer these and other questions, I remind you of a couple of things that were said on both sides of the Atlantic. These were;

A. The distress position transmitted by *Titanic* was "excellent" I.e. accurate.

B. There was a southerly - not easterly - current running across the scene of the disaster.

CHAPTER 37

IN OUR *HONEST* OPINION?

You will note that the word "honest" in the title of this chapter has a question mark after it. That is there because the opinions in question were those of politicians and political appointees.

I remind you of what was dished-out concerning our Captains back in the days and weeks following the disaster - of opinions which, to this very day, are perpetuated by the less forgiving, and the selectively blind.

First, the flowery language used by Senator Smith:

<u>Captain Arthur Rostron</u>

> *"Contrast, if you will, the conduct of the captain of the Carpathia in this emergency and imagine what must be the consolation of that thoughtful and sympathetic mariner, who rescued the shipwrecked and left the people of the world his debtor as his ship sailed for distant seas a few days ago. By his utter self-effacement and his own indifference to peril, by his promptness and his knightly sympathy, he rendered a great service to humanity. He should be made to realize the debt of gratitude this Nation owes to him, while the book of good deeds, which had so often been familiar with his unaffected valour, should henceforth carry the name of Capt. Rostron to the remotest period of time. With most touching*

detail he promptly ordered the ship's officers to their stations, distributed the doctors into positions of greatest usefulness, prepared comforts for man and mother and babe; with foresight and tenderness he lifted them from their watery imprisonment and, when the rescue had been completed, summoned all of the rescued together and ordered the ship's bell tolled for the lost, and asked that prayers of thankfulness be offered by those who had been spared. It falls to the lot of few men to perform a service so unselfish, and the American Congress can honour itself no more by any single act than by writing into its laws the gratitude we feel toward this modest and kindly man. The lessons of this hour are, indeed, fruitless and its precepts ill-conceived if rules of action do not follow hard upon the day of reckoning. Obsolete and antiquated shipping laws should no longer encumber the parliamentary records of any Government, and overripe administrative boards should be pruned of dead branches and less sterile precepts taught and applied

Captain Edward Smith.

Titanic though she was, his indifference to danger was one of the direct and contributing causes of this unnecessary tragedy, while his own willingness to die was the expiating evidence of his fitness to live. Those of us who knew him well - not in anger, but in sorrow - file one specific charge against him: Overconfidence and neglect to heed the oft-repeated warnings of his friends. But in his horrible dismay, when his brain was afire with honest retribution, we can still see, in his manly bearing and his tender solicitude for the safety of women and little children, some traces of his lofty spirit when dark clouds lowered all about him and angry elements stripped him of his command. His devotion to his craft, even "as it writhed and twisted and struggled" for mastery over its foe, calmed the fears of many of the stricken multitude who hung upon his words, lending dignity to a parting scene as inspiring as it is beautiful to remember.

Captain Stanley Lord

I am well aware from the testimony of the captain of the Californian that he deluded himself with the idea that there was a ship between the Titanic and the Californian, but there was no ship seen there at daybreak and no intervening rockets were seen by anyone on the Titanic, although they were looking longingly for such a sign and only saw the white light of the Californian, which was flashed the moment the ship struck and taken down when the vessel sank. A ship would not have been held there if it had been eastbound, and she could not have gone west without passing the Californian on the north or the Titanic on the south.

That ice floe held but two ships - the Titanic and the Californian. The conduct of the captain of the Californian calls for drastic action by the Government of England and by the owners of that vessel, who were the same owners as those of the ill-fated ship.

Contrast, if you will, the foregoing, inaccurate flowery nonsense with the cryptic findings of the UK Wreck Commissioner's Inquiry.

Captain Arthur Rostron

"The Court desires to record its great admiration of Captain Rostron's conduct. He did the very best that could be done.

Captain Edward Smith.

Captain Smith was not fettered by any orders and to remain on the track should information as to position of ice make it in his opinion undesirable to adhere to it. The fact, however, of Lane Routes having been laid down for the common safety of all, would necessarily influence him to keep on (or very near) the accepted route, unless circumstances as indicated above should induce him to deviate largely from it.

Without implying that those actually on duty were not keeping a good look-out, in view of the night being moonless, there being no wind and perhaps very little swell, and especially in view of the high speed at which the vessel was running, it is not considered that the look-out was sufficient.

Captain Stanley Lord.

The "Californian" saw distress signals. The number sent up by the "Titanic" was about eight. The "Californian" saw eight. The time over which the rockets from the "Titanic" were sent up was from about 12.45 to 1.45 o'clock. It was about this time that the "Californian" saw the rockets. At 2.40 Mr. Stone called to the Master that the ship from which he'd seen the rockets had disappeared. At 2.20 a.m., the "Titanic" had foundered. It was suggested that the rockets seen by the "Californian" were from some other ship, not the "Titanic." But no other ship to fit this theory has ever been heard of.

The ship seen by the "Californian" was the "Titanic," and if so, according to Captain Lord, the two vessels were about five miles apart at the time of the disaster. The evidence from the "Titanic" corroborates this estimate, but I am advised that the distance was probably greater, though not more than eight to ten miles. The ice by which the "Californian" was surrounded was loose ice extending for a distance of not more than two or three miles in the direction of the "Titanic." The night was clear and the sea was smooth. When she first saw the rockets the "Californian" could have pushed through the ice to the open water without any serious risk and so have come to the

> *assistance of the "Titanic." Had she done so she might have*
> *saved many if not all of the lives that were lost."*

As can be seen, in the case of the US Inquiry conclusions, the greatest numbers of words were used up in praising Captain Rostron, but in the UK, the greatest number of words were used in condemning Captain Lord. Not single words did any of them utter or write about Captain Moore of the *Mount Temple*.

Strangely enough, the man in command of the vessel which hit the iceberg and sank resulting in the deaths of over 1500 people is treated almost as an afterthought - almost as a sort of "Piggy-in-the-middle" character.

I leave the whys and wherefores for these finding for others to drool over, but to my mind these opinions were heavy in content but light-weight with regard to truth and reality and the previous chapter confirmed this. For what it is worth - my opinion is, that "horses" named "Politics" and "Press "overtook "Reality" and "Truth" in the race to produce a story acceptable to the public.

CHAPTER 38

TIME - THE GREAT LEVELLER

Before proceeding further, I want to clarify a problem which, from the very beginning, seems to have puzzled many *Titanic* Historians and caused them to come to incorrect conclusions. It concerns the subject of time keeping on board a British Merchant vessel. In particular, the correct time showing on *Titanic's* bridge clocks at the moment she hit the ice berg.

However, to consider this properly, we must understand the method of telling time and applying time changes on board such a vessel, as well as what the implications of these time changes were for those they affected most. I mean the members of the ship's crew - not her passengers.

The working day aboard a ship is divided into Day Work and Watches.

Day Workers performed their duties from dawn to dusk. Or from around 5 am until 10 pm. On the other hand, since ships do not stop for the night, the work of Watch-keepers was continuous. Thus their duties were shared in equal amounts of work and rest.

However, in the early days, sailors were simple men who could not read, write or tell the time, consequently, their lives were regulated by a sand glass and a code of bell sounds. The sand glass was turned over every half hour from the beginning of each Watch period. The moment this happened was indicated by a number of bell sounds, staring with one ring for the first half hour - twp for the first hour and so on. In this way, the number of rings indicated the number of half hours since the start of the Watch.

One (1) bell = first half hour

Four (4) bells= fourth half hour.....

Seven (7) bells = seventh half hour.

There were two more bell warnings and these were always sounded after seven (7) bells. These also measured time, but in a different way. They did not measure the passage of a period time but as a warning, thus:

One (1) bell meant fifteen minutes remained before the end of the Watch, and

Eight (8) bells = the end of a Watch period.

These last two were definitive - they indicated that whatever the planned length of a Watch - that planned length had:

A. in the case of One (1) bell: - The planned Watch time from the previous sounding of 8 bells has 15 minutes left to run
B. In the case of 8 bells: - The Total planned Watch time from the previous sounding of 8 bells has been completed.

By 1912, most if not all seamen were educated and some even had personal time pieces - i.e. clocks or watches. It follows, that if there were any surviving crew members whose evidence showed that after the time of hitting the iceberg, they had 15 minutes left off or on duty, heard One (1) bell sounded, or heard Eight (8) bells sounded, then a partial clock change had most certainly taken place.

Now apply the foregoing to the evidence of *Titanic's* Lookouts.

Lookouts Fleet and Lee who were on duty in the Crow's nest when the ship hit the iceberg, were also due to be relieved by Lookouts Hogg and Evans at Midnight. Here is what these crew members told their Questioners.

First Hogg who was due up in the Crow's Nest at partly adjusted Midnight.

Lookout Hogg on Day 7 US I nquiry

> *"I waked up, at 20 minutes to 12, with the confusion in the forecastle. I rushed up on the deck, and I saw there was not much confusion on deck, and I went below again, with some of my shipmates. I asked the time, then, of my mate, and he said, "It is a quarter to 12. We will get dressed and get ready to go on the ookout."*

Hogg was to relieve Fleet and Lee in the Crow's nest. The latter were to spend 2 hours 24 minutes in the Crow's Nest before getting relieved by Hogg and his mate

On Day 15 of the UK Inquiry Lee was closely question as to how long he remained in the Crow's Nest after hitting the ice berg until he was relieved by Hogg and Evans. Here is *his* reply:

> *17318. Then did you remain on the crow's-nest?*
> *- Yes.*
> *17319. Until eight bells?*
> *- Till eight bells went.*
> *17320. At eight bells, in the ordinary course, you were relieved?*
> *- Yes.*

Note that Fleet was relieved *"At eight bells, in the ordinary course"*. That answer is quite specific. If Hogg and Evans had relieved Fleet and Lee too early, then they would not have done so *", in the ordinary course"*. Nor would eight bells have been sounded and to suggest otherwise is nonsense.

However, if doubt lingers regarding a partial clock change - the following evidence given by Fleet's Watch-mate, Lookout Reginald Lee on Day 4 of the UK Inquiry must surely banish it from the minds of all but sceptical Flat-Earth Society members.

> *"2454. - I was not relieved till 12 o'clock.*
> *2472. …the men brought their bags up from there who were going on the 12 to 4 watch, because the watch was coming in there.*

2488. () After you saw that at 12 o'clock what did you do?
- I went on the boat deck.
2488a. Did you get any orders to go on the boat deck?
- No, but I heard the boatswain call the other watch
2490. That was the watch below; they were turned out, and
we all went on deck..
2492., the watch that had just gone below.
2493. That would be at 12 o'clock; they had just gone
below?- Yes.

If Lookout Lee saw members of the Midnight to 4 am Watch coming on duty when he went down at 12 o' clock then the 12 o' clock in question was the Midnight - 20 minutes after impact with the iceberg, and 20 minutes after his relief, Hogg, had been awakened by that impact

Apart from the foregoing which should be sufficient to convince a stone Buddha - there is the evidence of the following surviving crew members of *Titanic,* which, if carefully dissected, will show beyond any reasonable doubt that a partial clock change took place.

Bedroom Steward Alfred Crawford - Day 1 - US Inquiry.

I was on watch until 12 o'clock, and I was waiting for my relief
to come up. I was to be relieved at 12 o'clock. I heard the crash,"

Crawford was waiting for a relief when the crash came. If there had been no clock change then he his wait would have been a very long time - all of 43 minutes.

Stateroom Steward Andrew Cunningham - Day 9- US Inquiry.

"Yes, sir. It happened to be my turn for the middle watch, or
from 12 to 4. So I was excused from duty from 9 until the
time I was called to go on the middle watch.

Senator SMITH: were you on duty when this accident
happened?

Mr. CUNNINGHAM.: I was just called, sir."

On Day 7 of the US Inquiry, one of *Titanic's* youngest crew members gave the most convincing bit of evidence pointing to such a clock change.

John (Jack) Collins was not quite seventeen and a half years old when he stood before the US Inquiry on Day 7, Thursday, 25th April 1912.

The young Irish lad was signed-on to the Crew List of the *Titanic* as a Scullion in the First Class Galley and as such was a Day Worker.

As we have seen, Day Workers started work early every morning and would not get finished until 9 0' clock that evening.

Being a young "first tripper", Jack would have been very anxious to ensure that he arrived at work on time and did not sleep-in. Let Jack tell you as it was. The following is an extract of his evidence

> *"I stopped work at 9 o'clock on Sunday night, and I came up again and walked up and down the alleyway. I went into my bunk and fell asleep. That was about 10 o'clock - about a quarter to 10. I fell asleep, and was sound asleep, and exactly at a quarter past 11 I was wakened up. I had a clock by me, by my bed, and my clock was five minutes fast, and it was exactly a quarter past 11 when the ship struck the iceberg, and it wakened me."*

Jack's questioner was a little confused about the "my clock was five minutes fast" part of the evidence and after more careful questioning confirmed the clock of the witness was showing 11-20 pm when the impact of the berg was felt, but the true time was 11-15 pm.

As pointed out earlier, Day Workers set their personal time pieces back the full amount of any planned clock change before going to bed; young Collins was no different. It follows that if the planned set back was 47 minutes, then the Bridge clock and equivalent Greenwich Mean Times for the moment *Titanic* hit the iceberg would have been as shown in the following little table.

Fully Altered: - Ship 14th 11-15 pm. GMT 03-00 am 15th Part Altered: - Ship 14 11-39 pm GMT 03-00 am 15th

Unaltered; - Ship 15 12-03 am....GMT 03-00 am 15th.

Note that in the above, the time of impact on a partially adjusted clock is 11-39 pm. The popularly accepted time of impact is 11-40 pm.

Believe it or not - there remains historians who swear blind that a partial clock change did not take place before *Titanic* hit that big chunk of frozen water.

CHAPTER 39

APPLIED TIME

In the previous chapter, we saw how time was dealt with on board ship, and that in fact, Titanic's clocks had been set back 24 minutes just before she hit the iceberg. Now we will apply that knowledge to the rest of the evidence

On Day 5 of the US Inquiry, the man steering *Titanic* - Quartermaster Robert Hichens told his questioner:

> *"I stayed to the wheel, then, sir, until 23 minutes past 12. I do not know whether they put the clock back or not. The clock was to go back that night 47 minutes, 23 minutes in one watch and 24 in the other.*
>
> *Q Had the clock been set back up to the time you left the wheel?*
>
> *A: I do not know, sir. I did not notice it. ...I left the wheel at 23 minutes past 12, sir. I was relieved by Quartermaster Perkis.*

Hichens got it the wrong way round. In fact the Junior Watch - the 8 pm to Midnight Watch - was to work an extra 24 minutes and the Senior watch - the Midnight to 4 am Watch, was to get 23 minutes of extra duty. This was, and still is, normal practice on board ship.

He tells us that he was relieved at 00-23 am. (12-23am), If he was looking at an unaltered clock, then his relief was 24 minutes late. However Hichens was due to be relieved one minute before adjusted Midnight because it was considered good practice to do so. This would be, at 11-59 pm on a partially altered clock, and at that moment, an unaltered clock would have been showing 00-23 am (12-23 am). In other words: by his evidence, Hichens tells us that if he was looking at an unaltered clock, then his relief, QM Perkis, arrived at the proper time, to relieve him at wheel.

Two days later, on Day 7 of the US Inquiry, the same Quartermaster Walter Perkis, told his questioner:

> *I stayed there until I though it was time to turn out to relieve the deck at 12 o'clock."*

Watch Keepers were extremely careful that they did not go on duty before it was time to do so. Consequently if Quartermaster Perkis thought it was time to go on Watch, he would not have left the warmth of his bunk in the accommodation without consulting a time piece.

He was due on Watch at 23 minutes past Midnight on an unaltered clock. This being so, then we again have confirmation that Quartermaster Hichens was looking at an unaltered clock.

However, QM Perkis was not the only crew member who gave evidence indicating that a partial clock change had taken place shortly before *Titanic* hit the ice berg.

Third Officer Herbert Pitman was due to relieve 4th Officer Boxhall after the first part of the clock change had been completed. When he did so, he would have set the clock back the remaining amount of 23 minutes thus completing the 47 minute planned change.

In his evidence, 4th Officer Boxhall told his questioner that he was told to call the off-duty Officers, Lightoller, Pitman and Lowe. This he did, just before the crew arrived on the boat deck to uncover the boats, which was 20 minutes after the ship hit the ice berg. Previously, Pitman had been awakened by the impact with the ice berg and had gone on deck with Lightoller to see what the fuss was all about.

Here is what 3rd Officer Pitman told his questioner about that Boxhall call:

Day 4 - US Inquiry:

> *"A few minutes afterwards I thought I had better start dressing, as it was near my watch, so I started dressing, and when I was partly dressed Mr. Boxhall came in and said the - mail room - there was water in the mail room. I said, "What happened?" He said, "We struck an iceberg." So I put a coat on and went on deck, and saw the men uncovering the boats and clearing them away ".*

The expression *"near my watch"* had to have been near to 00-24 (12-24 am) April 15 on an unaltered clock which was the time Pitman was due to relieve Fourth Officer Boxhall on the bridge; and the time when Pitman would complete the planned clock change by setting the clocks back the remaining 23 minutes.

Anyone "just called" had 15 minutes left of free time before going on duty.

This evidence has been trashed because Pitman stated that he did not alter the clocks because there was more to think about. Only lack of understanding of bridge operations would suggest this.

Then there was.......

Leading Fireman Charles Hendrickson: Day 5 - UK Inquiry.

> *"Q4908...He asked me to get some men down to get the fires out. I went up top and saw a few and asked them if they would come down, and some went down.*
> *4909. Did you get some more men?*
> *- Yes.*
> *4910. You went forward to your quarters again?*
> *- Yes, they were the men belonging to the watch, the 8 to 12 watch.*
> *4911. The men whose watch it was below?*
> *- Yes."*

It cannot be clearer. Hendrickson was on the 4 to 8 Watch; if he saw members of the 8 to 12 Watch - and it was their 'Watch below' then the

8 to 12 Watches had been relieved, consequently a partial clock change of 24 minutes must have taken place at or immediately before *Titanic* hit the ice berg.

This and the previous chapter has established the correct time on *Titanic* when she hit the iceberg and now allows us to solve any other mysteries relative to time and navigation. However, before doing so, what about our gallant captains?

PART 7

CHAPTER 40

GLORY - CAPTAIN HENRY ROSTRON

I have never felt comfortable with the popular, larger-than-life super hero image of the captain of the steamship *Carpathia*.

Ever since the first time I read about Captain Arthur Henry Rostron and the part he and his ship played in the *Titanic* disaster of 1912, I've had not a few doubts picking away at the reasoning area at the back of my brain.

As well as the official records of his actions that early morning of April 15, 1912, there is something about the man, and his methods which seem alien to me. From the viewpoint of a professional mariner and one time Marine Accident Investigator something - or should I say 'some things' just do not ring true to form.

OK! I have to admit that I'm possibly the Owner, Captain and entire crew of the SS "Doubting Thomas". I also admit that the expression *'sour grapes'* might justifiably be aimed in my direction. After all, who in their right mind would attempt to cast a shadow over the credentials of a man who was feted by Governments on both sides of the Atlantic Ocean? A man, who, for acting as every decent seaman should have acted, was the proud recipient of:

1. A silver cup and gold medal from the *Titanic* Survivors,
2. The American Cross of Honour,

3.   A US Congressional Gold Medal,
4.   A signed letter of thanks from the President of the United States,
5.   A gold medal from The Shipwreck Society of New York and
6.   A medal fromThe Liverpool Shipwreck and Humane Society?

The foregoing list was by no means the end of the honours bestowed on him. Captain Rostron was also granted:

The freedom of The City of New York.
The Order of the British Empire (OBE).
A Knighthood and The French Legion of Honour?
Heavens! He was even made Aid-de-camp to his majesty King George 5th.

However, the icing on the *Titanic* cake for Rostron was; that his international recognition ensured life-long member of the inner circle of the Cunard Line senior officer's old boy network. It ensured that he would eventually become Commodore of the mighty Cunard Line fleet.

To top it all, he was photographed alongside Mrs Margaret Brown who is remembered by the world as the *Unsinkable Molly Brown.*

As Chairperson of the *Titanic Survivors Committee,* Mrs Brown presented Captain Rostron with a silver Loving Cup and a medal for every member of his crew.

Pause here for a bit of gossip.

Mrs. Brown was known as Margaret. The name Molly was an invention made in Hollywood.

Apart from the foregoing, Rostron was also the founder-member of a special Hollywood "Rat Pack", whose members Walt Disney and Frank Sinatra, also subsequently received a Congressional Gold medal. (I couldn't resist that - sorry!).

However I diverse.

So what of Captain Arthur Henry Roston himself…the man behind that plethora of honours? What of his actions that fateful morning? Let's try and paint a picture of the man. Was he a simple, honest seaman as portrayed by others?

In the book "Titanic Hero – The Autobiography of Captain Rostron of the Carpathia" Rostron described his first command as follows:

"My ship was the Brescia, the newest and best of the Cunard Fleet."

With that observation, the man showed his prevalence for embellishment and exaggeration. In fact, the SS Brescia was not the newest vessel. The newest vessel was the SS Pannonia. She was built in 1904, a year after *Brescia*. In truth, the SS Brescia was a four year- old cargo vessel when Rostron joined her and for these previous four years, had been plying her trade between the UK and Mediterranean ports. He was then 38 years of age and *Brescia* was very nearly the last ship he commanded.

During the very first voyage under the command of Henry Rostron, *Bresica* lost both bilge keels under mysterious circumstances.

Rostron and denied all knowledge of this happening although he must have known something was wrong; particularly when in a beam sea crossing the Bay of Biscay. Because bilge keels reduced the violence of a ship's rolling motion by acting as dampers. As any sailor will tell you, a ship without bilge keels would 'roll on wet grass'.

Rostron was not demoted after the bilge keels incident, but it would be another 4 years before Cunard would trust him with a passenger ship. Thus, in 1911, he was given command of the 8 year old RMS Pannonia. His next ship would be another veteran.

This was the nine year-old *Carpathia* which he joined on the 18th of January, 1912. At that time, Rostron was exactly one calendar month short of his 43 birthday. In fact, when *Titanic* encountered that fateful iceberg, he had about a year of passenger ship command under his belt.

James Bisset was Second Officer of the *Carpathia* at the time of the *Titanic* disaster. Many years after the event, he wrote in his book (*'Tramps and ladies -My Early Years in Steamers'*) that Rostron was known throughout the Cunard Line as *"The Electric Spark."*

This must have been in Rostron's latter days and after the *Titanic* incident. I say this because his late promotion to command suggests that he did not overly impress his employers during the early part of his sea-faring career. Before *Titanic*, he was definitely not earmarked for the 'fast track'. Perhaps he discovered that electric energetic ability later in life?

Bisset also wrote that Rostron was an extremely pious man- that he did not smoke or drink and was often given to prayer - a description which seems to be at odds with the *Electric Spark* image. It also clashes with the images caught on camera subsequent to the rescue of *Titanic's* survivors. These show a flamboyant, self confident, jovial individual who paid great attention to his public image. Have a look at the following, obviously posed photograph. Note the hand in pocket with thumb visible; the uniform cap at a rakish angle - the cigarette between the fingers. In modern parlance, he would be described as 'a *Poser*'.

(Photograph - National Archives reference Copy: 1566).
PIC 10

In later years, *Carpathia's* 2nd Officer Bisset, wrote many things in praise of Rostron. Then he would, wouldn't he? After all, he served with Rostron, shared in Rostron's *Titanic* glory and eventually received his first command in Cunard, almost 20 years later in 1931, when Rostron was Commodore of the Cunard Line.

So much for the man himself. Now consider the story of the part played by the SS *Carpathia* during the *Titanic* incident. Bear in mind that it comes almost entirely from a single source - the man himself - Captain Henry Arthur Rostron.

Here was a man who was described as an "electric spark" What did that description convey to a seaman?

I suggest to you that an electric spark is a sudden sensation, likewise, an individual who acts like an electric spark, acts suddenly and without apparent pre-thought.

This description most certainly matches the initial action of Rostron when he got the news concerning *Titanic*, as well as his actions when on the way to answer her distress call.

How else could you describe a man who was quite prepared to risk the lives of over more than thousand men, women and children by charging through a moonless, dark night toward a ship which was sending up distress signals after having hit an iceberg? A man who, without considering the adverse effect of his actions on other potential rescuers, fired distress rockets when going to the aid of a vessel in distress?

This same man, charged at full speed through a collection of icebergs for the last hour of his rescue mission.

As we have seen, Rostron first heard of the *Titanic* disaster shortly after midnight during the first hour of April 15, 1912. What truly passed through his mind at that moment...the moment when he is told that the biggest ship in the world needs help?

Bear in mind that at that time, Rostron did not know that *Titanic* was sinking or that there was any risk of life involved - just that she needed help?

To suggest an answer to the foregoing question, I can do no better than quote the words of Captain Stanley Lord of the SS Californian, as transcribed by author Senan Maloney from and interview between Captain Lord and Lesley Harrison in 1961

> *It was the height of every shipmaster's ambition in those days, and officers and crew too, to pick up a ship in distress. That means losing a propeller, losing a rudder and getting a tow... the wages were so small in those days that a man getting a few hundred pound salvage money, it was a godsend."*

So, with these words in mind, let's look behind the picture of sympathy and efficiency that Rostron painted at both Official Inquiries and apply them to the man himself.

I suggest to you that on hearing about the plight of *Titanic*, the following thoughts ran like an 'electric spark' ran through his mind:

> *Titanic had obviously stopped because of the ice. She gave no details of damage. She probably hit I the ice bow-on and her forepeak tank and perhaps even her forward hold would be damaged. It was therefore possible that she might not be unable to proceed under her own steam and might need to be towed.*
>
> *Regardless, she had very many people on board and they might have to be transferred to Carpathia. For that purpose she could use her own boats but if he got Carpathia's boats ready, the transfer could be effect in half the time.*
>
> *Then, like all shipmasters of the day, his mind turned to the question of salvage money.*
>
> *The thought of it was mouth-watering to say the least.*
>
> *He had no idea of the value of Titanic but his share of any salvage money would set him up for a very long time indeed. The fact that Sparks had said that*
>
> *Carpathia seemed to be the only vessel responding to Titanic's call for help was very encouraging indeed.*

Now let us examine Rostron's capabilities as a Navigator.

CHAPTER 41

ROSTRON THE NAVIGATOR

Earlier, we cleared-up problems concerning time keeping on the bridge of *Titanic*. We saw that establishing correct time was essential to understanding the navigation of the vessel. This is of no less importance when considering the movements of *Carpathia's* or any other vessel in the vicinity, before, during and after the disaster.

At the Waldorf Astoria Hotel, New York, on April 19 - the day after *Carpathia* arrived at New York and the first day of the US Inquiry - Captain Rostron told his questioners:

> *"At 12:35 a. m. on Monday I was informed of the urgent distress signal from the Titanic.",* the distress message from the *Titanic* was

> *"Come at once, we have struck a berg; it's a C.Q.D. O.M., position 41.46 N., 50.14 W."*

"The New York time at 12:35 was 10:45 p.m. Sunday night."

As can be seen, the distress signal contained position calculated by *Titanic's* 4th Officer, Joe Boxhall and the time differenece between *Carpathia* and New York was one (1) hour fifty (50) minutes. The New York time when this first contact was made is confirmed by the Wireless Log (Process-verbal) of the *Mount Temple* which was submitted in evidence on Day 10 of the US Inquiry:

"10-35 [EST] Carpathia answers M.G.Y. M.G.Y. says: "Struck iceberg; come to our assistance at once." Sends position.."

In his evidence, Rostron said the given distress position was 58 miles away and the course to steer to get there was North 52 West. If we use this information and the given distress position, we can easily work back to *Carpathia's* estimated position when she turned toward *Titanic* that morning of April 15, m 1912.

I have done this, and it turns out to have been at, or very close to, Latitude 41-10.0 North, Longitude 49-13.0 East. Was this correct? I firmly believe that it was and here is why.

Since the weather the previous evening was a calm sea, clear sky and sharp horizon, there is little doubt that *Carpathia's* navigators - like the Navigators on *Titanic* - obtained a very good, true or fixed, position. Therefore, the estimated position they calculated about 5 hours later at 12-35 am, would have been very close to the truth.

So, yes: I believe we can accept Rostron's start point for his rescue mission. However, did *Carpathia* follow the track indicated by Captain Rostorn?

The answer to that that question would be an emphatic NO! - Because Rostron did not find the survivors at the accepted distress position.

In fact, *Carpathia* was never at any time, near Boxhall's position. Instead, Rostron found the survivors at a position close to where we now know the wreck of *Titanic* is located, and that was due to the quick thinking of Joe Boxhall and his green flares and had nothing to do with the navigating skills of *Carpathia's* captain and officers.

Additionally; *Carpathia* arrived beside the survivors at 4 pm, which was half an hour earlier than the estimated time of arrival (ETA) advised by Rostron to the captain of the sinking *Titanic*

Not only that, but a plot of the evidence shows that instead of steaming 58 miles on the planned course of North 52 West, *Carpathia* steamed no more than 48 miles in 3 ½ hours, and she most certainly did not make good her intended track of N 52 W.

So what did the track of *Carpathia's* mercy-dash really look like?

To discover this, we will start from the beginning, and for the better understanding of readers without technical knowledge, I will illustrated *Carpathia's* movements progressively in a series of charts. First - her intended dash.

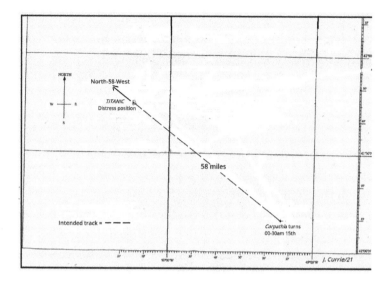

If *Carpathia* had arrived at the distress position calculated by *Titanic's* 4rth Officer Boxhall, then the above picture would hold good. However, the discovery of *Titanic's* wreck showed that Boxhall's distress position was wrong and that *Titanic* did not sink there but did so, over twelve miles to the eastward of that position.

It follows that the survivors must also have been in the vicinity of where the wreck now lies. Consequently, *Carpathia's* actual track from where she turned looks like this:

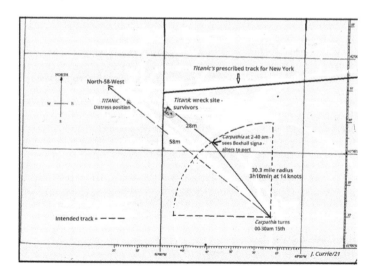

I am only able to construct this last chart because I know where *Titanic* actually sank; but did Rostron? It would seem not, because on Day 28 of the UK Inquiry when asked about the speed he made that night, he replied:

> "Ordi*narily about 14. We worked up to about 17 1/2 that night. That was about the highest speed we made that night.*"

Did Rostron actually believe that? Was he being truthful, or was he simply waffling? I am sure that his answer would have raised many eyebrows in the engineering fraternity.

In fact I suggest to you that this God-fearing man blatantly lied under oath and if any practitioner of navigation had looked closely at his evidence given by Captains Lord and Moore in the US, and Rostron's own evidence, they would have known this at the time.

In the US, evidence was received from a number of sources indicating that there was a barrier of ice between the given distress position and the position where *Carpathia* found the survivors, and no less that three vessels had been stopped on its western edge at the time. Lord of the *Californian* and Moore of the *Mount Temple* both expressed the opinion that the disaster happened well to the east of the given disaster position, but were ignored.

However, the damning evidence came from Rostron himself. It can be found in a wireless message sent by him to Captain Haddock of the *Olympic* during the afternoon of April 15 as Carpathia was making her way to New York. I quote:

> "*Captain Olympic - 7.30 G. M. T. 41.15 north longitude 51.45 west. Am steering south 87 west true, returning to New York with Titanic passengers. "ROSTRON."*

This message tells an experienced Navigator a great deal.

Since GMT is expressed in the 24 hour system, the equivalent Eastern (New York) Standard Time would have been 2-30 pm on the afternoon of April 15.

Rostron also gives the course he is steering for New York.

Since the weather was fine that afternoon, we can safely assume that the Navigators on *Carpathia,* like the Navigators on other ships in the area, would have obtained an excellent Noon position and at that time, the course of South 87 degrees West would have been set by Captain Rostron.

The clock would also have been adjusted to local mean time, which was about 3 hours 26 minutes SLOW of Greenwich Mean Time. If so, then the ship time when Rostron sent that message was close to 4 minutes past 4 pm on the afternoon of April 15 and he would have obtained his Noon position, 4 hours, 4 minutes earlier.

All of the foregoing means, that if we, as Navigators, have a position for 4-04pm and a course and speed from Noon that day, we can easily determine where *Carpathia* was at Noon on April 15, 1912.

A vessel on a course of S 87 W and steaming at 14 knots, when in the region of latitude 41 North, will change her Latitude by 0.7 minutes to the southward and increase her longitude by 18.5 minutes every hour. Consequently if *Carpathia* was making 14 Knots for 4 hours and 4 minutes, she would have changed her latitude by 3 minutes to the southward and her longitude by 1 degree 15 minutes westward. To find her Noon position, we simply apply these in reverse from the position given by Captain Rostron in his message to Haddock. Like this:

Carpathia at 4-04 pm.	Lat. 41°-15'N. Long.. 51°-45'W.
	D. Lat. <u>3'N D. Long. 1°-15'E</u>
Carpathia Noon 15th:	<u>Lat. 41°-18'N Long.. 50°-30'W.</u>

I will now incorporate the calculated Noon position in our chart.

Additionally, I will show the courses and distances steamed from 9 am when *Carpathi*a left the scene of the diisaster.

My effort is simply an educated guess. However, *Carpathia's* Navigators and her captain would have been able to do as I have done; and re-create their historic track back to its origin, using data from the Scrap Log.

In any case, since *Carpathia* must have been running at full speed of 14 knots from 9 am that morning, she would have covered a distance of at least 42 miles up until noon that day of April 15, 1912.

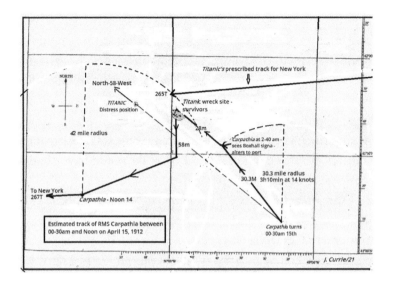

The above plot demonstrates very clearly, that instead of steaming 58 miles on her rescue dash, *Carpathia* steamed 10 miles less than that. In fact a total of 48 miles which divided by 3 hours 30 minutes steaming gives us an average speed 13.7 knots. Given that *Carpathia* altered course a few times during the last hour to avoid ice bergs, this seems a much more acceptable speed for an elderly lady such as she was.

My point in drawing attention to all of this is that Rostron must have retrospectively known the exact position of the disaster sight, because at Noon on April 14, he and his officers were perfectly able to do what I have just done, and work back to the departure position.

In addition, the distance from *Carpathia's* calculated April 15 Noon position to Boxhall's incorrect distress position is a mere 32 miles, which means that to get to Noon from there, *Carpathia's* full speed would have been just 10.6 knots.

Or at full speed of 14 knots her departure time would have been 9-42am, not 8-50 am as given by Rostron.

All of the foregoing begs the question - was Rostron genuinely unaware of what I have just demonstrated? Or did the man speak before thinking when he concocted this statement:

.25390. At what speed could you travel?

*- Ordinarily about 14. We worked up to about 17 1/2 that
night. That was about the highest speed we made that night.*

He even praised 4ᵗʰ Officer Boxhall, the author of *Titanic's* erroneous
distress position, for its accuracy.

Now either Rostron and all of his officers were the most incompetent
navigators afloat in 1912, or "Holy Willie" Rostron knowingly lied under
oath on both sides of the Atlantic.

I make a very unpopular suggestion, and that is, that if truth be known;
Arthur Rostron was a very average seaman who by sheer coincidence found
himself playing the major part in one of the world greatest maritime
tragedies. Reading between the lines, we get a picture of a man who, by
April 1912, had all but been forgotten. A man who, but for the *Titanic*
affair, would have sailed into obscurity.

I also think Rostron was a man who was clever enough to recognise
opportunity when it hit him between the eyes - a man who took full
advantage of the misfortunes of so many in order to politically further
his career.

A man who was involved in one of the world's greatest human tragedies
without exhibiting much in the way of personal human compassion.

To me he was a man who could have written the book on Publicity
and Marketing.

Indeed, it might be claimed that he was a man for whom the red
Hollywood carpet of fame must surely have been woven? It even crossed
my mind that had he fallen into a cesspit, he would have emerged smelling
of roses and encrusted in diamonds.

We are all entitled to our own opinions. I make no apology for
expressing mine regarding Captain Rostron. However, I do not for an
instant, dispute his ability to absorb knowledge. He was, after all, a
certified Extra Master and had well over 20 years experience sailing the
world oceans prior to the *Titanic* incident. I do, however, take issue with
the way he seems to have used that knowledge - in the way he handled
his ship during the period from just after midnight until 8-50 am on the
morning of April 15, 1912. Despite his vast knowledge of things maritime,
several actions he took during and after that time leave me a little uneasy.

So much for Glory!

PART 8

CHAPTER 42

DEATH - CAPTAIN
EDWARD SMITH

Edward Smith was a 62 year old mariner at the end of a very long, mercurial career.

When twenty years of age, he joined the White Star Line. Eight years later at the age of 28, he was given command of his first ship. Smith's knowledge of the sea was unsurpassed. He first served in sailing ships and subsequently moved on into the era of the steam ship. While doing so, he attained the highest maritime qualification of Extra Master.

His specialist knowledge was of the North Atlantic trade. So much so, that his employer, The White Star Line, consistently showed supreme confidence in the man by entrusting him with command of their brand new super passenger vessel, the RMS Olympic and subsequently, her younger sister, the RMS Titanic. It was said that *Titanic* was to have been his last command before he retired. However there is no proof tht this was the case.

Many myths have been written about Captain Smith's conduct relative to the *Titanic* disaster. These include:

1. He was over-confident.
2. He disregarded warnings of danger in the path of his ship.
3. He delayed altering course in the early evening of the day of the disaster.

4. He colluded with management to break the record time for a crossing
5. He was steaming too fast.
6. He dithered while the boats were being loaded and launched.

All of the fore-going is blatant rubbish of the first order and has been developed by those either too lazy to make a full investigation of the man's actions, or short in the knowledge that would allow them to do so.

I further suggest that the absence of any detailed analysis of the part played by him in the disaster is ample proof of this. However a simple analysis of the available evidence will show that, in fact, given the circumstances, Captain Smith acted in exactly the same way as any other experienced ship-master of the day would have acted when confronted with the same situation. So let's take these accusations concerning the man and destroy them one by one.

Excessive Speed.

The UK Inquiry found that the speed of *Titanic* immediately before she hit the ice berg was excessive and that the ice reports received by Captain Smith should have caused him to slow his ship down. To prove this they called to the witness box no less than fourteen active and retired ship - masters - captains who had specific knowledge of the area of North Atlantic where the disaster happened and more to the point, first hand experience of navigating in ice covered areas.

The plan back-fired; to a man, these witnesses confirmed the actions of Captain Smith by declaring that given the same circumstances, they would have behaved exactly as he had done. They would not have slowed down but merely increased vigilance.

On board *Titanic* that fateful voyage, was a passenger named Joseph B, Ismay. Mr. Ismay was not an ordinary fare-paying passenger. In fact, he was the Managing Director of the White Star Line and his declared purpose for joining the new ship on her maiden voyage to New York, was to ascertain the experience from the viewpoint of a passenger and to discover any shortcomings which might be improved upon relative to future new vessels.

GLORY, DEATH & DAMNATION

However, the "gossip-brigade" twisted Ismay's story to fit the excessive speed idea. They claimed that Ismay pressured Captain Smith into attempting a record run for the Company's newest vessel.

Proper analysis of the evidence tells us that nothing could have been farther from the truth.

Ismay was a business man and the desire of all such men back then was, as it is today, to stay in business and prosper. Although he was not a professional mariner, he had been in the marine business long enough to know that a new ship on her maiden voyage had to be "run-in". That is; her machinery and working parts were gradually worked up in such a way that any weaknesses and failures could be detected and rectified without major cost, or worse still, rendering the ship unable to perform the task for which she was built - to make money for the Shareholders.

Not withstanding the foregoing; it does not require a stretch of the imagination to guess what the Press reaction would be to such foolhardiness and the consequential damage to the White Star Line's reputation that any neglect of a foreseeable adverse situation would cause.

If you need any more proof-positive that such a record attempt was never contemplated you will find it in an unusual place, and that is within the sworn evidence given by the helmsman steering *Titanic* at the moment she hit the iceberg and that is Quarter Master Robert Hichens, who we know stated:

> *"The clock was to go back that night 47 minutes, 23 minutes in one watch and 24 in the other."*

So what kind of proof was that? I hear you ask.

The number of minutes of a clock alteration was governed by the estimated amount of change of longitude between Noons. Four (4) minutes of time is equal to one degree (1°) of Longitude. Therefore, 47 minutes clock alteration converts to an 11 degrees 45 minutes change of Longitude. We know what *Titanic's* longitude was at Noon on the 14th of April. So we simply add 11 degrees 45 minutes change of longitude to it to find the Longitude where Smith thought his ship would be at Noon the following day, April 15. We also know the tracks he planned to follow between these two Noon longitudes; therefore, we can calculate the distance Smith expected his ship to travel during the 24 hours and 47 minutes run time between them. Those of you who wish to check the maths will find the calculation in the Appendix. However, I can tell you now, that Captain Smith had absolutely no plans to increase speed at any time before Noon April 15. Because at that time, he expected his ship to be at or very close to Latitude 41°-22'North, Longitude 56°-19'West and have travelled a total of about 552 miles since Noon, the previous day - April 14. This equates to a speed of 22.25 Knots, which would be much the same as the days run at 75 rpm on his engines between Noon April 13 and the time of Noon on April 14.

As for Captain Smith's overshoot at the intended turning point? That did not happen either.

The distance to steam from the Fastnet Light at the south west tip of Ireland to the turning point of *The Corner* was 1618 Nautical miles. The distance from the starting point of the voyage south of Daunt Rock, Ireland to Fastnet Light is 55 miles. That is a total of 1673 nautical miles from when she left Queenstown until Noon, April 14.

On Day 5 of the US Inquiry, *Titanic's* 3rd Officer Herbert Pitman provided the Senate Committee with details of how far *Titanic* had actually travelled by Noon April, 14. These were as follows:

First day.........464 miles
Second day 519 miles
Third day <u>546 miles</u>
Total <u>1529 miles</u>

Since the total distance from Queenstown to *The Corner* was 1673 miles, this means that *Titanic* had a mere 1673 minus 1529 = 124 miles left until she was due to alter course at *The Corner* - directly for New York.

Captain Smith would have done exactly the same calculation, and he ordered the turn to take place at 5-50 pm that afternoon. If he had overshot the turning point by 10 miles, this means *Titanic* would have had to cover a distance of 124 + 10 = 134 miles in 5 hours 50 minutes - averaging a speed 23 knots which is absurd.

In fact, the evidence shows that he wisely, made an allowance for an expected head current. His only mistake was that he miscalculated the amount of leeway caused by the northerly wind, which was acting on *Titanic's* sail-like funnels.

In fact, calculations based on the available evidence show that *Titanic* turned short of, and to the southward of, the intended turning point known as *The Corner.*

Having consigned the excessive speed overshoot accusation rubbish to the bin of history, let's take a look at what was said about Captain Smith's treatment of ice warnings. Before doing so, it should be noted that a proper Ice Warning was specific to the presence of ice and included the position of the ship issuing the warning and the description of sea ice relative to that position.

We know for certain that Captain Smith personally received two messages which were not proper Ice Warnings, but personal messages which contained advice concerning ice; these were as follows:

At 9am April 14, 1912 - from the RMS "Caronia".

> *Captain, 'Titanic.' - Westbound steamers report bergs, growlers and field ice in 42° N. from 49° to 51° W., 12th April. Compliments. - Barr."*

At around Noon on the 14th from the RMS "Baltic".

> *"Capt. SMITH, Titanic:*
>
> *Have had moderate variable winds and clear fine weather since leaving. Greek steamer Athinai reports passing icebergs and large quantity of field ice today in latitude 41.51 north, longitude 49.52 west. Last night we spoke German oil tank Deutschland, Stettin to Philadelphia, not under control; short of coal; latitude 40.42 north, longitude 55.11. Wishes to be reported to New York and other steamers. Wish you and Titanic all success."*

However, we know of at least one proper Ice Warning that was overheard by *Titanic's* operator. Whether Smith ever saw that one - we will never know.

<u>At 6-30 pm from the SS "Californian" to the *Antillian.*</u>

Latitude 42.3 north, longitude 49.9 west. Three large bergs 5 miles to southward of us. Regards. Lord."

Before analysing what Smith did with the foregoing, we must consider what knowledge he would have applied to them. To do this, we must look at the problem though the eyes of mariners familiar with that part of the ocean.

What better way to do this, than to quote from the evidence of Captain Moore of the *Mount Temple* and 4th Officer Joe Boxhall of the *Titanic?*

First Moore: the following is from the transcript of Day 9 of the US Inquiry

> *"Of course, that ice had been in the Gulf Stream and was going with the Gulf Stream. The gulf stream, as we know, is always flowing to the east-northeast,"*

Then we have Joe Boxhall on Day 3 of the US Inquiry:

> *"Did you realize that you were out of the particular influence of the Gulf Stream? No, sir."*

Also, on Day 14 of the UK Inquiry, Fourth Officer Boxhall stated:

> *"invariably we find a strong easterly set there; very often we find that the Gulf Stream".*

CHAPTER 43

SMITH'S TREATMENT OF ICE REPORTS

As we have seen, both Captain Moore of the *Mount Temple* and *Titanic's* Fourth Officer Boxhall - both highly experienced Navigators - expected to be in the influence of the Gulf Stream at the location of the disaster. So why on earth would Captain Smith expect anything different? Even to this day, mariners in that area expect their ships to be influenced by an ocean current setting East-north East at a rate between one (1) and two (2) knots every hour. Nowadays, the current has been renamed and is called The North Atlantic Current. In my day - just after WW2 - it was called "The West Wind Drift", and when I was on the New York run in the 60's, it was still there. It follows that every captain in that area in 1912, including Captain Smith, would have expected the reported ice to be well to the North and East by the time *Titanic* arrived in the vicinity. Perhaps a little sketch will emphasise the point.

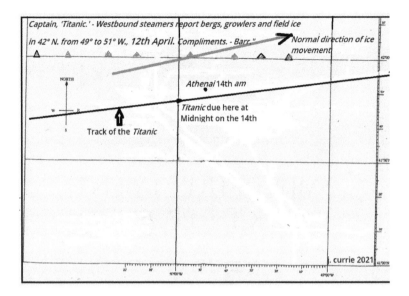

Captain, 'Titanic.' - Westbound steamers report bergs, growlers and field ice in 42° N. from 49° to 51° W., *12th April.* Compliments. - Barr."

Normal direction of ice movement

Athenai 14th *am*

Titanic due here at Midnight on the 14th

NORTH

Track of the *Titanic*

j. currie 2021

So, Smith did not, as the gossips would like you to think, ignore the fact that ice was seen in the vicinity. He expected the sea ice to behave in the way it always had done during the years he had sailed in that area, - move away.

Even if there had been leftovers from an earlier report, and there was even the slightest sea and swell, Smith knew that his Lookouts and Officers of The Watch would detect them in plenty of time to give it a wide berth.

However, he did not have the luxury of modern weather forecasting to help him predict future weather patterns. Unknown to him, the already high barometer would continue to climb and as it did so, the wind would drop completely away.

He could not foresee an even more unusual phenomenon for that part of the central North Atlantic Ocean - he could never have known or predicted that the swell would lengthen and decay and eventually, the sea surface would be reduced to an oily flat calm.

Thus, the elements which he had struggled with all his working life would prove to be his ultimate downfall.

Now you know two things:

A: That Smith did not ignore the ice warnings but treated them in accordance with long experience and normal expectations.

B: That based on long experience and universally accepted practice, Smith did not reduce speed.

From the evidence, we know that soon after dark, the wind dropped completely away. There was no moon, but the atmosphere was so clear that the stars could be seen setting on the horizon. In fact, but for a smallish, rogue iceberg, you might not be reading this now. Perhaps *Titanic's* Lookouts might have discovered in time that the "Mist" seen on the horizon was in fact low lying pack ice and consequently she was slowed down and survived with a lightly damaged bow? We will never know.

As with Captain Rostron, - so to Captain Smith's Navigation.

CHAPTER 44

CAPTAIN SMITH THE NAVIGATOR

A less easy to discover fact - and, but for a very small but significant bit of evidence, would have remained hidden, is that before *Titanic's* Fourth Officer Boxhall had calculated his widely accepted but totally incorrect distress position, Captain Smith had worked a different distress position. The source of this information can be found in the evidence given by Captain Moore of the *Mount Temple*, when on Day 9 of the US Inquiry, he told his questioner that shortly before he received Boxhall's distress position, his Wireless Operator had picked up the following message:

> *"Titanic sends C. Q. D. Requires assistance. Position 41° 44' north, longitude 50° 24' west Come at once. Iceberg."*

This was the first distress position calculated by Captain Smith which, like the later, accepted position calculated by Boxhall, was also totally wrong.

In fact, while Boxhall's position was 12.7 miles too far west, Smith's was almost 20 miles too far to the westward of the true distress position.

As a point of interest, you will not easily find Captain Smith's distress position recorded in any of the Process Verbal or official wireless message records that were used in evidence at the time of the disaster.

Since there was absolutely nothing wrong with Captain Smith's navigating ability, why was his position so far out from the true location of the disaster?

For an answer to that question, we had to wait a very long time - 50 years to be exact.

In 1962, *Titanic*'s Fourth Officer Boxhall was interviewed by the BBC. During the interview, he discussed Captain Smith's erroneous distress position and in the following way, explained the reason for Smith getting it wrong:

> *"I asked the captain 'shall I send a distress signal, sir?' he said "I already have sent a distress signal."*

Boxhall then asked Smith:

> *'but what position did you sent it from, sir?*

The Captain replied:

> *"from the eight o' clock DR"*

Boxhall responded with

> *"Well that was about - she was about 20 miles ahead of that, sir."*

Boxhall's statement infers that *the ship* was running 20 miles ahead of her estimated position. However, since Captain Smith's distress position was 20 miles a*head* of her true position - I.e. the locality of the wreck of *Titanic* - we must deduce that time had fogged Boxhall's memory and he should have told Captain Smith that in fact, it was the 8 pm DR which was 20 miles ahead of the true 8pm DR, and not the other way round. All of which tells us that if Smith had had use of the true 8 pm DR position at that time, then his distress position would have located the sinking *Titanic* close to, where her wreck was found by Robert Ballard in 1983 and where it lies to this day.

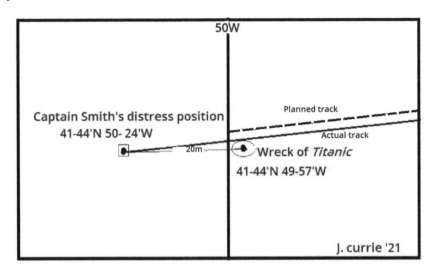

As for the source of Captain Smith's erroneous 8 pm DR position?

Watch-keeping officers on White Star Line vessels were required to enter the Dead Reckoning position for the ship at least twice each day. These were 8 am and 8 pm and there were specific places on the ship's Official Log Book for that purpose.

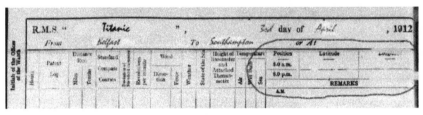

J. Currie

At this juncture, I don't intend to attempt to solve the mystery of who it was who made the incorrect entry used by Captain Smith - suffice to say that it was made by an Officer on the 6 pm to 8 pm Dog Watch and it was wrong. Consequently, Captain Smith cannot be blamed for it nor can he be blamed for using it.

Incidentally -solving the mystery of how Captain Smith arrived at his incorrect distress position suggest an alternative way of solving a few other problems concerning the navigation of *Titanic* that day of April 14, 1912.

As we have seen, *Titanic* was, as were most ocean-going vessels, quipped with a patent log; a device for measuring the distance a ship travelled through the water. The concept was very simple. It consisted of a fish- shaped brass rotator which was towed on the end of a very long rope from the stern of the ship. At the ship end, the rope was attached to a clock-work register, much like a car's odometer. The rotator had four brass fins which cause it to rotate at a fixed rate of 900 times for every nautical mile it was towed through the water, Thus, every time the rotator turned 90 times, a tenth of a nautical mile would be clocked-up on the register dial and a nautical mile would be registered for every 900 turns.

The amounts were cumulative and the register was re-set at Noon each day.

It has been suggested elsewhere that such a method of determining how far a ship had travelled was inaccurate. In fact, having used a Patent Log as a Navigator for very many years, I can tell you the idea is plain nonsense. In practice, if properly adjusted and calibrated, it was, as far as the degree of accuracy required at the time in question is concerned, a very accurate, useful navigation tool.

From the recorded evidence, we know the planned courses to be followed by *Titanic* between Noon April 14 and the time of hitting the iceberg. We also know the courses she would have followed had she arrived at where her Captain thought she was when she finally stopped. From the same source, we are also able to determine the value of Patent Log readings at specific times during April 14, and, what such readings *would* have been had *Titanic* actually arrived at the incorrect distress positions calculated by Captain Smith and his Fourth Officer. Consequently, by plotting from Captain Smith's distress position, back on the reverse of the course and at the average log speeds indicated, we can develop a fairly accurate record of *Titanic's* progress from Noon until she hit the ice berg.

To do this, we need actual and estimated Patent Log readings for the following times:

1. Noon, April 14, 1912.
2. 5-50 pm April 14, when *Titanic* turned for New York.
3. 6. 00, pm April 14, End of first Dog Watch.
4. Position by sights.
5. 8.00 pm April 14, End of second Dog Watch.
6. 8.00 pm DR used by Captain Smith.

7.   Impact with Ice Berg.

8.   Boxhall's distress position.

9.   Captain Smith's distress position.

Now let's try and find values for numbers (1) to (9). Here is a little picture of what we are looking for.

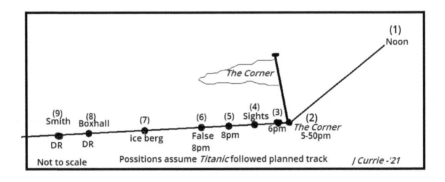

We start with a known position - in this case No.7 in the above plot.

As seen earlier - at the moment *Titanic* hit the ice berg, one of her Quartermasters - George Rowe - was stationed at the stern. Part of his duties while stationed there, was to read the Patent Log Register every two hours., and also at the end of each Watch- in Rowe's case, the end of the Log Book day of April 14. These readings were passed to the bridge by telephone .This enabled the Navigators to get an accurate estimate of ship's speed.

When Rowe felt the impact of the iceberg, his attention was drawn to it as it passed down the starboard side of *Titanic* - all else was swept from his mind during those moments. However, when the berg passed astern, Rowe remembered he had to read the Patent Log, so he went up onto the docking bridge where the Log Register was located and found that it was showing 260.0 nautical miles. The following is from Day 7 of the US Inquiry:

> "*as soon as the berg was gone I looked at the log and it read 260 miles. The log was reset at noon. I had charge of the tafrail log, which was a Neptune log*".

From this evidence, we know that the Patent Log was set at Noon that day and that Rowe's reading of it is a fairly accurate indication that *Titanic* had steamed a total of 260 nautical miles from Noon April 14 until she hit the iceberg. So we have ingredients (1) and (7) on our list. Incidentally, there was no obvious reason for Rowe to read the Patent Log at that moment, other than it being the end of The Watch. He had no idea of what was happening on *Titanic's* bridge. This reinforces the obvious - that when *Titanic* hit that ice berg, she had run a few minutes over twelve hours at full speed from Noon that day of April14, 1912 - the last full day of her life.

We also have an indicator as to what the Patent Log read at 6 pm that evening, and it comes from the evidence of *Titanic's* 5th Officer Hal Lowe.

As we have seen earlier, the Quartermaster at the stern had to read the Patent Log and report the reading to the bridge. Hal Lowe came on duty at 6 pm that evening of April, 14 - at the end of the First Dog Watch. One of his first duties would have been to record the patent Log reading for 6 pm as supplied by the stern Quartermaster. So what was that reading? The answer to that can be found out from Lowe himself. The following is from Day 5 of the US Inquiry:

> *"you take the average speed from 12 to 6 - that is giving her a run of six hours - We have the log -Twenty-one knots or under; it was really 20.95,"*

It follows that if Lowe calculated such a precise average speed of 20.95 knots over the previous six hours from Noon that day, then he did so by dividing the Patent Log reading for 6 pm by 6. Therefore, by multiplying the average speed of 20.95 knots by 6, we get the Patent Log reading for 6pm. Thus, we know that the Patent Log reading at 6 pm had to have been 125.7 nautical miles. That is number (3) of our list dealt with. We now have numbers (1), (3) and (7).

Titanic turned onto her final course for New York ten minutes *before* Lowe got the 6 pm Patent Log reading. Therefore, because we know she was averaging 20.95 knots at that time, we can deduce that ten minutes earlier, at 5-50pm, when she turned onto her final course for New York, the Patent Log read 3.5 miles less than it did at 6 pm. All of which means that at 5-50 pm when she turned, the Patent Log would have read 125.7

minus 3.5 = 122.2 nautical miles, which is number (2) on the list. We now have numbers (1), (2), (3) and (7).

The distance between where *Titanic*'s wreck now lies, and Fourth Officer Boxhall's distress position, is 12.6 miles, Therefore if *Titanic* had actually reached Boxhall's position, the patent Log would have read close to 260 + 12.6 = 272.6 nautical miles which is number (8) on the list. By the same token, if *Titanic* had reached Captain Smith's distress position. The Patent Log would have read 260+ 20 = 280 miles - No.9 on our list.

We now have estimated Patent Log readings for numbers (1), (2), (3), (7), (8) and (9) on the list. It is a while since we updated it, so what does it look like now? Here it is again, this time with the estimated Patent Log readings to date:

1. Noon, April 14, 1912 - 0.00 Miles
2. 5-50 pm April 14 when *Titanic* turned for New York-122.2 miles
3. 6. 00, pm April 14, End of first Dog Watch-125.7miles
4. Position by sights.
5. 8.00 pm April 14, End of second Dog Watch.
6. 8.00 pm DR used by Captain Smith.
7. Impact with Ice Berg - 260.0 miles
8. Boxhall's distress position - 272.6 miles
9. Captain Smith's distress position - 280.0 miles.

All that remains for us to find to complete our list, are values for (4), (5) and (6).To find the last two, we need to discover what course, speed and run-time Captain Smith used for his calculation between the false 8 pm and his distress position. So what were these?

If Captain Smith had used the correct DR position for 8pm that night, his distress position would have placed *Titanic* a little to the north, and close to where her wreck now lies. From this, we can deduce that the captain assumed that his ship was making good her planned course of 265True. Also, from the evidence, we know *Titanic* was making 22.5 knots from 8 pm onward, so we have values for course and speed. Now, all we need is a run time and then we have all three values that enable us to estimate the incorrect Patent Log reading used by Captain Smith.

The popular belief is that *Titanic* hit the ice berg at 11-40 pm unaltered ship time - 2-38 am GMT. However, as we have seen, a partial clock change of 24 minutes was made before *Titanic* hit the iceberg. So in fact, she hit the iceberg at 3 am GMT.

Captain Smith, like all navigators, worked in GMT. Consequently, when calculating *his* distress position, he would have used the GMT for 8 pm which was 10-58 pm and the GMT of impact.

To find the second GMT, he would have looked at the chronometer when he started his calculation and deducted about 15 minutes from the GMT showing on it to get the GMT of impact.

Thus he would have used a run time of 4 hours and 2 minutes.

A speed of 22.5 knots multiplied by a run time of 4 hours 2 minutes would have given Captain Smith a distance run between false 8 pm and impact with the ice of 91 miles

We have deduced that if *Titanic* had reached Captain Smith's distress position, the patent log would have read 280.0 miles

Consequently, if we subtract the run of 91 miles from that hypothetic reading of 280.0, we get 189 miles which, is an estimate of the Patent Log reading recorded in the Scrap Log at 8 m that evening - (6) on the list. However, according to 4th Officer Boxhall, this was a false 8 pm DR position, and was 20 miles too far a head of the proper 8 pm DR. position. Therefore to establish a proper estimate of the 8pm Patent log reading, we must subtract 20 miles from 189 miles. This gives us a more accurate, estimate of 169 nautical miles for the correct Patent Log reading for 8 pm that evening. (5) on our list.

We now have values for numbers (1). (2), (3), (5), (6), (7), (8) and (9) of the list, leaving (4) - the Patent Log reading for -30pm sights to be discovered. This will be done subsequently.

So now the all-but-one list looks like this:

1. Noon, April 14, 1912 - 0.00 Miles
2. 5-50 pm April 14. At *The Corner* turn -122.2 miles
3. 6. 00, pm April 14, End of first Dog Watch-125.7miles
4. Position by sights.
5. 8.00 pm April 14, End of second Dog Watch - 169 miles
6. 8.00 pm DR used by Captain Smith. -189 miles

7. Impact with Ice Berg - 260.0 miles
8. Boxhall's distress position - 272.6 miles.
9. Captain Smith's distress position - 280.0 miles.

Let's incorporate the foregoing times and estimated Patent Log readings into the plot and try and get a picture of the situation as it was during that period Noon to Midnight on April 14, 1912.

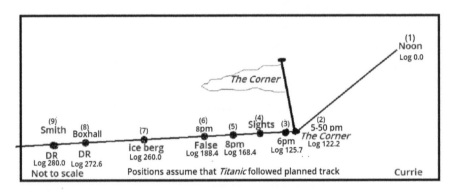

As can be seen, the above plot is relative to the planned track as laid down by International Convention and to be followed by the *Titanic*. However, she did not follow that track.

The track from Noon to *The Corner* was 236°.5 True. After she turned, it should have been 265°True. However, we know from the evidence of 5th Officer Lowe that *Titanic* was trying to make a course of 241°.5 True from Noon that day, this means that the April 14 Noon position placed her to the south and east of her planned track and that Captain Smith had altered course 4 degrees to the right so that *Titanic* would turn at *The Corner* exactly as planned and at 5-30 pm that early evening of April 14,

With the data accrued to this point, we are able to create a plot of estimated Patent Log reading from Noon that day and extended these to include the erroneous distress positions calculated by Captain Smith and his Fourth Officer. Thanks to the discoverer of *Titanic's* wreck by Robert Ballard, we also have a correct position for the wreck of the *Titanic*.

The accrued data has been plotted accurately on a proper North Atlantic Chart. I'm sure you will be astonished at the result.

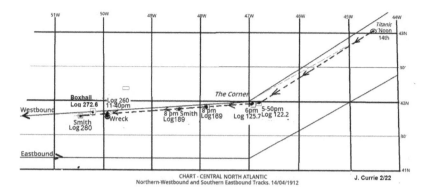

CHART - CENTRAL NORTH ATLANTIC
Northern-Westbound and Southern Eastbound Tracks. 14/04/1912

J. Currie 2/22

Log readings are estimates. However, if the above is within an acceptable margin of error, then *Titanic* never actually arrived at her intended turning point known as *The Corner,* but as expected, was held back by a current in the form of the eastern extension of the Gulf Stream. Nor only that, but she was also set southward by the northerly wind that had been blowing hard against her starboard side and four enormous sail-like funnels for most of the day. Consequently, she only covered a distance of 46.2 miles in the period between 5-50 pm when she turned and 8 pm which means that she only averaged 21.3 knots during that time.

From the foregoing, it should be obvious to a blind man in a dark room that there was absolutely nothing wrong with Captain Smith's navigation and that had he been fed with the correct data, he would have calculated the distress position to within a mile. It is also obvious that he used the correct course, speed and run time from 8pm that evening.

To summarise: Captain Edward J. Smith was a competent, highly experienced Mariner and Navigator who followed the protocol of the day.

Like his contemporaries, he did not slow down for ice nor did he alter his intentions. Nor did he - contrary to popular belief - intentionally over-run his intended turning point of *The Corner* at 5-50pm. Also, despite having logged an average speed of 22.1 knots up until Noon April 14, he made allowance for an expected head current when calculating the time to turn onto the final course for New York. We know this because we know the distance *Titanic* had to cover from leaving Queenstown to *The Corner,* and the distance she still had to run from Noon April 14 until she arrived there.

It follows that to find the proper time when he should turn his ship at *The Corner*, Captain Smith had to divide 124 by the speed he expected *Titanic* to make from Noon that afternoon.

Since he decided to turn her at 5-50 pm, we simply divide 124 by that number of hours and minutes (5 hrs. 50 minutes) to get his expected speed during that afternoon, which was 21.25 knots. From this, and because *Titanic* was averaging 22.1 knots up until then, we can deduce that Smith most certainly expected to meet a head current of a little over 1 knot and his 4th Officer expected the same thing. This is what Boxhall said at Q 16955 on Day 12 of the UK Inquiry:

> *".invariably we find a strong easterly set there; very often we find that the Gulf Stream".*

If Smith erred at all that afternoon of April 14, it was that he under-estimated the current strength and the wind leeway influencing the course of his ship

CHAPTER 45

THAT OTHER "WRONG" DISTRESS POSITION

We have dealt with the problem of Captain Smith's incorrect distress position and demonstrated how it happened, but what about the one calculated by *Titanic's* Fourth Officer Joseph Boxhall - you know - the distress position that was declared "excellent" by *Carpathia's* Captain Rostron, and the one everyone headed for but proved (by the finding of *Titanic's* wreck) to be 12.7 miles too far west.

How on earth did a man like Boxhall - an Extra Master with so many years experience - get it so wrong?

To discover this, we must understand the method he and Navigators of the day used back in 1912, and appreciate the conditions under which Boxhall was working.

From the sworn evidence, we know that just after 7-30 pm that evening of April 14, the Officer-of-the-Watch, Second Officer Lightoller, took sextant observations of six stars - three to the south and north, for latitude and three eastward/westward for longitude. After he had done so, the Watch senior Navigator, 3rd Officer Pitman, commenced the lengthy series of calculations which, when completed, would establish an exact position for *Titanic,* when Lightoller's sextant observations were made.

Pitman started the calculation process, but it was getting close to 8 pm - almost at the end of his Watch, so he did not have nearly enough time to finish them.

Consequently, they were completed by 4th Officer Boxhall during the 8 to Midnight Watch and the result given to Captain Smith some time after 9pm that evening.

Each Officer kept his own personal Work Book. It was, in fact, a running navigation record, and included details of where *Titanic* was, in terms of Greenwich Mean Time, at any one place during the voyage. Consequently, Boxhall had ready access to the results of Lightoller's 7-30 pm sights - which, incidentally, according to Pitman, put *Titanic* right on her planned track for New York.

So, when he went back to the chartroom to work his distress position, after calling the rest of the officers, Boxhall had a known, fixed position and the GMT when it was obtained. These were the basis upon which he would be able to calculate *Titanic's* distress position.

He also needed a course made good an average speed from 7-30 pm sights, and a GMT of when *Titanic* stopped due to hitting the iceberg.

When he had completed calculating that 7-30 pm sights position, Boxhall would also have known the time and distance that *Titanic* had steamed from the previous known position, which was at Noon that day. This would have provided him with an average speed up until 7-30 pm. Additionally; he would have calculated the course being made good between 5-50 pm (when *Titanic* had been turned onto her final course for New York) and 7-30 pm sights. According to his evidence, this was 266°True. Since there was no plan to alter course, he would use that course in his calculation.

Thus, from his workbook, Boxhall would have obtained three bits of vital information which he needed and which were essential to calculating an accurate distress position for *Titanic,* these were:

1. The coordinates of a fixed start position.
2. The course being made good from the fixed start position.
3. A Greenwich Mean Time for 7-30 pm sights.

In addition to these three, he would need:

4. An average speed. Between the fixed start position and when *Titanic* stopped.

5. A Greenwich Mean Time for when *Titanic* finally stopped.

We know what speed Boxhall used, because in his evidence, he stated that due to the perfect conditions of flat calm, he assumed that the ship was making her optimum speed, therefore he used a speed of 22 knots.

In other words, he estimated a value for speed rather that use a speed indicated by engine revolutions or by Patent Log reading.

Historians have argued that *Titanic* averaged more than 22 knots from Noon that day, but Boxhall's evidence provides us with clear, unequivocal proof that the speed *Titanic* had made between Noon until 7-30 pm that evening, (deduced from the fixed position obtained) had to have been less than 22 knots, otherwise, due to the perfect conditions, Boxhall would have used a speed *greater* than 22 knots.

This is borne-out in the plot shown previously where the indicated average speed between 6 pm and 8 pm was 21.3 knots.

So, Boxhall had all the ingredients necessary to calculate a distress position - all except one - the GMT of when *Titanic* stopped for the last time. This was absolutely necessary to obtain the running time between the GMT of the 7-30 pm sights and stop time. He would get that time from the Scrap Log and/or the Movement Book which were in the Chart room and wheelhouse; so what was noted therein?

We know from the evidence of Quarter Master Hichens that immediately after *Titanic* had come to a halt after that frantic attempt to avoid the iceberg, First Officer Murdoch ordered Sixth Officer Moody to make a record of the helm and engine orders which had been given during that hectic few minutes. However, because these times were written after the event, their absolute accuracy could not be relied upon but would have been close enough for the purpose of calculating a distress position.

In fact, there would have been a series of recorded times, starting with the time of hitting the ice berg, followed by the first engine order and finishing with the final "STOP" order on the engines. The first recorded time is popularly accepted as 11-40 pm. From Engine Room personnel evidence, we know that engine movements from moment of impact until the final STOP order took six (6) minutes. Therefore, the final STOP notation in the Scrap Log should have been about 11-46 pm. Boxhall said he used 11-45 pm.

For the twenty-odd minutes after the ship stopped, everyone was running about performing a multitude of duties. Not until all this frantic activity had settled-down to a steady pace, would Boxhall have been able to return to the chartroom and calculate the ship's position. We know from his evidence this was just after Midnight- after he had called the other officers. Before then, he would have had little time to consult with 6th Officer Moody and 5th Officer Lowe - the two officers who were responsible for applying the planned two-stage clock change of 47 minutes. As we saw in Chapter 38 of this work, there is uncontroversial proof that the first stage of the planned clock alteration had taken place just before *Titanic* hit the iceberg. Consequently, my best guess is that since it was after midnight when Boxhall eventually had time to perform the task of calculating a distress position, he was in a hurry and did not perform the detailed calculation using the Greenwich Mean Times in his work book, but simply used the calculated position in that book together with the Greenwich Mean Time equivalent for 7-30p. (10-28pm) He also assumed that the 11-45 pm was unaltered ship time, and was therefore equal to 2-44 pm GMT unaltered time, and - since Pitman had been called, - added the full clock change of 47 minutes to get a GMT equivalent of 3-31 pm for when *Titanic* stopped.

Thus he used a run time of 10-28 pm GMT to 3-31 am GMT = 5 hours 02 minutes - a speed of 22 knots, which equates to a run distance of 110.7 miles.

As we have seen in the previous chapter, the Hypothetical Patent Log reading for Boxhall's erroneous distress position would have been 272.6 miles; if we subtract 110.7 miles from that. We get an estimated patent log reading of 161.9 miles for the time of Lightoller's 7-30 pm star sights. Is this a coincidence? Or does it fit with another bit of evidence - once again given by 5th Officer Lowe, who on Day 5 of the US Inquiry stated?

> *"I worked the course from noon until what we call the*
> *"corner"; that is, 42 north, 47 west. I really forget the course*
> *now. It is 60° 33 1/2' west - that is as near as I can remember -*
> *and 162 miles to the corner.*

It has been argued by *Titanic* Historians that Lowe got his numbers mixed-up, and that in fact, he simply got the distance number the wrong way round and really meant "and 126 miles to the corner". All very convenient, but I suggest that in fact, Lowe mixed up his memory with a later event when, as Junior Navigator, he would have called aft for a patent log reading to be used to calculate a DR (estimated) Position which is always necessary for working accurate sextant observations. Lowe would have called for that on completion of 7-30 pm sights - about 7-40 pm.

Incidentally: we know that Boxhall was aware that a partial clock change had taken place before the ship hit the iceberg, because on Day 10 of the US Inquiry, he told his questioner, Senator SMITH:

At 11.46 p.m., ship's time, it was 10.13 Washington time, or New York time."

This is a difference of 1 hour 33 minutes.

Once again, certain *Titanic* historians have jumped on this answer because it is inaccurate, in that a partly adjusted *Titanic* clock time would have had a 1 hour 38 minutes difference instead of Boxhalls' 1 hour 33 minutes difference. As I have already pointed out; Boxhall did not normally work in terms of the New York Time -EST - Eastern Standard Time kept at New York. He and all other marine Navigators worked in Greenwich Mean Time and in Local Mean Time aboard ship based on Longitude.

Navigators always worked in longitude time and the longitude time for New York Boxhall and all other Navigators used, had a difference of 4 hours 55 minutes from GMT, not the 5 hours different between GMT and Eastern Standard Zone Time used by lands people. Thus, when Boxhall was asked to make that time comparison, he knew that the equivalent GMT for 11-46 pm was 3-22 am. Consequently he subtracted 3 hours 22 minutes GMT from 4 hours 55 minutes (not from 5 hours). This gave him the time difference disputed by historians - 1 hour 33 minutes.

So there you have it.

Because we have established the arguments Boxhall used to calculate his distress position, we can determine an estimated position for where Lightollers sights located *Titanic* just after 7-30 pm that evening. I have done so and the details can be found in the Annex.

However, the results suggest that Second Officer Lightoller's 7-30 pm star sights located *Titanic* 37 miles westward of *The Corner* and 2 miles south of her intended track, not on the track, as claimed by Third Officer Pitman; and near to the position of Latitude 41-54'North, Longitude 47-47'West. I have plotted this on the following chart to illustrate the point

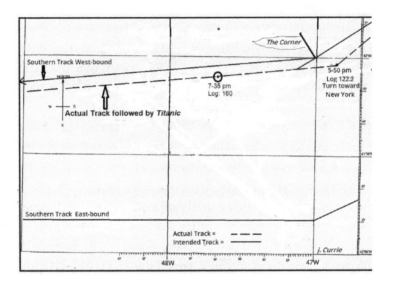

To summarise: Boxhall made four basic errors. These were:

A: He assumed *Titanic* was on her pre-planned track and had over-shot *The Corner* before she turned at 5-50 pm. Consequently:

B: He used the wrong Course from the 7-30 pm sights position to the distress position.

C: He assumed the wrong speed from the 7-30 pm sights position to the distress position.

D: Even although, he knew that a partial clock change had taken place at or just before, the time if hitting the iceberg, he wrongly assumed that the clocks had been fully set-back. Consequently, he used the wrong run time from Lightoller's fix position to the stop position.

Having observed this, none of us should condemn the man. Our good fortune is not to have found ourselves in similar dire circumstances and had our skills tested in a similar way.

Ironically; when Boxhall died in 1962, his body was cremated and in accordance with his wishes - scattered at his erroneous distress position.

PART 9

CHAPTER 46

DAMNATION- CAPTAIN STANLEY LORD

History is full of tales concerning incompetent, drunken ship captains but Captain Stanley Lord was, in fact the exact opposite. Despite this, and unlike the villains of the past whose bad reputations were written about *after* they died, Lord was damned and branded as such at the height of his career and had to carry that damnable brand to his grave almost 50 years later. Worse still - in the minds of some people, he is *still* damned and presented as the villain of the piece.

So who is right, was Captain Stanley Lord of the *Californian* a villain or a victim? Make your own mind up after reading the following.

On his way up to the dizzy heights of command, Captain Stanley Lord was described by his lecturers as "a brilliant student". He obtained his Master and Extra Master's Certificates at the age of twenty three and within six years, his then employer, the Leyland Line, demonstrated their confidence in him by promoting him at the unusually young age of twenty nine, to command a cargo vessel named *Antillian* which by then, was seven years old.

At the time of the *Titanic* disaster Lord was within five months of his thirty sixth birthday. By then, he had been in command for seven years, and had been captain of the SS Californian since March in the previous year of 1911. Consequently, up until April 14, 1912, the man's ability as a commander and navigator could never have been in any doubt.

Much has been written about Lord's personality as a man and as a commander, most of it derogatory and damaging. However those who have penned such nonsense exhibit their lack of knowledge in doing so, as well as having a penchant for gossip. What they did not know, and still do not know, is that in the old days, the Master of a vessel wrote a character report for each of his junior officers when they paid off the ship at the end of the voyage. This was sent to the Company and a copy went to The Board of Trade.

It would subsequently constitute part of the assessment of each candidate's suitability to be the holder of a Certificate of Competency.

According to *Titanic* author, Senan Maloney; Captain J. D. McNab, the Chief Examiner for The Board of Trade Examiners at Liverpool, described Stanley Lord as "a brilliant student".

Following the disaster and the findings of both Inquiries into the *Titanic* disaster, the same Captain McNab was asked to write an Employment Reference for Lord. This he did and thanks to Senan, part of it is reproduced hereunder:

> *"His testimonials for good conduct and ability at sea being invariably of the highest order and I have ever heard him spoken of as a humane and clever officer and commander."*

It should be borne in mind that the above reference was written by a person who was an employee of the British Board of Trade - the very organisation which commissioned the Inquiry into the *Titanic* disaster - an Inquiry, the findings of which, contradicted Captain McNab's assessment of Captain Lord. So why would McNab, in turn, contradict his employer?

Very strange indeed!

The picture painted by McNab was hardly the image of the incompetent, dour, self-centred, grim-faced, ogre-like character depicted by so many of the man's accusers who were coincidently McNabs bosses.

CHAPTER 47

LORD - THE NAVIGATOR

Before the *Titanic* disaster, Captain Lord had never been on the North Atlantic run during the ice season. His only experience of meeting sea ice was when he was sailing in the southern hemisphere. Consequently, due to the previous receipt of ice warnings, he was being even more than normally cautious during that evening of April 14, 1912.

At 8 pm, when his Third Officer Groves took over the bridge Watch from Chief Officer Stewart, Lord joined Groves on the bridge and doubled his lookouts in the bow and in the Crow's Nest, Two hours and twenty minutes later, these precautions paid off - *Californian's* progress was abruptly curtailed by a barrier of pack ice. It stretched out of sight as far north and south as he could see.

When the ship came to a complete stop, Lord calculated her DR (approximate) position. To help him do this, he had an accurate latitude by Pole Star obtained by his Chief Officer Stewart 3 hours earlier, so he used that as his starting point.

He had also obtained an accurate Noon position for April, so he already knew his course and speed from then until they met the ice. Because of the foregoing, the calculation for the stopped position was fairly simple and straightforward and with little possibility of error. It was therefore entered into the Log Book as:

Latitude 42° - 05'North, Longitude 50° - 07'West.

However, at Noon that day, the position by observation of the sun was found to be Latitude 52°-05'N, Longitude 47°-34'W. Consequently, Lord had altered his course a little to the southward, with the intention of bringing his ship back onto her intended course, which was to be due west along the 42nd parallel of latitude.

He was therefore probably surprised when the Chief Officer's Pole Star sight showed that in fact, *Californian* had not changed her latitude since Noon and had been maintaining a true course of due West.

Despite the recorded abilities of the man, one of the criticisms and accusations levelled at Captain Lord was that his navigation was either faulty or by implication, that the ship's Official Log Book was altered to show an improper position when *Californian* stopped at 10-21 pm on the evening of April 14, 1912.

The basis for this accusation was, and still is to this very day, a need to establish beyond reasonable doubt, that *Californian* was in plain sight of those on the sinking *Titanic*. Because once that was established, the task of proving Lord's negligence and inhumanity in disregarding the persistent pleas for assistance would be a simple one.

In the next chapter, I will deal with the accusations concerning separation distance, however, for now; we are considering the man's navigation expertise.

From the evidence given by Captain Lord, it is obvious that his intentions on the morning of April 14, was to navigate his ship in the usual way - by obtaining a latitude by Pole Star during the 4 am to 8 am Watch and thereafter, establishing a longitude by sun observation some time after breakfast.

Normally, this would not create any problems on such a bright sunny morning as it was. However, Lord had estimated that *Californian* would reach the turning point at *The Corner* between these two early and late morning observations. Consequently, he simply assumed that *Californian* was on her proper course for *The Corner* when the earliest observation was taken.

At that time, if *Californian* had been on the recognised Great Circle track to the turning position at *The Corner* from the entrance to the English Channel, his course would have been about 235True.

We also know from the evidence, that Captain Lord had estimated that *Californian* would be at *The Corner* at 9-40 am that morning.

If his First Officer had obtained a latitude at say 5-30 am. and the estimated speed of *Californian* was 11 knots, then the plot would look like this:

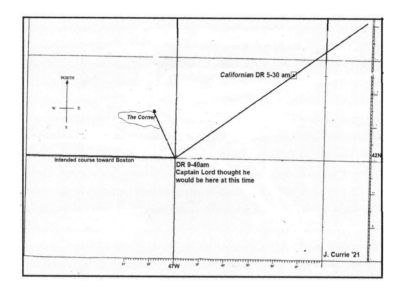

After breakfast, a longitude of 47°-25'West was obtained. We know this because on Day of the US inquiry, Captain Lord told his questioner that he tried to contact *Titanic* at 10-50 pm that evening -25 minutes after *Californian* had stopped for the ice, and that *Californian's* clocks had been set when they had obtained a Longitude of 47-25'W. Such a Longitude is 18.6 miles due west of *The Corner*. If *Californian* was making 11 knots and she turned at 9-40am, then the longitude of 47-25'W was obtained 1 hour, 42 minutes after she turned - at 11-22am that morning.

As we have seen - at 12 o' clock, the altitude of the sun placed *Californian* at the latitude of 42°-05 minutes North. Then, the course was set to 269°True, which is one degree south of due West.

On that course, if there was nothing influencing the compass or the ship herself; *Californian* would slowly have returned to her originally intended track of due West along the 42nd parallel of Latitude and have been at the position of Latitude 42°-00'North, Longitude 53°-34'West the next Day, April 15.

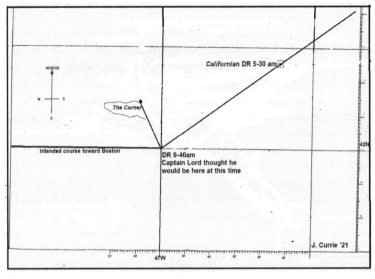

J.Currie

Further indication of this intention, was the approximate position given at 6-30pm that early evening.

At that time, ice bergs were seen south of the track and Captain Lord reported his position relative to them was by wireless message to the SS "Antillian".

"Latitude 42 3 north, longitude 49 9 west. Three large bergs 5 miles to southward of us…. Regards. Lord."

Note the reduction in latitude since Noon that day. It is obvious that this position was an estimated one based on the Noon position, estimated speed and an assumption that the ship was making a track one degree south of due West.

Unfortunately this anomaly between the Noon latitude and latitude at 6-30 pm was pounced upon by Lord's detractors as an example of bad navigation, or worse still- of an attempt by him to pervert the course of justice. As proof, they cited the official record of this sighting, submitted by Lord at the end of the voyage to the US Hydrographic Office which showed the latitude as 42- 05 'North…2 miles to the northward of the original message recorded by the Wireless Operator. What they failed to comprehend was, that such official notifications were submitted in retrospect, and by the time the official notification was filled-in, which would have been after April 14,- after the true latitude had been established by Chief Officer Stewart .

At 8pm that evening, of April 14, a DR 8 pm position would have been entered into *Californian's* Scrap Log. Since it was calculated less than an hour after Stewart had obtained his Pole Star latitude, the 8 pm DR latitude recorded, would have been the same - 42-05'N.

When *Californian* finally stopped because of the ice...two hours twenty-odd minutes later, it was a very simple task, for Captain Lord to calculate a DR position for that stopped position. In fact, the Navigation Apprentice, James Gibson could have done the same thing with his eyes shut. Have a look at this.

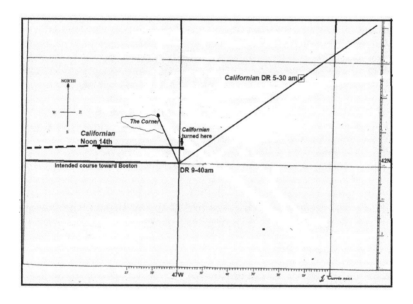

Further indication of this intention, was the approximate position given at 6-30pm that early evening.

At that time, ice bergs were seen south of the track and Captain Lord reported his position relative to them was by wireless message to the SS "Antillian".

> *"Latitude 42 3 north, longitude 49 9 west. Three large bergs*
> *5 miles to southward of us…. Regards. Lord."*

Note the reduction in latitude since Noon that day. It is obvious that this position was an estimated one based on the Noon position, estimated speed and an assumption that the ship was making a track one degree south of due West.

Unfortunately this anomaly between the Noon latitude and latitude at 6-30 pm was pounced upon by Lord's detractors as an example of bad navigation, or worse still - of an attempt by him to pervert the course of justice.

As proof, they cited the official record of this sighting, submitted by Lord at the end of the voyage to the US Hydrographic Office which showed the latitude as 42- 05 'North, which was 2 miles to the northward of the original message recorded by the Wireless Operator. What they failed to comprehend was, that such official notifications were submitted in retrospect, and by the time the official notification was filled-in, which would have been after April 14,- after the true latitude had been established by Chief Officer Stewart .

At 8pm that evening, of April 14, a DR 8 pm position would have been entered into *Californian's* Scrap Log. Since it was calculated less than an hour after Stewart had obtained his Pole Star latitude, the 8 pm DR latitude recorded, would have been the same - 42-05'N.

When *Californian* finally stopped because of the ice...two hours twenty-odd minutes later, it was a very simple task, for Captain Lord to calculate a DR position for that stopped position. In fact, the Navigation Apprentice, James Gibson could have done the same thing with his eyes shut. Have a look at this.

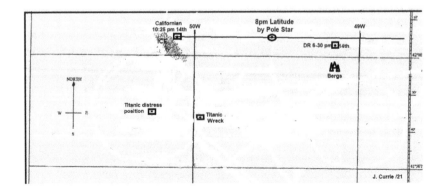

The above situation was verified by Ice Reports submitted by no less than five other vessels on the same day in a time span of less than twelve hours. These were the SS "Mesaba".

The SS "Trauutenfels"

SS "Pisa",

SS "Ahtenai"

SS "Bretagne".

All five actually sighted the bergs seen by those on the *Californian*.

The first two, also met the same barrier on the same day at the same place where it was encountered by the *Californian*. In fact, the SS "Trautenfels" was stopped by it four miles to the Southeast of where *Californian* was stopped by it and the *Mesaba* had to divert 20 miles to the south to go around it

As can be seen from the plots, the *Californian* was nowhere near the *Titanic* when she hit the ice berg. Not only that, but they contradict the claim that there was a south-setting current in the area. In fact they suggest a movement toward the north.

So what was the true separation distance between the two vessels?

CHAPTER 48

HOW FAR APART WERE THEY?

Lord's technical ability as a Commander and Navigator had been officially tested and found faultless by his superiors, so could never have been in any doubt. Yet, there are many, to this very day, who cannot accept these findings, and strive to prove, that in fact, his navigation and that of his officers was so bad that the officers could not read a sextant or compass properly and that *Californian* was in fact, as much as 16 miles off-course and that was why she had stopped within sight of the sinking *Titanic*.

No lesser a being than Lord Mersey, the King's Wreck Commissioner actually committed this nonsense to the annals of history when in his final report following the Official Inquiry into the disaster, he wrote:

> *These circumstances convince me that the ship seen by the "Californian" was the "Titanic," and if so, according to Captain Lord, the two vessels were about five miles apart at the time of the disaster. The evidence from the "Titanic" corroborates this estimate, but I am advised that the distance was probably greater, though not more than eight to ten miles."*

This was, and still is, an outrageous, public lie.

For a start:- the transcript of his evidence at the UK Inquiry in London shows us that Captain Lord told him no such thing.

Lord Mersey had at his command, the technical assistance of some of the most competent marine minds of the day, backed up by the entire UK Marine fraternity. He also had access to the evidence taken at the US Inquiry during the previous weeks.

Through Mersey, all these experts had access to every single iota of sworn evidence given on both sides of the Atlantic.

Consequently, the idea that any one of them would have advised him of such a separation distance beggars belief.

In fact, the idea that anyone with even a basic understanding of nautical science could have reached such a conclusion after carefully analysing all the available evidence given at the time, is totally incomprehensible and belongs among the Tales of Aesop.

Not only was it a lie back in 1912, but it became obviously so, 80 years later when, at the request of the then UK Government Minister of Transport, the case was re-examined by the then, recently formed Marine Accident Investigation Branch (MAIB) of the UK Coastguard.

The first attempt by the MAIB was farmed out to a retired Marine Inspector of The UK Department of Transport. This turned out to be a rehash of the 1912 version, and the man simply rubber stamped the Lord Mersey nonsense.

However, to give credit to the Chief Inspector of the MAIB; he was not convinced; therefore he had his Depute carry out a greater in-depth evaluation of the evidence.

The second, more thorough effort concluded that *Californian* was not 8 or 9 miles - but more like 18 to 20 miles - from the sinking *Titanic,* and, in addition, offered the possibility of there having been a third vessel involved.

Despite the progress made, the last of these MAIB investigations was moulded as a form of compromise with Mersey's utterances.

It was fatally flawed in that it ignored and/or failed to include, or emphasise, four most significant parts of the sworn evidence given, which, if these had been properly considered, would have proved beyond all reasonable doubt, that the ship seen from the sinking *Titanic* could not have been the *Californian* and that the separation distance between these two vessels at the time of the disaster was greater than 22 miles.

These significant bits of evidence were as follows:

- The sworn evidence of Captain Lord regarding the movements of a vessel which stopped about 4 miles to the southeast of the stopped *Californian* at 11-30 pm ship time - 9-40 pm EST on April 14.
- The sworn evidence of survivors from the *Titanic* that
  a) They did not see the lights of a ship before or after *Titanic* hit the iceberg and was stopped at or about 11-46 pm ship time *Titanic*.
  b) That lights were not seen ahead of the sinking Titanic for a period of more that 20 minutes after she had finally come to a halt.
  c) That they saw a moving ship when *Californian* was already stopped.
  d) That they saw a red sidelight on the nearby vessel at the time *Californian* was showing a green one to her nearby ship.
- The sworn evidence regarding helm orders given by *Titanic's* 'surviving Quartermasters, Hitchens that only one helm order was given as part of the iceberg-avoiding manoeuvre.
- The sworn evidence given by the *Californian's* 2nd Officer and Deck Apprentice regarding the 3-30 am sighting of *Carpathian's* "rockets of comfort" on their visible horizon at 3-30 am on the morning of April 15, 1912.

The first three of these are crucial to the argument, in that proper analysis of the evidence relative to them will show that the vessel stopped near to the *Californian* after she had stopped could never have been the *Titanic*. The fourth bit of evidence proves, beyond any doubt whatsoever, that the true separation distance between *Titanic* and the *Californian* was much greater than proposed and in keeping with the declared navigation of the latter.

CHAPTER 49

ANALYSIS OF SEPARATION EVIDENCE

In the last chapter I drew your attention to four (4) sources of evidence which prove that the vessel seen by the survivors from the *Titanic* as she was sinking, could not have been the SS Californian. I will now conduct an in-depth analysis of this evidence which will show you exactly why that was the case, beginning with:

No 1: From *Californian.*

On Day 8 of the US Inquiry, Captain Lord told his questioner;

"I was talking with the engineer about keeping the steam ready, and we saw these signals coming along, and I said "There is a steamer passing. Let us go to the wireless and see what the news is. He came and lay at half-past 11 ...alongside of us...within 4 miles of us."

This conversation with the engineer took place on a lower deck, starboard side of the *Californian* around 10-50 pm that evening, after *Californian* had been stopped for about 25 minutes. At this point, non mariners should know that when a professional uses the expression "alongside us" he means very close - or within a few miles.

Lord also told questioners on both sides of the Atlantic that the ship he saw was showing a green light right up until she stopped and he stopped watching her - until 11-30 pm.

On the other hand, when *Titanic* stopped, she was showing her port-red light, not her green one, to the vessel in plain sight.

Then Lord told his questioners that his Third Officer had used a powerful, Morse signalling lamp at least four separate times before midnight - in an attempt to discover the name of the vessel stopped nearby. This was corroborated by his Third Officer. These signals were completely ignored by the vessel in plain sight.

In fact the evidence clearly shows that there were no vessels in sight from *Titanic's* bridge during those first twenty minutes.

At 10-50 pm - 9 pm EST on *Californian*, the time on *Titanic* would have been 11-02 pm and she had another hour to run before she hit the iceberg which at that time, was 22.5 miles ahead of her. This means that if Lord and his Engineer were seeing the White Star Liner at 10-50 pm, she was at least 36 miles away and at best 28 miles away which is patently absurd. I'm sure the eyesight of Lord and his engineer was good, but not *that* good.

However as earlier mentioned - there are those who conveniently do not accept that *Titanic's* clocks were partially changed before she hit the iceberg. I say "Conveniently", because if *Titanic's* clocks had not been partially changed, then when Lord and his Engineer first saw the approaching vessel, *Titanic* would have had 38 minutes or about 16 miles to run before she hit the ice berg. Even then, the idea is absurd.

You will recall that the MAIB report put *Californian* at 18 to 20 miles from the sinking *Titanic*. If so, then these two "hawk-eyes" on *Californian* first saw *Titanic* when she was 29 miles away.

However, after all this - even if there had been no clock change and *Titanic* stopped 9 miles from *Californian*; Lord and his engineer would have first seen *Titanic's* lights with the naked eye at a distance of over 18 miles again, a ludicrous idea.

I have concocted a little sketch to illustrate how ridiculous the assertions concerning separation distances between the two ships were. In it, I show separation distances at 5 mile intervals between *Californian* and the sinking *Titanic* and the relative separation distances between the two of them an hour before *Titanic* met her destiny with the iceberg.

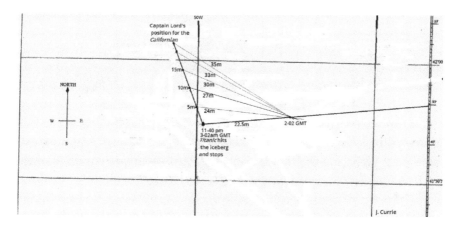

The above clearly shows that there is no way that the vessel seen approaching the stopped *Californian* at 10-50 pm that night by Captain Lord, his engineer could possibly have been the *Titanic*.

No.2: From *Titanic*.

The vessel seen to arrive near to the stopped *Californian* was being observed by Captain Lord for at least 40 minutes before it finally arrived nearby This being the case, then by the same token - unless everyone was asleep on that vessel - the lights on the *Californian* would most certainly have been in sight of the approaching vessel's lookouts and bridge officer on duty as that vessel approached; and would have been so, for at least the same period of time as they were being seen from the *Californian*. There is no way around such a conclusion.

However, the foregoing scenario does not match the sworn evidence of *Titanic's* surviving Lookout Fred Fleet who was up in the Crow's Nest from 10 pm that evening until Midnight - 20 minutes after hitting the ice berg.

On Day 4 of the US Inquiry, Fleet had the following conversation with his questioner:

"Q had you reported anything at all, do you remember?

> *Fteet: <u>There was nothing to be reported</u>...We were looking all over the place, all around...<u>There was no lights at all when we was up in the crow's nest.</u>"*

Can there be any doubt about what that man was telling his questioner?

<u>No.3 The moving vessel</u>

At midnight - twenty minutes after hitting the iceberg and fourteen minutes after *Titanic* had stopped, the officers and deck crew were on her boat deck preparing the ship's boats and alerting the passengers. Fourth Officer Boxhall returned to the bridge where he got permission from Captain Smith to calculate a (second) distress position and take it to the wireless room. Around that time the lookouts who had relieved Fleet and Lee at Midnight, or someone else, reported sighting a light ahead of the sinking liner. This was the very first indication of there being *any* vessel within sight of the sinking *Titanic* - after the first distress call had been sent out, and long after the ship had come to a halt.

The following are the relative parts of the sworn evidence of Fourth Officer Joe Boxhall given on Day 3 of the US Inquiry and Day 13 of the UK Inquiry respectively - he was describing what he saw when the light ahead was reported.

> *Boxhall: "By the way she was heading she seemed to be meeting us. Senator SMITH: .Coming toward you?*

> *Boxhall: Coming toward us.......And then, <u>as she got closer, she showed her side light, her red light.</u>*

> *after seeing the men continuing with their work I saw all the Officers were out, and I went into the chart room to work out its position.*

Then at the UK:

> *1390. Was it after that you saw this light?*

Boxhall - It was after that, yes, because I must have been to the Marconi office with the position after I saw the light.

15391. You took it to the Marconi office in order that it might be sent by the wireless operator?

15392. And then you saw this light which you say looked like a masthead light?

- Yes, <u>it was two masthead lights of a steamer..</u>"

Note that Boxhall was describing a moving vessel, whereas, *Californian* had been stopped for an hour and 50 minutes.

Boxhall also mentions seeing a red sidelight. This was also seen by *Titanic's* 5th Officer Lowe as he was preparing to launch lifeboat No.1 and a few minutes after Boxhall had fired the first of *Titanic's* distress signals. There is no doubt that those ob Californian saw Titanic's distress signals, but at that very same time, the *Californian* was showing a green light in the direction of *her* nearby vessel and most certainly not, a red one..

<u>No. 4 The Dipping distance.</u>

At 3-30 am the rescue vessel *Carpathia* was about 8 miles from the location of where *Titanic* sank. The evidence tells us she was firing "rockets of comfort" every fifteen minutes. These were seen at extreme range- i.e. right on the horizon of those who saw them from the upper bridge of *Californian*.

If *Carpathia was firing* standard rockets rising to a height of 350 feet above her decks, then the extreme range of such rockets was 21.5 nautical miles.

The horizon of those on the *Californian* was 8.5 nautical.

Combined - these extreme ranges indicate a separation distance between *Californian* and *Carpathia* of 21.5 + 8.5 = 30 miles.From the evidence, we know that at the time the rockets were seen, *Carpathia* was 8 miles from the disaster site. Eight (8) miles subtracted from the extreme range of 30 miles, shows that *Californian* was 22 miles from that site.

Another little sketch will, I hope help to make this crucial point.

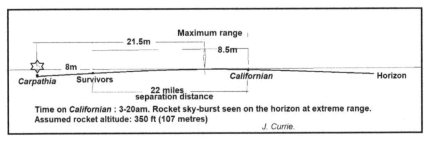

J. Currie 2022

Although the foregoing is overwhelming proof that the vessel stopped nearby to *Californian* that night could not have been the sinking *Titanic* and that there was nothing wrong with Captain Lord's navigation; those who would condemn him have ignored it all and have even gone to the lengths of "bending" the evidence to suite the findings of Lord Mersey. I used the term *bending* in the fullest sense as will be seen in the next chapter.

PART 10

CHAPTER 50

BENDING THE EVIDENCE

There is no doubt that Immediately before *Titanic* hit the iceberg, *Californian* was stopped away to the northward and on the White Star liner's starboard bow. - In a direction which was far-off to the right of the direction in which *Titanic* was travelling. Nor is there any doubt that a vessel was seen on *Titanic's* port bow by survivors, as she was sinking. However, if *Titanic* turned hard left - southward - in an attempt to avoid danger, and then stopped pointing south west, and *Californian* was stopped to the north-west of her - how on earth did *Californian* get to be seen on *Titanic's* port - left bow and not on the opposite - starboard bow?

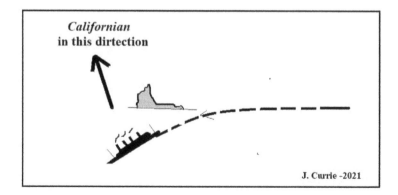

All very neat and convenient, but utter nonsense, and here is why.

On Day 3 of the UK Inquiry, the man who actually received and obeyed the helm orders - Quartermaster Hichens - was specifically questioned on a second helm order the following was his emphatic answer:

"*1316. It is Question* She never was under a port helm?

- She did not come on the port helm, Sir - on the starboard helm."

At this point, it should be emphasised that back in 1912, helm orders were the opposite of what they are today. Thus: instead of as today, hard a port means hard left rudder, back in 1912, it meant hard right rudder, and hard -to starboard meant the opposite to what it means today.

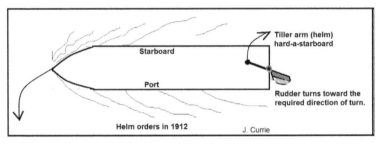

J. Currie 2022

All very confusing, but bear with me. Not only the evidence of QM Hichens, but the evidence of Second Officer Boxhall reinforced the fact that only a single helm order was given.

On Day 13 of the UK Inquiry Boxhall told his questioner that he overheard the following conversation between First Officer Murdoch and Captain Smith at the moment the latter appeared on the bridge immediately after *Titanic* hit the iceberg:

> "Q15355. - *The first Officer said, "An iceberg, Sir. I hard-a-starboarded and reversed the engines, and I was going to hard-a-port round it but she was too close. I could not do any more.*"

In the foregoing evidence, the emphasis is mine. The content may be interpreted in two ways - none of which support a zig-zag avoidance attempt.

In fact, what Murdoch was telling his captain was, that the intention was to turn the ship left to clear danger, but the ship (not the berg) was too close and the attempt failed.

The clue in that answer is the intention of the witness. The First officer "was going" to do something - he didn't do it. What more is needed - perhaps a sound video taken at the time? Really? Imagination is a great tool but can be counter-productive on occasions - this was one of them.

Apart from the foregoing, the physics of a ship turning precluded the possibility of *Titanic* ever having been able to stop her left hand (hard-a-starboard) turn and convert it into a right hand one. Here's why.

Back in 1912, ships like *Titanic* had steam-driven steering gear activated by the steering wheel on the bridge. Although it was very efficient, there was a slight delay between movement o the steering wheel and corresponding movement of the rudder. Consequently When Quartermaster Hichens received that berg-avoiding helm order, he would have spun the steering wheel as fast as he could from about mid-ship to hard-over- left. This would have taken him about five (5) seconds. *Titanic's* bow movement - as with every ship -would lag the application of the wheel. However, from a slow start, her bow-swing would have rapidly increased to a constant rate.

The moment a ship starts turning, she immediately starts to lose speed. The rate at which a ship slowed down when the helm was set hard over and with engines on Full Ahead was found during her sea trials. At that time, a Turning Circle Trial at full speed was carried out. While the results of such trials varied from vessel to vessel, there was one commonality. It was found that a ship making full speed would complete a turning circle equal in diameter to about six(6) times her length, but when she had completed but half of that circle and without touching the engines, her speed would fall by almost 50%.

Then there is the small matter of turbulence.

A ship's rudder will operate efficiently down to slow speeds as long as the water flowing past it is constant and undisturbed. However, *Titanic's* engines were stopped at the same time the helm order was given. This meant that three very large propellers came quickly to a halt directly in front of the rudder.

Although the ship was still moving at 22 knots, her propellers were not...they were being dragged along with her as useless appendages. We can only imagine the turbulence and turmoil around the rudder from the moment these great blades halted, but I'm sure some test tank results will show that the rudder very quickly became useless and a would remain so until normal water- flow past it was restored.

In simple terms: because of the rapidly reducing speed, the turning motion of the giant hull and the ensuing turbulence around the stern area caused by propeller drag, it would have been impossible for *Titanic's* rudder to convert a hard left turn to into a hard right turn.

It should also be appreciated that a ship's rudder only instigates a turn. Consequently, if a turn has to be stopped - checked - and a reverse turn put in its place, only an efficient rudder can do this, and as we have seen, *Titanic's* rudder was certainly not efficient after a very short space of time.

However, having pointed this all out to the doubting Thomases of the world - there certainly was, a second helm order given, but as the witness to it, stand-by Quartermaster Olliver told his questioner; it was given when the iceberg was "way-down astern" - too late to have been part of any iceberg- avoiding plan.

This begs the question as to why First Officer Murdoch would give such an order when danger had passed and knowing that the ship was rapidly slowing down and the rudder was becoming useless.

I suggest the answer to this question can be found in the evidence of Coal Trimmer Thomas Dillon who was in the engine room at the time and noted the engine movements from start to finish during the emergency.

On Day 5 of the UK Inquiry, he told his questioner:

> *3719. You just heard it ring. Then a few seconds after that*
> *you felt a slight shock? - Yes.*
> *3720.- They stopped.*
> *3722.- They went slow astern. - About two minutes.*
> *3726. And then did they stop again? - Yes.*
> *- They went ahead again.- For about two minutes.*
> *3729. Then did they stop the boat after that? - Yes."*

These engine movements tell a ship handler that Captain Smith stopped his ship and then briefly ran his engines ahead before finally stopping them.

There is only one reason he would do that and it would be to use his rudder, and the only reason he had for using his rudder at that early stage after hitting the ice, would have been to bring his ship back on her original heading, ready to resume passage, if a "no damage" report was received.

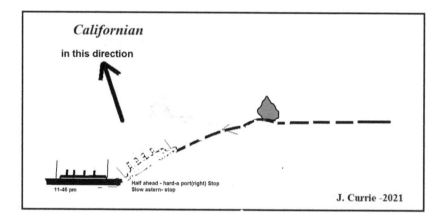

At this point, those who are still in doubt will point to a serious anomaly in the evidence given by *Titanic's* helmsman Hichens - his reference to a change in heading of two points - two and a quarter (22.5) degrees - when *Titanic* had turned away from the iceberg. Let's put that nonsense to bed as well.

CHAPTER 51

THE TWO POINT TURN

The two-point to the left evidence, is yet another example of manipulation to reinforce the *Californian* on *Titanic's* port bow myth.

On day 3 of the UK Inquiry, the man steering *Titanic* at the time of hitting the iceberg - Quartermaster Hichens - told his questioner:

> *.952. Did you begin to get the helm over?*
>
> *- Yes, the helm was barely over when she struck. The ship had swung about two points.*

Note the he states that the ship had swung two points during the application of the wheel; a statement which - since such an action took no longer that 5 seconds - is in itself, also absurd as we will see.

Louise Patton, wife of Chris Patton, last Governor of Hong Cong and granddaughter of *Titanic's* surviving 2nd Officer Charles Lightholler, has written about a story, alleged to have been passed on to her by her revered ancestor. It seems that her grandfather told her that QM Hichens had turned the steering wheel the wrong way and that this had been the cause of the disaster - (and brought *Californian* on the port bow) but did he?

Other *Titanic* historians have gone to great lengths, as did Lord Mersey, to examine this first turn of the great ship - even to the extent of finding out, by experiment using her sister ship, how long such an action would have taken, and concluding that it took 37 seconds.

Somewhere within the foregoing lie the elements of the truth, unfortunately those who seek it, have either misinterpreted what they heard, read, or simply concluded before properly examining the evidence.

In the case of Louise Patton, we have to remember that she was born in 1944 and that she was only eight years old when her grandfather died. Consequently she may not have accurately remembered the story she was told and, like so many - myself included - did not know that helm orders were not officially classified (reversed) until the mid-1930's.

As for the 37 second timing of two points (22.5 degrees)? Pure academic nonsense when matched to the evidence. Unless, of course, you believe that QM Hichens took 32 seconds longer than normal, to spin the steering wheel to the left, or that he lied about the interval between receiving that first helm order and the moment of impact with the iceberg, which, according to him, was as long as it took to set the steering wheel hard over.

Everyone has completely disregarded or discounted the one thing that would most certainly have immediately affected, and continued to affect, the direction in which Titanic's bow was pointing, and that was contact with the iceberg.

To suggest, as has been done previously, that this had little or no affect on the heading of *Titanic's* bow is simply more nonsense.

To get a true picture of the event we must factor-in the effect on *Titanic's* heading due to contact with a relatively immoveable object - the ice berg.

Titanic enthusiasts have completely dismissed this as trivial and of no contribution to the behaviour of the ship during the time she was in contact with the ice. Their reasoning being that it was merely a *brush-past*.

In doing so, they exhibit a lack of knowledge as to how little is the amount of energy required to alter the direction of travel of a floating object.

What they fail to consider is the fact that the energy expended during *Titanic's* brush with the berg was enough to spring the seams along the starboard side… enough to sink the biggest ship in the world.

Such energy *had* to obey Newton's Third Law which states that for every action there is an equal and opposite re-action. This means that for every force, there is an equal force in the opposite direction to the original force. Consequently there would have been a force pushing on *Titanic's* starboard side as long as it was in contact with the ice.

However, in the case of *Titanic* there was a third element which complicates matters - the source of the force. *Titanic* herself - was moving at an angle relative to the point of resistance.

I don't intend to bore you with the physics of a moving ship versus a stationary object. I am not clever enough to do so. Instead - I would ask you to consider what happens to the bow of a moving ship when it is restrained on one side? For instance - what happens to the bow of a moving ship when a breast rope is attached to a quayside? Perhaps a little sketch will best illustrate the point.

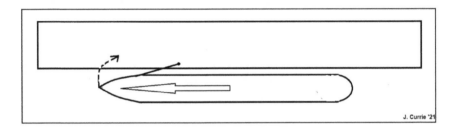

Note that when the shoulder is restrained, on a moving ship - no matter her speed - the bow will swing toward the source of the restraint - not away from it.

Similarly, when the shoulder of *Titanic* was restrained by contact with the berg, her bow would have swung toward - not away from - the source of restraint; Something like the following.

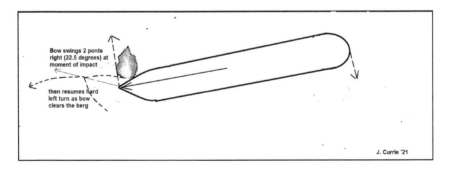

If the above is correct, then the moment of contact, the bow would swing suddenly to the right - the two point turn of QM Hichens (but in the direction of the tiller - to starboard).

However, *Titanic* was making 22.5 Knots with her rudder hard -over and beginning to turn the left - away from danger at that moment. Because of this, her starboard side would be trying to close with the iceberg once again. In fact, we have witness evidence which points to this phenomenon.

On Day 13 of the US Inquiry, First Class Passenger George A. Harder told his questioner:

"I could feel the boat quiver and could feel a sort of rumbling, scraping noise along the side of the boat.

When I went to the porthole I saw this iceberg go by. The porthole was closed. The iceberg was, I should say, about 50 to 100 feet away. I should say it was about as high as the top deck of the boat."

Mr Harder and his wife were in Cabin E-50 on the starboard side - exactly mid-ship. If the ship had been closing with the ice berg, the latter would have been scraping his porthole.

Harder was not the only witness who saw the iceberg abeam and out from the ship's side after impact.

On Day 2 of the UK Inquiry, Able Seaman Joe Scarrot told his questioner:

"I saw an iceberg that I took it we had struck. It would be abaft the beam then - abaft the starboard beam.

352. Was it close to?

- No, it seemed the ship was acting on her helm and we had swung clear of the iceberg".

For Scarrott to have made that observation, the iceberg must have been out from the ship's side. Additionally; for him to have seen it from where he was, it could not have been astern of the ship.

Even if a second helm order had been given immediately after the first - there was no time for the ship's side to have swung away from the danger as described by Scarrott.

In plain language - if *Titanic* had been turning away from the iceberg and was still under left rudder (hard-a-starboard helm), she would be almost hard-up against the iceberg all along her starboard side.

We know she was not because QM Rowe at the stern saw it pass by about 10 feet out from where he was standing.

We also know from QM Olliver that the second helm order was not given before that time. So what else could have swung the stern clear of danger long enough for the ship to pass clear other than contact with the berg?

For those of you who are not nautically minded, we can consider the phenomenon relative to shore-side activity. Consider a child's chute or the water chute in a swimming pool.

When sliding down one of these you ensure you don't touch the sides. However, when sliding down one of these feet- first; if a hip or shoulder touches the side, the feet of the individual - like the bow of Titanic - will swing toward the side of contact.

To summarise:

Titanic's bow certainly did swing two points at the moment of collision with the iceberg, but to the right - not the left...to starboard - and it did so because of contact with relatively immoveable object.

That unintentional turn was soon rectified by the speed of the ship combined by the initial rudder action. First Officer Murdoch did not attempt to zig-zag, slalom-like, around the danger. He did not, as he told his captain, have time for such a fancy manoeuvre.

More to the point, it was a physical impossibility for *Titanic* to have been turned so as to bring the *Californian* almost right ahead. Consequently the vessel seen on *Titanic's* bow was most certainly not the SS Californian.

The crime here is that back in 1912 and as late as 1992; if the will had been there to discover the truth, they had all the necessary evidence readily available to find it.

Consequently, there would not have been any need to besmirch the characters and capabilities of the men on the *Californian*.

However, there is no doubt that a vessel was seen by the survivors of the disaster. Nor is there any doubt that the vessel in question was moving.

So who might that mystery vessel have been? Why did her captain ignore the signals of the sinking *Titanic?*

I will try to answer these questions in the following chapters - but first - for those "Doubting Thomas's" and "Ah but" merchants among you, I will deal with the accusations against Captain Lord of the *Californian.*

CHAPTER 52

COWARDLY, *CALIFORNIAN?*

The most serious accusation against Captain Lord and his men was that although they saw distress signals - they ignored them. Was that despicable behaviour true - is it still true? Let's establish a few facts for the record.

First of all, what is a distress signal?

You might think this to be a silly question, but I can assure you it is not. Sad to say, the answer to it shows that in their anxiety to condemn, most people ignore the obvious.

For a distress signal to be effective, it must draw and hold the attention of a potential rescuer. More to the point, it must not be able to be mistaken for any other signal that is not a distress signal.

Back in 1912, pyrotechnic signals did not always mean a ship was sinking, but could mean a number of things. These included a whole range of distressful events - a lost rudder, a fire on board, lost masts, or any of a large number of impediments to a ship's voyage.

In 1912, there was, as there is today, an internationally recognised series of Day and Night signals for a vessel in distress. At night these included:

A. Flames as from a burning tar barrel.
B. A gun firing at intervals of about 1 minute.
C. Rockets at short intervals rising to a height of 3 or 4 hundred feet above the sea and giving off a shower of stars or balls of any colour.

D. In lieu of signal (B) - a signal rising to 600+ feet above the sea, emitting a loud report and a shower of stars of any colour

Titanic was supplied with both (C) and (D).

Now match the foregoing definition to what Captain Lord was told and what his Officer of the Watch saw during the early hours of the morning of April 15, and see if what was seen fits any of the above.

According to Second Officer Herbert Stone: ten minutes after midnight on April 14, when he relieved Third Officer Groves on the upper bridge, there was a vessel abeam to starboard showing one masthead light, a red side light and two or three small indistinct lights. He was told by Groves that the vessel in question had been stopped in that position for over half an hour and that regular attempts to contact her using *Californian's* powerful signalling lamp had been ignored by those on the bridge of the other ship. Shortly after that, Groves left the Upper Bridge and went off duty.

About 20 minutes after Groves had left, Captain Lord contacted Stone on the upper bridge by voice-pipe and asked him for a situation-update. Stone advised him that all was well and the nearby vessel remained stopped at her original position and continued to ignore attempts to contact her by signal light.

Five minutes after he had spoken with his captain, Stone was pacing up and down when his attention was drawn to a soundless flash in the sky in the direction of the nearby vessel. There was no lingering shower of stars of any colour.

He focussed his binoculars in that direction and shortly afterwards was rewarded by seeing a flash in the sky in the same direction this time, at about half the height of the nearby vessel's masthead light, seemingly low on the horizon and beyond the nearby vessel. It too was soundless, but this time it was followed by a shower of white stars which slowly descended seaward - again - match the foregoing to The Rules.

As can be seen from The Rules, the standard distress signal of the day rose to a great height above the vessel firing it before it emitted a shower of stars, and these would be seen between 300 and 400 feet above the vessel firing them. And at least 200 feet above her masthead light. On the other hand, if the nearby vessel had been firing signals as described in Rule (D), the stars would have been seen close to 500 feet above the nearby vessel's masthead light. Not only that, but the shower of stars would have commenced with an extremely loud 'BANG' which was audible at a minimum of 10 miles; so what the heck was Stone seeing?

To further confuse 2nd Officer Stone; he knew that if the nearby vessel was in trouble, she would not have waited so long to call for help. Why, then, if they were in trouble, had those on board her consistently ignore the frequent attempts to contact her during the hour she had been stopped? All of these questions must have raced through the mind of *Californian's* young Second Officer.

Everyone who has been trained in the UK Merchant Service as a Deck Officer will tell you that there was a little rhyme of advice given by lecturers at UK Nautical training establishments and it was *"If in doubt - get the Old Man out",* and that is exactly what the Second Officer of the *Californian* did. He did not recognise what he was seeing, so he immediately called down to Captain Lord and reported the phenomenon. He did so BECAUSE THERE WAS DOUBT IN HIS MIND.

Dare I say it? It's not rocket science.

It cannot be over-emphasised and should be kept firmly in mind, that at this stage, the vessel in question had been happily stopped in the same place for over an hour.

The popular belief then was, and still is in some quarters, that on receiving that first report, Captain Lord should have immediately left where he was and made his way up to join Stone on the upper bridge. I will comment on this later.

When Stone reported to his captain, he informed him of something which did not immediately awaken a memory in the captain's mind - something which did not fit with anything Captain Lord had ever seen.

Because the use of low trajectory rockets as a means of communication was common in 1912: that was the first idea that entered his mind. Consequently, the captain ordered his officer to continue to observe and make contact in the normally accepted way - by signal light-and thereafter, report any further developments.

There was no more he, the captain could, or should, do at that point.

In compliance with his orders, Stone continued to watch the vessel and - as with all competent bridge officers - to take bearing of her, using the ship's standard compass. The reason for this was to establish movement - following the principal that if two vessels are stopped near to each other and subject to the same external influences, then they will remain in a constant direction from each other. However, if one or other moves, then the bearing (direction) between them will change.

To Stone's astonishment: almost immediately he had finished his report to the captain, the bearing of the nearby vessel began to change; consequently she was moving.

Even more puzzling was the fact that while this was happening, he continued to see another six rockets in the same direction. In fact, it seemed to him that she was firing the things while turning in a wide - through South - circle and toward the south-westward.

By the time he saw the last rocket, which would have been close to 1-30 am, the vessel had completely turned around and was heading through the ice barrier and thereafter, continued in that direction at an ever-increasing speed.

At 2 pm, all Stone could see was the vessel's stern light in the southwest, so he sent Apprentice Gibson down to report the sequence of events to the captain.

Shortly after Gibson arrived back on the upper bridge, the mystery vessel had completely vanished toward the southwest and all was quiet.

At this point, seekers of the truth should consider honest answers to the following questions:

Q1: How should a ship captain respond, if an officer reported the positive sighting of one strange signal in the direction of a nearby ship which had been lying quietly nearby for the previous hour?

And

2: If rockets are seen apparently from a nearby source which subsequently moves away and disappears - what is the point in reporting such an event other than closing a chapter in a day?

I can assure you, any experienced Master would answer as follows:

A1: Ascertain the cause and report immediately thereafter.

A2: Since there is no danger to the observer's ship - simply to keep an interested party informed.

"Ah, but," - as many have asked - "why didn't Captain Lord get up off his settee when the first positive identification of a pyrotechnic signal was reported to him?"

The same questioners should also ask: how could Captain Lord or his 2nd Officer have known in advance that there would be a series of such signals? What guarantee did Lord have that if he did go to the upper bridge and join Stone, that any more such signals would be seen?

The 'should have gone and looked' nonsense has been perpetuated by armchair experts who have little understand of the nature of the job, or by those who for political reasons, ignore the facts of a seafaring life.

It has even been suggested by those who know better, that Lord should have called his Wireless Operator and had him find out if the nearby vessel was in distress. Such an idea beggars belief.

The foregoing also requires an honest answer to the following question:

If the nearby vessel was in distress, yet ignored the constant efforts by *Californian's* officers to contact her by signal light - what on earth makes anyone believe that a wireless operator would have made any difference? Heavens! While all this was going on, *Titanic* was desperately trying to attract the attention of the vessel that was ahead of them and in full sight yet not a blink of a signal lamp was seen aboard that vessel. Nor was it seen by anyone on the *Californian* looking at *their* nearby vessel.

Nelson's words with telescope to a blind eye - "I see no ships."- come to mind.

What Captain Lord was told and what his Officers witnessed, was beyond normal comprehension.

As young 2nd Officer Stone advised deaf ears at the UK inquiry:

"8037. - A steamer that is in distress does not steam away from you, my Lord."

Unfortunately for Stone, "My Lord" was not listening to him. The latter had already made his mind up which was obvious from his remark:

"You do not give answers that please me at present".

If he had been honest, the same "Lord" would have completed his remark with:

"because I have already made up my mind as to what was going on at that time and what you are telling me does not fit my conclusions."

To get a feeling for the official mind-set then, and even today, compare the foregoing with the opinions of the armchair experts who loudly declare that as soon as Captain Lord was told about the first rocket he should have had his wireless man called and made his own way up to join Second Officer Stone on the upper bridge.

It is significant that among all those who have made this silly suggestion - not one has given a though to the consequences of doing so. However let's explore the implications should Lord have actually done such a thing.

First of all, the *Californian's* wireless man had earlier told his Captain that only one vessel was within wireless range, so there was no guarantee that the nearby vessel had wireless.

Since Captain Lord had sent an ice warning earlier - as soon as he saw that vessel approaching; might not anyone else within range hearing it have replied? After all, that seemed to be the normal practice among operators.

If *Californian's* Operator had been called and had tuned-in his equipment after the second, positive sighting of a rocket, it would have been close to 1 am on *Californian* and 11-15 pm New York, Eastern Standard Time.

We know from the wireless logs of the *Olympic, Baltic* and *Mount Temple* that at that time, the operator on *Titanic* was in conversation with the operator on the *Olympic* and that they were discussing the situation. Consequently, the operator on *Californian* would have had to wait until that conversation was over before he was able to establish contact ant learn the extent of *Titanic's* predicament. He would then have obtained *Titanic's* position and reported it to Captain Lord.

Captain Lord would have plotted the distress position given and immediately noted that it was on the other side of the nearby ice barrier, and almost 20 miles away, to the south-westward of his ship. To add to the confusion, he would also see that it was not in the same direction in which the rocket signals were being seen, which, as we know, was in the direction of a ship which was only 5 miles away to the south-eastward. This would cause Lord to have his wireless operator verify the distress position.

Such verification would have taken time, during which, we know from the evidence, that almost immediately after the first positive sighting, the vessel nearby to the *Californian*, began to move off her location…her bearing was changing. She would have had started moving in the direction of the nearby ice barrier and the sinking *Titanic*. Not only that, but shortly after that time, *Titanic* would cease transmitting and she would be sinking rapidly at her distress position. Do you get the picture?

Now, after that speculative nonsense let's further examine what we are told by the evidence.

Before doing so, it is worthwhile noting that even although Captain Lord had called his wireless man at the time in question, and had taken immediate action at that time and headed for *Titanic*'s distress position - he would have failed in his rescue attempt. Because, as was the case later that morning, he would have still have arrived at the wrong position and found himself on the wrong side of the ice barrier, in a lonely, empty patch of ocean while *Carpathia* was already on the scene almost 13 miles away and almost out of sight. So back to reality.

There is no doubt that the signals seen by Stone and Gibson in the direction of the nearby vessel *were* from *Titanic*. However, proper analysis of the evidence given by Captain Lord an his Officers as well as the evidence given by survivors from the disaster shows very clearly that the vessel which stopped so close to the *Californian* at 11-30pm that night could never have been the White Star liner *Titanic*, So who was that mysterious stranger and was she the only one in sight? Consider the following.

At 11-30 pm - at the time Lord saw his approaching vessel stop - his 3rd Officer Groves advised him that there was a vessel approaching *Californian* from the south.

Groves had positively seen it at 11-15pm and estimated it to be 12 miles away at that time. Later, he told the UK Inquiry that his vessel was showing two(2) white masthead lights and turned away to show her red side light. However, although like all ships, *Titanic* had a green and a red sidelight, she had but a single white masthead light. Not only that, but since he observed it over half an hour and in that time reduced its distances from 12 to 6 miles; *his* vessel was making about 12 knots, whereas, *Titanic* was making 22.5 knots and would have been approaching from the east. Groves also said that his vessel turned away and put out her lights.

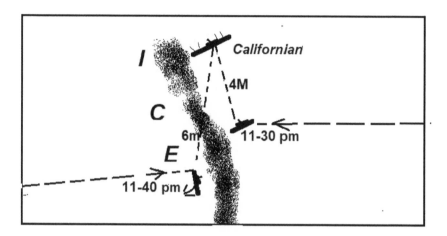

From the foregoing, it seems that there were not one, but two mystery vessels to the southward of the stopped *Californian*.

CHAPTER 53

THE BREAK-UP

There are conflicting survivor stories concerning the final minutes of Titanic's short life - the brief few minutes before she finally slipped bellow the surface.

Some claimed that the great ship tipped over by the bow and slipped, intact, below the surface.

Others claimed that in these final moments, she tried to return to life, but broke her back in the attempt.

The argument was settled when her remains were found on the sea bed, 6000 feet below where she last graced the world with her presence. Only then, was the story about her breaking her back proved to be the correct one. In fact she was found in two major pieces surrounded by a field of smaller bits termed as 'debris'.

There are many versions of how exactly the great ship broke apart near the surface and descended downward thorough the depths to finally come to rest on the sea floor in the positions seen in the following photograph. The exact mechanics of how it all came about is an academic exercise which I leave to those who find such mental exercises stimulating. As far as I am concerned, the most important outcome of the find is simply the confirmation of the evidence given to the effect that *Titanic* did not sink intact.

Why the differing opinions at the time?

I suggest that those up against the ship in complete darkness were unable to see the entire length at the time of sinking, while those at a distance were able to take in the whole picture.

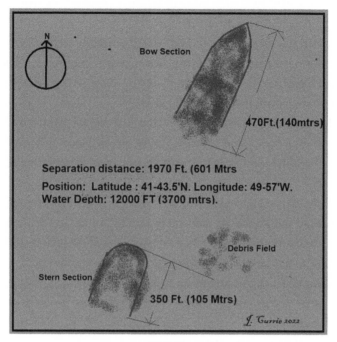

PIC 11
Source: encylopediatitanica.org

So what were the mechanics of the break-up?

Like all ships built of steel, *Titanic* had five main strength members. Two of these were the extra thick line of steel shell plating know as "Sheer Strakes." These ran from bow to stern on either side of "C" deck -the main deck. Then there was her giant keel, also running from bow to stern and on each side of it, her Garboard Strakes - bottom cousins to the aforementioned Sheer Strakes.

This configuration was designed to counteract the bending stresses imposed in the hull as the ship was alternately supported at the bow and stern and then in the middle by passing head seas and swells.

However, the aforementioned strength plates were not designed to counteract the enormous bending stress of almost half a ship suspended for any time out of the water and the other half trying to lift a wedge of the sea on top of it.

Just imagine a sea-saw with one end wedged under a truck load of cement and a 400 lb (181.5 kilo) individual perched on the other end. Something had to give, and it certainly did.

However, the sheer strake did not simultaneously part on both sides of the ship. Witnesses recalled hearing two distinct 'explosions'. These were more than likely the first two failures of the sheer strake; but why would they not break simultaneously on both sides?

Evidence from survivors tells us that just before failure of the sheer strakes, the ship was listed to port. Consequently, not only was the ship "hogged - bending along her fore and aft line, but she was also being bent athwartship.

It follows that on her starboard side, she was bending in two directions. Consequently the starboard side sheer strake failed first with a BANG. This was almost immediately followed by a second BANG as the port side sheer strake succumbed to the fore and aft bending moment.

You might think the foregoing to be a bit far-fetched, however, there is visual proof of this, and it can be seen in the most unlikely place - Las Vegas, Nevada.

Back in 199, an expedition to the wreck site of *Titanic*, recovered a large section of the ship's side plating measuring twelve feet high by twenty six feet long and weighing close to fifteen tons. It came from an area on the starboard side at "C" deck.

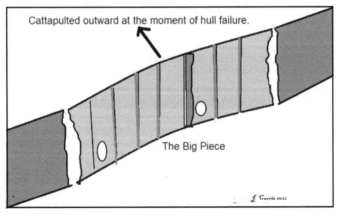

(PIC 12)

As can be seen in the above photograph of the arrival of the *Big Piece* at its destination - the section recovered was bent outward by a great force which caused the side plating to fracture verticallyThe side plating in question contains part of the main strength member - the sheer-strake., and scrutiny of the ship's plan of 'C' Deck shows that this part was once the outside of Cabins in the region of C79 to C 83. These cabins were situated 120 feet aft of midship and directly over the forward end of the main engines; in fact, almost directly over the point where *Titanic's* hull came clear of the sea and at the location of the weakest point in the hull structure - the vertical void at the forward end of the main engine room. The following is a rough representation of the area in question. Adjacent windows, portholes and other features have been omitted for clarity.

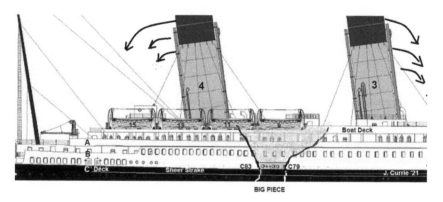

BIG PIECE

After that initial failure, the port side sheer strake would have parted and thereafter the failures of the main hull would propagate upward and downward, taking the path of least resistance. As this was happening, the strain on the superstructure expansion joint would have been too much and the superstructure would catch up with the failing main hull.

Cabins C79 to C83 were less than 40 feet from the Barber's shop and the staircase leading up from B Deck. Consequently, proof of this location being the initiation point for catastrophic break in the hull structure can be found in the evidence of First Class passenger Major Peuchen, who told the US Inquiry on Day 4:

> *"in passing the wreck the next morning - we steamed past it - I just happened to think of this, which may be of some*

> *assistance to this inquiry - I was standing forward, looking to see if I could see any dead bodies, or any of my friends, and to my surprise I saw the barber's pole floating. The barber's pole was on the C deck, my recollection is …*

Supporting evidence for this came from survivors in a lifeboat.

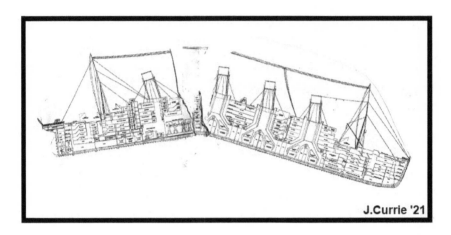

J.Currie '21

After *Titanic* had disappeared below the surface, Fourth Officer Lowe, who was in command of lifeboat 14, gathered a number of occupied lifeboats together and had them tie up to each other. Thereafter, he picked a prize crew of seaman and one passenger and headed back to the place so recently vacated by *Titanic*. When boat 14 arrived there the bodies were so close-packed that they had to push there way through them. They did this, because they saw a man kneeling on a detached staircase. This could not have been any other than the one leading from B Deck up to "C" deck and the Barber's shop.

CHAPTER 54

THE MYSTERIOUS WAIF
OF THE WAVES

In Chapter 49, we have seen that there were at least two mystery ships seen from the *Californian*. However, these and the other two were stopped.

The most import mystery ship of all was the moving one seen from the bridge of *Titanic* as she was sinking - the one everyone was so anxious to identify as the *Californian*. Obviously, it was not!

Lord Mersey's initial remit was to supply the British Board of Trade with the answers to twenty six (26) questions and that the name *Californian* was not mentioned in a single one of these. However, he had thereafter received copies of the evidence from the US Inquiry and doubtless had read the popular press. It follows that The King's Commissioner of Wrecks already had all the necessary information with which to form opinions.

In reality, Lord Mersey had already made-up his mind concerning the culpability of the captain of the *Californian*. Consequently, no attempt was made by him to discover the identity of a mystery vessel as an alternative to the *Californian* - despite the fact, such evidence was available had there been the will to uncover it.

The basic qualifications for "Mystery Ship" were as follows:

1. She must have been to the westward of the ice barrier before Midnight on April 14.

2. She had to have been a steamship with two white masthead lights and to have been moving southward along the western edge of the ice barrier from midnight on April 14.

In previous chapters, we have seen that *Californian* did not fit the requirements, so was there such a vessel? Is there - and more to the point - was there at the time, evidence of such a vessel? The answer to these two questions is a resounding YES!

While perusing the work of Dr. Paul Lee, I came across the following Ice reports. They make very interesting reading:

> *"April 14:*
>
> *This message was sent from La Bretagne to captains of Europe bound ships: "Met with ice field and icebergs from 42N and 49 to 50W Compliments Mace." This message was also sent to the Captain of the Marengo at 8.08am, the Olympic at 11.00am, Campanello at 12.00pm and Pennsylvania at 14.08.*

And; from the underlined vessel's captain:

> *"SS Campanello - 42.00 N 50.16 W to 41.10 N 49.00 W"*
>
> *"April 14-15: encountered heavy pack ice, large bergs and field ice, drifting south"*

/titanic/ice.html

The foregoing information allows us to develop a plot of the movements of the *Campanello*. However, before doing so, it should be understood that the fact that at Noon on the 14th, the *Bretagne bothered to send Campanello* a warning at all, concerning ice on the 42nd parallel, proves that the latter was west of the ice barrier at Noon that day, and *Capmanello's* own ice reports shows she was following the 42nd parallel of latitude.

The SS Campanello was a four masted steamship built in 1901. In 1912 she was owned by the Uranium Steamship Company and running between Rotterdam, Halifax Nova Scotia and New York. She left New York around the same time as the *Carpathia* and was returning to Holland.

From her Ice report, she seems to have been avoiding the regular steamship tracks and taking the most direct route to her destination, hence her report of being at latitude 42° North on April 14.

However, she seems to have encountered the same ice barrier which would subsequently stop the *Mount Temple,* and consequently, circumnavigated it to the southward. We know she did so, because the next day, as we can see from her ice report, she was eastward and south of the ice and at latitude 41°-10 North Longitude 49° West. Yet, there is a mystery about this vessel, which does not fit with the ice reports.

Eight days later, on April 23, *Campanello* is reported at being 140 miles west of Bolt Head in Devon, England. This report has been used to show that the mystery vessel could not have been the *Campanello,* thus removing her from the list of likely culprits.

However, the distance from her April 15 ice report position to her reported position west of Bolt head is 1810 nautical miles. At a speed of 13 knots, she should have been there no later than April 21st.

In addition; the distance from New York to Rotterdam is 3270 nautical miles. Consequently, if *Campanello* left New York around Noon on April 11, 1912, she should have been near to 42°North 50°-16 West about 11-30 pm on April 14 and was due at Rotterdam around 6 m on the morning of April 22nd 1912.

If she was due at Rotterdam in the early hours of April 24, then she had lost about 2 days on the voyage. A reconstruction of her movements developed from these ice reports is plotted as follows:

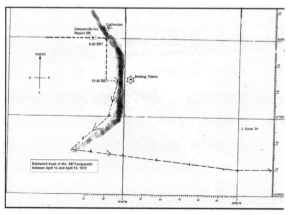

J. Currie

The evidence so far, begs the question: Other than those on *Titanic* - did anyone else see the *Campanello?*

In the previous chapter we discussed the evidence of *Californian's* Third Officer Charles Groves. Might the vessel he saw approaching *Californian* have been the very same *Capanello* looking for a way eastward?

Any reasonable individual can conclude but one thing, and that is that the vessel seen by Groves was not the same vessel seen earlier by Captain Lord. Nor was it the same vessel which was constantly under observation between 11-30 pm on April 14 until it finally vanished around 2-30 am on the morning of April 15. So what other vessel was on the west side of the ice barrier before Midnight?

I believe that Groves was so occupied by his vessel which was approaching from astern direction that he and Captain Lord missed the fact that there were two mystery vessels.

The first one had stopped to the southeast at 11-30 pm and had approached from the eastward.

The other one had approached from the westward - saw *Californian's* lights and headed for them. When her captain met with the western edge of the ice barrier, he turned away to the southward.

While this was happening, Groves was below, reporting to Captain Lord.

Groves returned to the upper bridge, just in time to see his approaching vessel turn away and 'put her lights out'. Shortly after, Lord joined him and the two of them were then looking at the vessel which had stopped ay 11-30 pm.

Groves also stated that his vessel was a passenger ship -*Campanello* was a passenger ship. He said his passenger ship turned away - *Campanello* would have turned away. However, according to popular belief, *Titanic* turned toward the *Californian.*

All very plausible you might think - but if it was the *Campanello,* why did her captain - the captain of that moving ship seen by those on *Titanic* - ignore the distress signal and Morse light cries for help?

I suggest to you for one very simple reason, and that was that he did not recognise them as such.

Think about it!

The captain of the *Campanello* - like all ship captains that night - was aware of a an ice barrier ahead of his ship; in fact he had already seen two west- bound ships - *Californian* and her nearby, mysterious, neighbour - stopped by it on its eastern side. It was a beautiful night; the stars could be seen setting on the horizon. Visibility was so good that he could easily make out the western edge of danger. Consequently, on seeing the other two vessels, he decided to head due south and find a way around it.

All the reports he had had combined with his experience on that run told him that a clear passage would be found to the south of the barrier, so he headed south.

By that time, his solitary Wireless Operator had gone to bed and it was getting on for midnight. That was when he first sighted the *Titanic* on the far side of the ice.

By then, she had been stopped for almost half an hour and would have been ablaze with lights right down to her water-line. Perhaps the captain of the *Campanello* thought *Titanic* was not stopped, but making her way south of the ice? After all, both vessels were nearly end-on and there was a long delay between mutual sighting and the firing of the first distress signal.

In addition - because they were almost end-on to each other - when *Titanic* began to used her signal lamp, it would have been hard to see against the blaze of light around it as well as the distraction caused by the opening and closing of brightly-lit doorways.

However, we are discussing a very dangerous situation - a passenger ship being navigated through an ice-infested sea on a very dark night. It should therefore be kept in mind that the attention of *Campanello's* captain and his men, like those on *Carpathia* and *Californian*, would have been completely occupied with looking after themselves and their own ship - that is - dodging the ever-increasing presence of ice flows.

Eventually, the captain of the *Campanello* would know that he could not go through the ice at the place opposite the brightly lit, ship ahead of him, so he would turn away to the south-westward and continue his passage around the ice barrier.

CHAPTER 55

THE MARCONI CONSPIRACY?

Students of the *Titanic* disaster will be very familiar with the part played in it by the Wireless Operators of the following vessels.

	Wireless Equipment
Titanic (MGY)	Marconi
Californian (MWL)	Marconi
Mount Temple (MLQ)	Marconi
Carpathia (MPA)	Marconi
Baltic, (MBC)	Marconi
Olympic (MKC)	Marconi
Frankfurt (DFT)	Telefunken.
Birma (SBA).	De Forest

The three letters after in brackets after the ship's name, indicate that the ship was equipped with wireless and was a unique wireless call sign allocated to each vessel.

Those with the first letter 'M' indicated that the wireless equipment and Operators on that particular ship were supplied by the Marconi Wireless Telegraph Company. Other countries used either the first letter of the equipment supplier or the name of their country. Thus, the prefix letter "D" stood for 'Deutsland'. In fact, the *Deutsland* was equipped with

Telefunken equipment, .and the *Birma* was a Russian vessel equipped with American equipment designed by Dr De Forest in the USA.

It should be noted that all of the men who operated the equipment were not employed by the shipping companies who owned the ships, but were employees of the Wireless Company who allocated them ships and who paid their salaries. However, when at sea, those Wireless Operators, like everyone else, were under the direct command of the captain of the ship, and his orders were paramount.

In 1912, the use of wireless on board ships at sea was in its infancy. Many ships - particularly smaller vessels - did not have wireless and the use of night and day visual signals between all ships - even those with wireless - was still very much in use. In fact, visual signalling as an alternative to electronic communication remains an alternative to this day.

Although Guglielmo Marconi's Company had the major part of the marine business he had, as can be seen, two major rivals. These were the Telefunken Company of Germany and The United Wireless Company of America the suppliers of the De Forest system.

Between these three there was great rivalry. A careful examination of the wireless evidence submitted to the US and UK Inquiries, exposes that rivalry and will reveal what, to all intents and purposes, cannot be described in any way, other than as form of corruption and conspiracy which I believe was entirely due to that rivalry. However, to prove this, we must delve deeply into the relevant verbal and written evidence given, during the Public Inquiries on both sides of the Atlantic; and into Hansard, the recorded proceedings of the United Kingdom Houses of Parliament.

First we will examine the witness records.

On Day 9 of the US Inquiry, Captain James Moore of the Canadian Pacific vessel, SS Mount Temple, very clearly, and in detail, told his questioners that within a short interval, his Wireless Operator received two different distress positions from *Titanic*. This was the very first indication from any source, that there had been more than one call for help.

On Day 8 of the UK Inquiry, Captain Moore once more, reminded his questioner of that first distress position, but was seemingly ignored. In fact, this first erroneous distress position was completely buried until it was talked about by *Titanic's* surviving 4th Officer Boxhall during a BBC radio interview in 1962.

By that time, it was too late to be of any significance to the outcome of the official Inquiries into the disaster, but why was it buried in the first place?

On Day 10 of the US Inquiry, Captain Moore provided the Inquiry Committee with a copy of the *Mount Temple's* PV - Process Verbal - Wireless Log. There was no mention of that first distress position in it, but, there was a record of it.

When Captain Moore received the message containing reference to that first distress position - a message which had been initialled and sent to him by his Wireless Operator at the time of receipt - he did not discard it, but kept it in his pocket.

In the UK, the members of the Inquiry noticed the absence of that first message in the *Mount Temple's* wireless log, so they questioned her wireless operator John Durrant.

He explained that that first message was not official - that he had simply overheard it, hence did not formally record it.

The Americans didn't even bother to call Durrant to the stand.

All this seems a simple explanation as to why there was no official record of it - simple, until we remember what Captain Moore said in the US about keeping that "overheard" message.

The following is the relevant part of *his* evidence - evidence which shows that there was, and still is, to this day; a formal record of that very first distress call:

> *"At 12:30 a.m. on the 15th I was awakened by the steward from my sleep with a message from the Marconi operator, sir. I immediately switched on the light and took a message that the operator sent up to me which said that a message that the operator sent up to me which said that the Titanic was sending out the C. Q.*

> *D. message, and in the message it said "iceberg."*
> *Q: Have you the message?*
> *A: Yes*

> *"Titanic sends C. Q. D. Requires assistance. Position 41° 44' north, longitude 50° 24' west Come at once. Iceberg.*

This is just a message he picked up, sir. He happened to hear it. He was sending this up at once to me.

Q: Can you file that with the reporter?.
Yes, sir. He makes a remark at the bottom, "Can't hear me."
Q: On this message?
Yes, sir. You will see it on the bottom there - "Can't hear me."
Q: What is the initial under that?
That is my operator's, sir."

So there was in fact a record of this first distress position and the Final Report of the US Committee tells us it was filed as *"Exhibit Moore - No.1"*. It is probably still there, in Washington DC.

Now consider the official Wireless Log of the *Mount Temple* submitted in evidence on Day 10 of the US Inquiry

"10-25 - Titanic sending C.Q.D. Answer him, but he replies: "Can not read you, old man, but here my position, 41.46 N., 50.14 W. Come at once. Have struck berg." Informed captain.
10-48 - Frankfurt answers M.G.Y. M.G.Y. gives him his position and asks "Are you coming to our assistance?"

As can be seen, there is no mention whatsoever about the first distress position and the record indicates that the *Frankfurt* - a Telefunken Operator vessel - did not answer *Titanic's* calls for help for 23 minutes after the Marconi Operator had things in hand.

However, the foregoing official record completely contradicts Marconi's own employee and *Titanic's* surviving Wireless Operator Harold Bride, who, on Day 10 of the US Inquiry, very clearly told his questioners:

"Q: Now let us fix exactly the first message you received after you sent out your first C.Q.D. call. What was the first reply you received?
Mr Bride: The first reply we received was from the Frankfurt.
Q: What ship did you next hear from?
Mr Bride: The Carpathia, sir.

Q: *How long after this last message from?*
Mr Bride: *Mr. Phillips just called "C.Q.D.," and gave our*
position and the Carpathia responded immediately."

So, the first distress call is missing from official records which show that *Mount Temple* was first to hear *Titanic's* distress signal, *Carpathia* was second to answer it and it took the 'sleepy' operator on *Frankfurt* a full 23 minutes before he thought something was wrong. However, as can be seen, this does not fit with the damning contradiction given in the sworn testimony of the *Titanic's* surviving Operator Bride, who very clearly stated the Telefunken-equipped *Franfurt* was first to answer the cry for help… not the Marconi-equipped *Carpathia*.

There is much more to this mind- bending maze of contradiction found in the evidence given by Marconi employees.

Carpathia's Marconi Operator Cottam, did not, as claimed, hear *Titanic's* call for help and answer it, because in his evidence, the man very clearly told his questioner he heard that desperate call purely by chance. On Day 1 of the US Inquiry Cottam stated:

"Q: *He [Capt. Rostron] said you were about to retire?*
A: *Yes, sir.*
Q *And caught this message rather providentially?*
A: *Yes, sir.*"

So, would the foregoing paint a picture of competence to anyone contemplating fitting a ship with Marconi equipment and Operators?

Think about it! Here we have the world worst maritime disaster involving the world's largest ship - a ship which had Marconi equipment and Operators on board. There were three potential rescue vessels - all of which were equipped with Marconi wireless and manned by Marconi Operators. Of these three:

1. The operator on one potential rescuer was sound asleep in bed,
2. The Operator on another, caught the first distress call but didn't bother to record it.
3. The operator on the principal rescue vessel did not hear the distress call because he was too busy listening to the news.

Carpathia, with her cargo of misery, docked at Pier 34, Manhattan, New York at 9-30 pm on April 18, 1912. Her Marconi Operator, Cottam first gave evidence to the US Inquiry Committee on Friday April 19.

Analysis of the evidence to this point, shows there was much to be kept private concerning the performance of Marconi Employees as the disaster unfolded.

It is obvious that a certain manipulation of records and tampering of evidence took place and it started before the day Cottam gave his evidence. We know this because of the following private wireless message Guglielmo Marconi sent to his employee - Cottam:

> "*from Seagate to (personal to operator,):*
>
> *Meet Mr. Marconi and Sammis at Strand Hotel, 502 West Fourteenth Street. Keep your mouth shut. Marconi*"

However, if the foregoing exhibition of 'Smoke and Mirrors' does not point to evidence manipulation and witness tampering, consider the following.

The Associated Press was first to break the news that *Titanic* was in trouble, they had been notified by he Marconi station at Cape Race, Newfoundland.

On Day 13 of the US Inquiry the General Manager of the Association, Melville Stone told his questioners that the following message had been received:

> "*CAPE RACE NEW BRUNSWICK - Friday night, April 14.*
>
> *At 10:25 o'clock to-night the White Star Line steamship Titanic called "C.Q.D" to the Marconi wireless station here, and reported having struck an iceberg. The steamer said that immediate assistance was required.*
>
> *Half an hour afterwards another message came, reporting that they were sinking by the head, and that women were being put off in the lifeboats.*

The weather was calm and clear, the wireless operator reported, and gave the position of the vessel as 41.46 north latitude 50.14 west longitude."

Obviously the geography was wrong - Cape Race is in Newfoundland. However, note the time of that message was 10-25 pm and the coordinates given were those of the revised distress position; there is no mention of the first, incorrect position.

This same message containing exactly the same information was provided to the General Manager of the White Star Line at his New York home in the early hours of the morning of April 15 - long before the first edition newspapers carried their headlines.

The deceit didn't end there, the records of the Marconi Station at Cape Race - the source of this information were also subjected to "artistic licence".

So what was the truth? What coordinates matched what time?

Perhaps the answers lie in a report by Journalist Sue Baily in the Canadian Press on April 6, 2012? Sue wrote:

"The actual Marconi logs at Cape Race were lost to fire or were accidentally thrown out, according to differing historical accounts.

But a log later replicated from those notes by one of Gray's assistants, Robert Hunston, documents in eastern standard time the last messages between Titanic and other ships."

A copy of that replicated log begins:

"The Titanic disaster as viewed from Cape Race by wireless

April 14, 1912

10:25 pm (EST) [12:15 am on Titanic]J.C.R. Godwin on watch hears Titanic calling C.Q.D. giving position 41.44 N 50.24 W about 380 miles SSE of Cape Race.

10:35 pm: Titanic gives corrected position as 41.46N 50.14W. A matter of 5 or six miles difference. He says "have struck iceberg".

10:40 pm: Titanic calls Carpathia and says "We require immediate assistance". Gray on duty.

10:43 pm: Titanic gives same information to Californian, giving Titanic's position.Caronia circulates same information broadcast to Baltic and all ships who can hear him.

10-55-pm tells German steamer "Have struck iceberg and sinking". e Ca

All done and dusted you might think, and you were meant to think so, but any resemblance to fact is purely coincidental. Look at the coordinates recorded against the time of 10-25 pm. They do not match the coordinates given against the time of 10-25 pm as given to the Press Association.

Not only that, but how likely is it that a simple Wireless Operator would have taken time to plot positions and calculate distances?

Then we have the record of a communication with *Californian* at 10-43 pm EST, when we all know for absolute certainty that at that time the *Californian's* Operator had been in bed for over an hour.

Also note the 10-40 pm communication with the *Carpathia- 5 minutes after the time recorded by Mount Temple*

Finally; the piece de resistance the "German Steamer" without a name - presumably the *Frankfurt*. It is shown as last to respond - a full 30 minutes after the first distress call.

Incidentally; this does not agree with the wireless log of the *Mount Temple* or the Associated Press report which gave 10-25 am as the time for the amended position.

It doesn't end here. There seems to have been one, young, insignificant fellow present at the Cape Race Marconi station that night, and his name was Jimmy Myrick.

The Myrick family had been lighthouse keepers at Cape Race from 1886 when Jimmy's grandfather took-on the job. At the time of the *Titanic* disaster, Jimmy's father was the Lighthouse-keeper, and it has been reported that Jimmy was a 14 year-old Apprentice Wireless Operator.

The story told by the Myrick descendents of Jimmy, as related to them by him many years later, is that on the night of the disaster, he -Jimmy - was alone in the receiving room of the Cape Race wireless station. The Second Operator - a man named Godwin - was on duty, but was absent from his post. Suddenly, Jimmy heard *Titanic* transmitting her very first distress position together with the coordinates 41-44 north latitude 50-24 west longitude, and immediately went in search of his superior. He met Godwin on his way back and both returned to the transmitting room. Shortly after that, - at 10-25 pm - Godwin received the second, amended distress position.

In his old age, Jimmy told the family that Marconi had them all sworn to silence - quoting the Official Secrets Act .How true was that story?

To answer that question, we should keep in mind, that the existence of that first distress position was not common knowledge at the time. The only public mention of it had come from the evidence of Captain James Moore of the *Mount Temple*, so how would young Myrick have known about it unless he heard it, or saw it written down.

However, as we have seen, the written evidence from Cape Race was conveniently lost and there was only one, single bit of written evidence of it, presented to the Courts of Inquiry. It did not appear in any of the Marconi records submitted in evidence, yet it most certainly existed.

There is yet another story about the first distress call heard from *Titanic*.

In 1912, there was a Weather Station on Cape Hatteras. Many years after the Titanic disaster, the station was being demolished, and the demolishers discovered old paper-work stuffed behind a wall - allegedly for insulation. When going through these, they discovered a crumpled wireless message form. They smoothed it out but because of age were unable to read what was written on it. However, after forensic? Work, it was possible to make out what was written on it, so someone made a clear copy along the bottom of it as follows:

"Received Hatteras Station at 11-25 pm. Titanic calling CQD giving reading 41-24 about 380 miles S.S.E of Cape Race. At 11-35 pm Titanic gives corrected position as 41.46

North, 50.14 West, a matter of 6 miles different. He says have struck iceberg."

Source:

In fact, the Cape Hatteras "copy" written for clarification at the bottom of the alleged original message form, is an almost verbatim copy of a retrospective account of the Cape Race wireless log written much later by Marconi Operator Robert Hunston who was not even on watch at the time.

Whoever did the 'transcribing, botched the job. Apart from the time of the message being an hour later; it is a hybrid, containing the first half of the Latitude coordinate and the second half of the Longitude coordinate of the first distress message. Have a look:

"10:25 pm (EST) [12:15 am on Titanic]

J.C.R. Godwin on watch hears Titanic calling C.Q.D. giving position 41.44 N 50.24 W about 380 miles SSE of Cape Race.

10:35 pm: Titanic gives corrected position as 41.46N 50.14W. A matter of 5 or six miles difference. He says "have struck iceberg".

What you are seeing in the translation of the original, illegible, Cape Hatteras telegram sent by the operators, Daily and Hoskins to their head office in New York, is an interpretation of it which was written much later.

According to author James D Charlet, when the New York Office received that first notification, their superior

"severely chastised the senders, thinking it was a hoax. In his response, he [the head man at New York] *said that the senders were troublemakers who were just "clogging up the lines," and that they,* [the Hatteras Station Operators] *were to refrain from any further communications."*

If this is correct, then only one message was passed-on from Cape Hatteras to New York and there were no further communications between that station and *Titanic* after the first one.

When it was 11-25 pm EST at Cape Hatteras, *Titanic* was sending out her amended CQD (See *Mount Temple* process-Verbal). Apart from that, the translation at the foot of it could not have been written before the Hunston re-write. Consequently, this is yet another manipulation of the truth.

There is yet another bit of evidence which points to the malicious manipulation of the truth performed by Marconi and his servants. It is related in full by author Senan Malony in his excellent article "Birma's Wireless bears Witness"

The SS 'Birma' was a Russian ship which had recently left New York, bound for Rotterdam. Her captain also responded to *Titanic's* cry for help.

The *Birma* did not have Marconi or Telefunken wireless equipment, her wireless and Operators were supplied by another of Marconi's bitter rivals - The United Wireless Company of America who promoted the De Forest wireless system. The history of wireless in America tells us:

"John W. Griggs, of New Jersey, who is president of the Marconi Wireless Telegraph Company of America. He says:

The managers of the Marconi's Wireless Telegraph Company, Limited, and of the Marconi Wireless Telegraph Company of America, deem it their duty to the public to deny absolutely and unequivocally that the United Wireless Telegraph Company has acquired control of more than 51 per cent of the Marconi's Wireless Telegraph Company, Limited, and to deny that the United Wireless Telegraph Company controls a majority of the stock of the Marconi Wireless Telegraph Company of America.

Source: *Electrical World*, November 24, 1906, page 984.

Obviously, there was no love lost between Marconi and his American rivals. Nowhere is this more obvious than in the content of a letter written by *Birma's* wireless Operator Joe Cannon to his parent and the action taken by *Birma's* captain, Ludwig Stulping. In his letter to his parents concerning the part played by *Birma* in the *Titanic* disaster, Joe wrote:

"it is a known fact that Marconi company will give no information to any ship not Marconi, unless in distress .....all day, and days following, we were refused any information."

Captain Stulping was so enraged about the actions of Marconi personnel during the time surrounding the disaster that he made an unscheduled stop at Dover and gave his story to a reporter from the Daily Telegraph Newspaper. Consequently, the disgraceful actions of Marconi became public knowledge.

Despite this, the members of the Wreck Commissioner's Inquiry and the Commissioner himself, buried the dreadful truth.

I have put before you all of the available evidence I can find, and shown you the considerable number of inconsistencies in both the verbal and written evidence concerning the wireless communications and in particular -distress messages.

Did the world believe that Marconi and his senior managers capable of such deceit?

To answer that question, I refer you to Hansard - The official record of all UK Government Parliamentary debates, dating back for over 200 years. The relative record begins:

"Marconi Wireless Telegraph Company, Limited

Volume 42: debated on Friday 11 October 1912

The agreement between the Marconi Wireless Telegraph Company and my right hon. Friend the Postmaster-General has been criticised on two grounds—first, that it is a bad bargain, an imprudent bargain; and, second, that it is a bargain which is tainted with corruption."

It seems that there was most certainly doubt in the minds of many people in high places back in 1912.

I rest my case.

PART 11

CHAPTER 56

SETTING THE HISTORIC
RECORD STRAIGHT

So much rubbish has been written and filmed about the *Titanic* disaster that I find it difficult to know where to start. "Why not from the beginning?" I hear you ask. I agree with you.

Conspiracy theories are as old as Fish Wife's Tales…they all originate from the same source…ignorance!

Show me a disaster and I'll show you a "flat-earth" conclusion concerning it.

In the case of *Titanic* - conspiracy theories and old wives tales concerning that ill-fated vessel are as numerous as the rivets with which she was constructed.

In the previous chapters I have hopefully dealt with the harmful ones - the ones that besmirched, and continue to besmirch, the memory of honest sailor men who simply did their duty as best they could, according to the then practices of sailor men, and under conditions most of us can only imagine.

Of lesser importance - other Old wives tales include:

A. After the incident in the early part of 1912, when *Titanic's* sister ship *Olympic* was rammed by HMS 'Hawk' in the Solent - *Olympic* was taken to her birthplace at Belfast where *Titanic* was being built, and in order to maintain continuity of business, *Olympic* was switched with the almost completed *Titanic*.

B. There was a fire in one of *Titanic's* coal bunkers. This fire weakened the bulkheads thus accelerating her end.

C. The rivets used in constructing *Titanic's* hull were brittle due to the cold, causing the rivet-heads to pop-off (shear).

D. The plan was to arrive early at New York, beating the voyage time set by *Olympic;* therefore *Titanic* was being driven at high speed through a known Ice Field.

E. Captain Smith allowed *Titanic* to over-shoot the planned turning point of *The Corner* by ten (10) miles to avoid meeting ice.

F. Captain Smith knowingly charged at full speed into a dense ice field.

G. The lifeboats should have been launched fully loaded with passengers.

H. The SS Californian stopped within sight of the sinking *Titanic*.

Much of the foregoing nonsense has already been extensively dealt with in previous chapters; however, in case I missed something, I think they deserve a closer examination.

CHAPTER 57

DE-MYTHTIFICATION

(A): for Absurd.

To understand the absurdity of the "switch" theory and much more of the nonsense written about *Titanic*, we must first be made aware of the complexities in creating a ship.

Ships were built "under survey". This simply means that they had to be constructed according to a laid-down set of Rules. Consequently, the entire creation of the vessel from conception to completion at the end of successful Builder's Trials was subjected to meticulous scrutiny by experts in their fields. Such expertise included the disciplines of Naval Architecture, Ship Construction and Marine Engineering as well as all the subsidiary skills necessary to build the perfect vessel.

A UK owned ship was constructed in accordance with the various Merchant Shipping Acts of Parliament in force at the time. Not only did the ship have to conform to these Rules, but its owners had to be citizens of the United Kingdom and its Colonies. The ownership was split into 64 equal shares and each shareholder had to be British.

As wells a as ships having to comply with Government legislation; if they were insured, they were usually built in accordance with Rules of Class set out by the Insuring authorities. In the United Kingdom, this was Lloyds Register of Shipping. When this was the case, a ship was said to have been "Built to Class".

We know that *Titanic* was not "Built to Class"; in fact, it was claimed during the UK Inquiry that her owner's requirements often exceeded the minimum requirements of the Classification Society.

My point in drawing attention to the foregoing is to emphasise the need for very careful scrutiny of a new vessel by specialised Inspectors from concept to final, Official Registration. It follows that if at any time during her construction, there was an interruption or a divergence from the norm, then one or several Inspectors of different disciplines would have been immediately aware of it.

You will note that I have not even mentioned the more obvious reasons for this idea being plain silly. By this I mean the cooperation of thousands of workers in a subterfuge, and the physical differences between the two ships, primary of which was that the bridge of *Titanic* was 3 feet wider that that of *Olympic*. Nor have I touched on the formalities of Ship Registration.

During the entire time *Titanic* was under construction at the Belfast Yard of Harland and Wolff, she would have received daily visits from at least one of the aforementioned Official Surveyors. Each visit would create an official report which would be entered into accumulative record of construction. This record would be produced as proof during the registration procedure which was done at Liverpool. It would also be needed to create Insurance Cover and we know that there the hull of *Titanic* was insured for $5 million US.

It follows that for such a "switch" to have taken place, every Government and Insurance Official would need to have been bribed to silence. In addition, all official documentation generated for *Olympic* would need o be transferred to *Titanic* which, in itself, would be a criminal offence under Shipping Legislation.

As I said, *Titanic's* bridge was almost a metre wider than that of the *Olympic*, and in addition, her A Deck was partly covered -in by steel bulwarks surmounted by vertically opening windows. Because of this, and to maintain her gross and deadweight tonnages for Port tonnage dues purposes, shipyard workers would have had to add a great deal of extra top- hamper which would also have affected her stability. The whole idea beggars belief.

Now then! What about that fire in the bunker?

(B) For Bunker Bunkum and Balderdash:

Anyone who has ever carried a coal cargo in a ship or has had a reason to store coal in bulk, knows about this phenomenon and it is not confined to coal, because when I was a boy, it was once a common call-out for rural fire services to extinguish hay stack fires caused by the same process - internal heating.

The process of spontaneous combustion is not a true fire, in that there are no flames involved unless the seat of it is exposed to the atmosphere. When this happens, it gets all the oxygen it needs to become a fully fledged, blazing fire.

In 1912, most steamship boilers were coal-fired; consequently, ships had cavernous storage spaces called bunkers (houses on land had them too

Spontaneous Combustion takes place deep inside a coal bunker or hold - usually at the bottom and close to a bulkhead. It occurs when coal is loaded wet or becomes wet. Then, oxidation takes place and the coal starts to heat up, if the heat is not dissipated, ignition temperature is reached and the coal will glow or eventually explode. Not a pleasant thought.

Titanic had 22 coal bunkers as well as an addition coal-storage hold and storage aft for galley coal used in the kitchens.

Before the ship sailed from the UK, wet coal had been loaded into these bunkers and in particular the starboard bunker in boiler room 5. There, it had been stacked up against the Water Tight Bulkhead "E" separating boiler Rooms 5 and 6.

Water tight bulkheads are not ordinary bulkheads, Apart from the obvious; they are also in creased in strength from top to bottom by increasing steel plate thickness and further strengthened by full-height, narrowly spaced, vertical steel angle stiffeners.

When the potential danger of a spontaneous combustion fire in bulk coal or other material was discovered, the normal practice aboard ship was to work the coal out of the danger area in a controlled way.

In the case of the fire aboard *Titanic;* as the stokers took out the coal a shovel-full at a time, a man would play a hose on top of the ever-diminishing heap. - the idea being that if the red hot glowing coal - seat of the fire -was exposed to the atmosphere, the hose would prevent full combustion and extinguish the fire.

This process began on *Titanic* before she left Southampton and by Saturday, April 13, the coal had been cleared from the bunker.

Afterward, it was noted that the heat of the fire had caused the steel plate of the water tight bulkhead to expand. However, due to the restrictions caused by the vertical stiffeners; the bulkhead plating simply bulged between them. The shipyard-applied protective paint coatings had, of course, vanished, so a coating of oil was given to the damaged areas to prevent any future corrosion, and until a proper repair could be made.

The idea that in some way the foregoing contributed to the demise of *Titanic* is ludicrous to say the least.

First of all, it did not occur in an area where the water tight integrity or strength of the ship was threatened in any way. Nor did it occur in a critical part of a particular strength member.

Additionally, the temperature at which coal starts o combust is in the region of 230 C whereas, steel retains its integral strength up to much higher temperatures and its structure only changes instantly when its temperature is suddenly, not gradually changed.

C) For Cracking rivets:

In the same way - the brittle (Martensitic) steel rivet theory is also a non-starter.

Steel and iron rivets were located in place by heating and hammering into shape. From the day they were submerged in the sea, their temperature would never have fallen below freezing. There could not have been any change to their molecular structure - no matter what the outside sea temperature was, because steel is a conductor of heat and a boiler room is very hot.

(D) For a Daft Idea:

Now we consider Captain Smith's record breaking attempt - yet another bit of fanciful nonsense.

Some of you who are old enough, might remember the days when a new car had to be "rub-in"? If not, allow me to remind you of it.

Fifty years ago, the proud owner of a new car "ran it in". They seldom exceeded a speed of 45 mph for the first 1000 miles, and even had notices on the rear window asking other drivers "Please pass - running in".

Long after the modern car dispensed with this practice, ships at sea still followed the practice of "running-in" during the maiden voyage. Back in 1912, marine engineering was making giant leaps forward, but not to the point where they disregarded the wise practice of running-in or bedding-in the machinery. *Titanic* was no different from any other new ship. In fact she was only the second of her class and her 'big sister' *Olympic* wasn't even a year at sea when *Titanic* made that first, and sadly, last voyage. Her owners didn't even have an example to follow.

Apart from the nuts and bolts of the situation - consider the commercial aspects of it.

Think for a moment, the repercussions following a maiden voyage during which, the biggest ship in the world broke down due to engine failure before she reached her final destination, and it was found that cause was over-taxing of the engines in an attempt to arrive a few hours early. The lawyers and Insurance world would have had a field day.

Look at it from another angle.

There was one very significant bit of evidence referred to earlier, and that was the planned clock change of 47 minutes. That change equates to a change in longitude of 11 degrees, 45 minutes of longitude or in terms of distance expected to travelled between Noon, April 14 and Noon April 15 - 545 miles which means there was no planned speed run, and Captain Smith expected his ship to average a maximum of 22 knots over that period; much the same as she had done during the previous day's run.

(E) For Extra Ten Mile Rubbish.

It was claimed that to avoid the ice, Smith altered his plans and over-shot the turning point of *The Corner* by 10 miles. This too, is blatant nonsense.

At Noon on April 14, *Titanic* ad 124 miles to run before she was due to turn onto her next course. To get there by 5-50 pm, she would have averaged a speed of 21.3 Knots. However, if, as claimed, she turned 10 miles south of *The Corner* at 5-50pm - the time when she did turn - then she would have covered a total of 124 + 10 = 134 miles in 5 hour 50 minutes and would have been averaging 23 knots all that afternoon of April. 14.

In fact, the speed of 21.3 Knots shows that Captain Smith used his local knowledge and expected his ship to slow down due to meeting the Gulf Stream pushing her backwards throughout the afternoon of April 14.

More to the point - he and every captain following that Southern Route did so to avoid meeting ice - that was what the route was supposed to do, so there was no reason to slow down. He had not received a warning of ice on or to the south of that track.

(F). Fatal Ice Warnings?

The evidence shows that Captain Smith received two messages containing second hand information regarding concentrations of ice. Specifically; these were not Ice Warnings, but general messages containing reference to ice.

The first of these was two days old and mentioned ice stretching east - west, along a 44 miles stretch of ocean which was 10 and 12 miles to the north of his planned track.

The second message mentioned ice in the same vicinity, but gave the position of a ship which was 9 miles south of where the ice had been reported two days earlier.

However, the normal practice when giving ice reports was to give the ship's position, not that of the ice, so this second advice simply confirmed ice in that vicinity, consequently, it could not be relied upon as being accurate.

Both of the aforementioned messages contained historic, second-hand information. Combine this with the fact that Captain Smith - like all other mariners - expected ice in that area, to move in a north easterly direction, so this second message containing the word 'ice' was treated by him as confirmation of the first one.

If any fault could be placed at the door of Captain Smith and his officers, it was one of assumption - assumption that the sea -ice would behave in the way it had always behaved. In fact, plots of ice reports produced by Paul Lee covering the Month of April, 1912, proved that these assumptions were correct.

(G): Deficit in the Lifeboats:

One of the most ill-informed bits of assumption comes from those who push the idea that *Titanic's* lifeboats should have been filled to capacity before launching, and if this had been done, many more would have survived.

Nothing can be farther from the truth. In fact, there was a real chance that the very opposite might have been the result of doing so, and many more would have been lost.

It has all to do with how *Titanic's* lifeboats were deployed.

Although she was fitted with the very latest in davits (crane arms), which greatly reduced the time taken to make the boats ready, each one of *Titanic's* lifeboats still relied on two individual, manila rope lowering systems - one at each end of a boat.

These acted through a block and tackle system but ultimately the entire load was suspended on a single rope at each end of the boat and the boat was lowered by slacking them off individually.

However, if the slacking off was uneven, the boat would also become uneven; end -to-end. When that happened, a rope at one end would be stopped "snubbed" - suddenly. This would result in a hock load in the rope; the greater the load - the greater the shock. If that shock load exceeded the strength of the rope, it would break. The boat would then be suspended by a single rope at one end and the contents tipped into the sea below them.

The greater the height of the boat above the water when this happened, the more likely would be the death toll among its passengers.

After this, the boat would then be rendered useless.

A full size lifeboat on *Titanic* had a capacity of 65 persons. Using the standard weight of 140 lbs/person, this means that the suspended weight of boat and contents would be within the safe working load of the rope used. However, a sudden shock due to an abrupt halt in the lowering process would break one or both ropes.

Titanic's designers and officers knew this; consequently, the safest method of embarkation of survivors was followed.

Much has been written, and will continue to be written about the tragically short life of - RMS 'Titanic' - "The Big Boat with The four Chimneys".

The dreadful tragedy has spawned numerous books, films and Television Documentaries, and I dare say, the story will continue to tantalize the imaginations of the masses for many years to come.

Unfortunately it is the public thirst for Fish-wives Tales, romantic nonsense and conspiracy, as well as intrigue mystery and imagination which drives most of those who produce and create a lot of what is offered for public consumption.

However, if this little offering of mine helps to blow away a few of these silly notions which cloud the truths of historic reality since that fateful day in April, 1912 - that day when all those poor, innocent individuals and brave seafarers lost their lives - then my effort will not have been in vain.

If nothing else, I hope me endeavours will at least help to improve the vision of those who earnestly seek the truth.

Captain Jim Currie.

ANNEX

(i) Tables

RISING OR DIPPING DISTANCE (M)
OF TERRESTRIAL OBJECT
OR COMBINED HEIGHT OF EYE AND HEIGHT OF OBJECT

H. E. 30	35	40	45	50	Height of Object	55	60	65	70	75	8
13.6	14.1	14.5	15.0	15.4	40	15.8	16.2	16.5	16.9	17.2	17
14.0	14.5	15.0	15.4	15.8	45	16.2	16.6	17.0	17.3	17.7	18
14.4	14.9	15.4	15.8	16.3	50	16.7	17.0	17.4	17.7	18.1	18
14.8	15.3	15.8	16.2	16.7	55	17.1	17.4	17.8	18.1	18.5	18
15.2	15.7	16.2	16.6	17.0	60	17.4	17.8	18.2	18.5	18.9	19
15.6	16.1	16.5	17.0	17.4	65	17.8	18.2	18.5	18.9	19.2	19
15.9	16.4	16.9	17.3	17.7	70	18.1	18.5	18.9	19.2	19.6	19
16.3	16.8	17.2	17.7	18.1	75	18.5	18.9	19.2	19.6	19.9	20
16.6	17.1	17.5	18.0	18.4	80	18.8	19.2	19.6	19.9	20.2	20
16.9	17.4	17.9	18.3	18.7	85	19.1	19.5	19.9	20.2	20.6	20
17.2	17.7	18.2	18.6	19.0	90	19.4	19.8	20.2	20.5	20.9	21
17.5	18.0	18.5	18.9	19.3	95	19.7	20.1	20.5	20.8	21.2	21
17.8	18.3	18.8	19.2	19.6	100	20.0	20.4	20.8	21.1	21.5	21
18.4	18.9	19.3	19.8	20.2	110	20.6	21.0	21.3	21.7	22.0	22
18.9	19.4	19.9	20.3	20.7	120	21.1	21.5	21.9	22.2	22.6	22
19.4	19.9	20.4	20.8	21.2	130	21.6	22.0	22.4	22.7	23.1	23
19.9	20.4	20.9	21.3	21.7	140	22.1	22.5	22.9	23.2	23.6	23
20.4	20.9	21.3	21.8	22.2	150	22.6	23.0	23.3	23.7	24.0	24
20.8	21.3	21.8	22.2	22.7	160	23.1	23.5	23.8	24.2	24.5	24
21.3	21.8	22.3	22.7	23.1	170	23.5	23.9	24.3	24.6	25.0	25
21.7	22.2	22.7	23.1	23.6	180	24.0	24.3	24.7	25.0	25.4	25
22.1	22.6	23.1	23.5	24.0	190	24.4	24.8	25.1	25.5	25.8	26
22.6	23.1	23.5	24.0	24.4	200	24.8	25.2	25.5	25.9	26.2	26
23.0	23.5	23.9	24.4	24.8	210	25.2	25.6	25.9	26.3	26.6	27
23.4	23.9	24.3	24.8	25.2	220	25.6	26.0	26.3	26.7	27.0	27
23.7	24.2	24.7	25.1	25.6	230	26.0	26.3	26.7	27.1	27.4	27
24.1	24.6	25.1	25.5	25.9	240	26.3	26.7	27.1	27.4	27.8	28
24.5	25.0	25.4	25.9	26.3	250	26.7	27.1	27.4	27.8	28.1	28
24.8	25.3	25.8	26.2	26.7	260	27.1	27.5	27.8	28.2	28.5	28
25.2	25.7	26.2	26.6	27.0	270	27.4	27.8	28.2	28.5	28.8	29
25.5	26.0	26.5	26.9	27.4	280	27.8	28.1	28.5	28.9	29.2	29
25.9	26.4	26.8	27.3	27.7	290	28.1	28.5	28.8	29.2	29.5	29
26.2	26.7	27.2	27.6	28.0	300	28.4	28.8	29.2	29.5	29.9	30
26.5	27.0	27.5	27.9	28.4	310	28.8	29.2	29.5	29.9	30.2	30
26.9	27.4	27.8	28.3	28.7	320	29.1	29.5	29.8	30.2	30.5	30

Time Table of Events

GMT	EST	SHIP	EVENT	P.Log	Date
14-58	9-58 pm	12-00	Noon - April 14, 1912.	00.0	14th
	11-58	2-00 pm		42.0	14th
	1-58	4-00	1st Dog Watch	84.0	14th
15-40	3-48	5-50	Alter course at *The Corner*.	122.2	14th
		6-00	2nd Dog Watch	125.7	14th
22-33	5-36	7-35	Evening position by observation stars	160.0	14th
22-58	5-58	8-00	Change of Deck Watches.	168.4..44	14h
22-58	5-58	8-00	Captain Smith's DR position	188.4	14th
22-58	6-58	10-00	Change of Bridge Watch	213.8	14th
01-38	8-58	12-00	Bridge clock retarded 24 minutes.	258.8	14th
01-38	8-58	11-36	Partly adjusted time starts.		14th
03-02	10-02	11-40	Collision with ice berg.	259	14h
03-08	10-08	11-46	Ship stopped and sinking.	260	14th
03-12	10-12	11-50	Captain Smith works distress position - 41-44'N..50-24W...	Projtd 280.0	
03-17	10-17	11-55 p	First distress call transmitted. All hands to lifeboat stations		14th
0 3-18	10-18	11-56	*Frankfurt* answers *Titanic* *Mount Temple* hears CQD		14th
03-22	10-22 pm	Midnight	Change of Deck Watches		14th
03-26	10-25 pm	00-03 am	Second Distress call Transmitted: 41-46'N...50-14'W.	Projtd 272..0	15th
03-40	10-40	12-26	*Mount Temple* turns for *Titanic*		15th
03-45	10-45	00-23	*Carpathia* received distress call		15th
03-48	10-48	00-26	Launch Boat 7		15th

GMT	EST	SHIP	EVENT	.Log	Date
03-54	10-54 pm	0-32	Launch Boar 5		15th
04-07	11-07 pm	0-45	First distress signal fired.		15th
03-10	11-10	0-48	*Olympic* contacts *Titanic*		
04-47	11-47 pm	1-25	Last signal fired.		15th
04-52	11-52 pm	1-30	Launch boats 10 & 4		15th
04-57	11-57 pm	1-35	Launch boats 2 & 10		15th
05-02	00-02 pm	1-40	Launch Collapsible C		15th
05-12	00-12 pm	1-50	Launch Collapsible D		15th
05-22	00-22 am	2-00	Launch of Collapsibles B & A progress		15th
05-25	00-25	2-03	*Titanic* sinks		15th
07-20	02-20	4-10	*Carpathia* arrives beside Boat 2		15th
07-44	02-44	4-30	*Mount Temple* stopped by ice.		15th
08-20	03-20	05-00	*Mount Tempe* gets underweigh.		
08 -25	03-25	5-05	*Mount Temple answers Californian*		15th
08- 40	03-40	5-20	*Frankfurt* Answers *Californian*		15th
09-00	04-00	5-40	*Californian* contacts *Virginian*		15th
09-20	04-20	06-00	*Californian* crosses ice		15th
09-40	04-40	06-20	*Californian* answers *Birma*		15th
11-30	06-30	7-30	*Californian* passes *Mount Temple.*		15th
11-10	06-10	8-00	*Californian* heads for *Carpathia*		15th
11-40	06-40	8-30	*Californian* near to *Carpathia*		15th

(iii)

Calculations

A:

Titanic's Great Circle Distance - Fastnet to *The Corner.*

From Fastnet at - Latitude 51°-22'N Longitude 09°-36'W
To: *The Corner* - Latitude 42°-00'N. Longitude 47°-00'W.

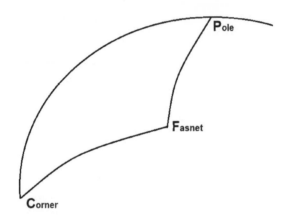

Formula: Hav Distance = HavP. sin PF. sin PC + hav(PC -PC).

Angle P = 09°-36' ~ 47°-00' = 37-24	(Log Hav: 9.01196
Line PF = 90°-00 - 51°-22 = 38°-3	(Log sin: 9.79542
Line PC = 90°-00 - 42°-00 = 48°-00'	(Log sin: 9.87107
Log Hav.	....8.67829
Convert Log Hav. 8.67829 to a Nat. Haversine.	= 0.04768
PF ~ PC = 38°-38 ~ 48°-00 = 9°-22' Nat Hav.	= 0.00669
Natural Haversin Distance	= 0.05437
Nat. Hav. Distance in degrees and minutes	= 26° 58'.

Since 1 minute arc = 1 mile, the Great Circle distance from 1 mile south of Fasnet Rock Lighthouse to *The Corner* is therefore 60 x 26 + 58, which is equal to 1618 nautical miles.

<u>(B) Titanic distance to Steam - Noon April 14 to *The Corner.*</u>

Titanic's 3rd Officer Pitman provided the following run details to the Chairman of the US Inquiry. In it he detailed each day's run from the moment Daunt Rock was abeam to starboard on the day *Titanic* left Queenstown until Noon on April 14, 1912. These were as follows:

Day 1 - 484 miles.
Day 2 - 519 miles.
Day 3 - 546 miles

<u>Total - 1549 nautical miles.</u>

This total included the 55 miles run from Daunt Rock to the Fasnet light. Consequently, if we deduct that amount from Pitman's Total, we can find the number of miles *Titanic* steamed on her Great Circle course until Noon April 14, and consequently - how far she was from *The Corner* at Noon on April 14

In addition - if we know the course set at Noon that day, we can calculate *Titanic's* Noon position.

Total distance Run:	1549.0
Run: Daunt Rock to Fasnet	55.0
Total distance run on GC Track:	1494.0 miles.
Total distance run on GC Track:	1494.0 miles.
Total length of GC Track	1618.0 miles.
Distance left - Noon to *The Corner:*	124.0 miles.

<u>(C) *Titanic's* April 14 Noon position.</u>

Arguments: Course 240.5° True minus 180° = 060.5°True. (reverse of course from Noon stated by 5th Officer). Distance 124 miles = distance left on Great Circle Course.

Formulae:

1) Difference between Longitudes divided by DMP (DMP = Difference of Meridional Parts) equals the Log Tangent of the course.
Transposing the above: D. Long = DMP times Log tangent course.

Log DMP...............1.92993
Log Tan. Course........0.24736
Log D. Longitude: 2.17739 = 150.4 minutes = 2°- 30.4 minutes

2) Distance steamed equals the Difference between latituded multiplied by the Log secant of the course.
Transposing the above: Distance divided by Log secant course = D. Latitude

Log Dist.: 2.09342
Log Sec. Course: 0.30766
Log D.Lat 1.79576 = 62.6 minutes = 1°- 02.6 minutes

The Corner: Latitude. 42°- 00'N. MP: 2766.1   Longitude. 47° - 00.0'W
               D.Lat. 01°- 02.6'N   D. Long. 02° - 30.4'E
Noon 14th Latitude. 44°- 02.6'N. MP:2857.2   Longitude. 44° - 29.6'E
Ship time *Titanic*: 12-00...GMT: 02-58 pm. EST: 09-58 am.

(D) 5th Officer Lowe's Calculations:

One of the most important witnesses to the navigation of *Titanic* during the period between Noon April 14 and 8 pm that evening was 5rd Officer Herbert Lowe, although much of that man's evidence has been ignored or completely missed by researchers.

Lowe and his colleague 6th Officer Moody were occupied with a specific task, and that was to record the difference between ship speed according to the number of propeller revolutions and ship speed by measurement. They were building a reference table known as a Slip Table. To do this, they would receive regular reports from the engine room regarding the number of propeller revolutions for a given time and compare these with actual distances travelled. To find the latter information they would use fixed positions and/or Patent Log readings at regular intervals. Adjustment would be made at the time of obtaining a true position.

<u>Slip Calculation - Commencement of the 6 pm 2nd Dog Watch</u>.

Distance by Patent Log since 4 pm = 41.9 miles.
Average speed = 20.95 knots. Propeller pitch: 35 feet. RPM 75.
6 pm. Total engine RPM since 4 pm. = 9,000
Engine distance: 4pm to 6pm = 9000 x 35 ، 6080 = 51.81 miles in 2 hours.
Engine Speed = 25.9 Knots. Log Speed = 20.95 Knots. Propeller slip = 4.95 miles/ hr.
Percentage Slip = 4.95 x 100 ، 25.9 = 19.1% slip. Indicative of a head current.

<u>(E) The *Titanic* 7-30 pm star position.</u>

The position of *Titanic* was ascertained after 7-30 pm that evening. The sextant observations of the Stars was made by 2nd Officer Lightoller when he returned from dinner at 7-30 0pm. Consequently the position found indicated where *Titanic* was between 7-35 pm and 7-40 pm.

According to 4th Officer Boxhall, six stars were used - 3 for latitude and 3 for longitude, thus each would be a check against the other. The star chart for the time indicated that the following stars would have been available:

Pole Star - Arcturus - Sirius - Regulus - Spica - Virgo etc.

What we know is that the position obtained, proved that the *Titanic* was making less than 22 knots up until that time. We know this because 4th Officer Boxhall used an estimated speed of 22 knots to calculate his distress position using the 7-30 pm position as a start point. He used that speed because he assumed that from 7-30 pm onward, *Titanic* was making her absolute optimum speed due to the flat calm weather conditions that prevailed thereafter.

Since we do not have the name of the starts used or their altitudes, we cannot exactly re-create Boxhall's calculations. However, from the estimated Patent Log readings shown on the Table of Events, and his evidence regarding speed and course made good, we can re-construct a fairly accurate representation of *Titanic's* 7-30 pm position by running back eastward in reverse from his distress position.

Boxhall's CQD:	272.6 miles
Estimated Patent Log reading at 7-38 pm:	160.5 miles
Distance run:	112.1 miles
Boxhall's distress position	Lat: 41°- 46'N. Long: 50°- 14'W.
Co.068°True x 112 miles	D.Lat: 00 8'N. D.Long: 02°- 38'E.
7-30 pm Star Sight position.	Lat: 41°- 54'N Long: 47°- 36'W. (Estimated)

(F) Captain Smith's Distress position.

By Calculation, Captain Smith's distress position is 20 miles west of the true distress position, and according to the evidence of Joe Boxhall, Captain Smith used the wrong 8 pm DR position as the start point when he calculated his distress position. Consequently, if we add 20 miles to our estimated 8pm DR position, we will get the 8pm DR position used by Captain Smith. In addition, if Captain Smith used partly adjusted time, then his run time was 4 hours 24 minutes - not only can we calculate the distance he used, but also the ship average speed he used. So let's do it.

Calculated 8 pm DR position:	Lat.41°-54.3'N.	Long. 47°-52.0'W.
20 miles on 265 True:	D.Lat. 1.7'S	D.Long. 26.8'W.
Captain Smith's 8pm DR	Lat.41°-52.6'N.	Long . 48°-18.8'W.
Captain Smith's Impact pos.	Lat.41°-45.0'N.	Long.. 50°-23.0'W

From the foregoing: Course made Good = 265 True, distance: 92 miles; Av. speed: 21.5 k.

To the above impact position, Captain Smith would have allowed a mile south and west for his final distress position which was Lat. 41°-44.0'N., Long. 50°-24'W

E) Fourth Officer Boxhall's Distress Position Calculation.

Unaltered impact time	11-40 am
Clock adjustment ±	47 Minutes.
Impact time:	12-27 am.
Diff GMT	03.22
Impact	03-31 GMT. (15th)
Star sights time	10-33 GMT (14th
Run time	4 hrs 58 min at 22 knots = 109.3 miles.
	Course: 086 True.

Impact position;	Lat. 41°-47.0'N.	Long.: 50°-13.0'W.
	D.Lat. 7.6'N	D.Long 2°-27.0'E.
7-30 pm sights?	. 41°-52.6'N	47° - 46'W

(F) <u>Reconstruction of Pole Star observation made by Chief Officer Stewart</u> of the *Californian* <u>during the evening of April 14.</u>

Height of eye: 55 feet.	Observed Alt.	41° 01.08'
Air Temperature 33 degrees Farenheight.		
Barometer: 31.5 inches. Dip of Horizon		7.27'
		40°53.81'
Refraction		1.21'

True altitude		40° 52.60'
LHA Aries: 130° 24.9' (North)		
From previous page:	True altitude	40° 52.60'
	subtract	1° 00.00'
		39° 52.60'
GHA Aries:	173° 00.7'	A +	1° 12.00'
Increments:	7° 31.2'	A 1	+ 0.40'
GHA Aries:	180° 31.9'	A 2 +	1° 00.00'
DR Longitude: 50° 07.0'W		LATITUDE	42° 05.00'North.

The ship time of 7-40 pm is assumed and is derived from the evidence of Chief Officer Stewart who stated *"Not only that, I had the Pole Star at half past ten".*

Stewart also stated that he had it at about 7-30 pm ship time. However, since he worked in GMT and the ship's clock was 3 hours 10 minutes SLOW of GMT. the time of the Pole Star sight 10-30pm GMT. has been used. This is more in keeping with the prevailing conditions when 2nd Officer Lightoller took his sights on the *Titanic,*

(G) 3rd Officer Pitmans calculations.

Pitman made a glaring mistake when calculating the distance from Noon April 14 until 5-50 pm, the time when *Titanic* was due to arrive at *The Corner* and alter her course for New York.

In his evidence, to the UK Inquiry on Day 13, he stated:

> *"15183 I thought that the course should have been altered at 5 p.m…"*

So how did he arrive at that conclusion?

We know from the same evidence that Pitman was using a ship speed of 21.5 knots; this means that he calculated the distance from Noon until 5 pm as 5 x 21.5 = 107 nautical miles. However, the distance to *The Corner* from Noon that day was 126 miles on a course of 240 True.

In fact, the calculation as to when *Titanic* was to be turned at *The Corner* would have been done by Captain Smith. Consequently, the only person with notes on that calculation would have been Smith himself. If another Officer had wished to check the captain's findings, that officer would require to do his own calculations.

Pitman also knew the ship's position at Noon that day and her expected position at 5-50 pm. If he had calculated the distance between these two points, he would have got the proper answer.

However, it seems that he did not actually calculate that distance but used what were known as the Traverse Tables.

To find the distance between 2 points using these Tables, Pitman would first determine the difference of Longitude in minutes between the known Noon position and the known longitude of *The Corner.* Using that difference between these two, he would have obtained and argument from the table called "Departure". Since he knew the course being steered from

Noon, this would allow him to determine the course and distance from Noon to The Corner and, using a speed of 21.25 knots, give him a time of arrival at *The Corner.*

Noon Position: Lat. 43-01'N. Lon . 44°-33'W.
Position of *The Corner* Lat. 42-00'N. Long. 47°-00'W.
            D.Lat. 1-01'S D.Long. 2°-27' W.

Pitman would convert the D. Long. to minutes of arc (147') and enter the Traverse Table at 42 degrees with that number. This gave him a value of 109 for "departure". His next step would be to convert the D. lat to minutes - 61' and with these values enter the Traverse Table again, to obtain a course and distance. If he had completed the whole operation, he would have obtained a course of 240° True and a distance of 124 miles. However, it seems that he did not do so, and used departure of 109 as a distance and a speed of 21.5 knots which gave him a steaming time of 5 hours from Noon Hence his answer to UK Inquiry question 15183." *I thought that the course should have been altered at 5 p.m..."*

Then with this information and the course to be steered, you consult the appropriate mean Longitude page - In his case the 43 degree table.

On the other hand side of the Longitude Table, you find the value for difference of longitude and read off the value for "departure" adjacent to it. . With this value, you then consult the Course Table and directly read off the appropriate distance between the two positions.

We know from his Junior that the course to The Corner was 240 True. Thus, Pitman had the 2 arguments to obtain the distance between the Noon Position and *The Corner.*

Pitman would have consulted the 43 Degree table for Longitude, using a difference of longitude of 62 minutes (the latitude difference between Noon and *The Corner.*) There he would have found a departure value of

Calculation (1) - DR when course altered.

Course 240True, Speed 21.5 knots. Distance 17.9 miles (overshoot)
The Corner   Lat. 42°-00'N Long.   47°-00'W
                        D.Lat. 09'S D.Long.   20'W

DR 8-48 pm GMT - 5-50 pm ship.   41°- 51N   47°-20,'W
Calculation (2) - DR Alter Course to DR for Sights
Course 265° True, Speed 21.5 knots. Distance 38.7 miles.
Run 1 hr 48 min at 21.5 knots. Course 265 True
DR 8-48 pm GMT(5-50 pm ship).   41°- 51'N   47°-20'W
                        D.Lat.   00°- 03'S D.Long. 00°-51'W
DR 10-36pm GMT (7-38 pm ship). .   41°-48'N   48°-11'W
Calculation (3) Sights to DR 8 pm
Course 265° True, Speed 21.5 knots. Distance 4.3 miles
DR 10-36pm GMT (7-38pm ship).   41°-48.0'N   48°-11.0'W.
                        D.Lat. 00°-00.4'S D.Long. 00°-06.0'W.
DR 10-58 pm GMT (8pm ship)   41°-47.6'N   48°-17.0'W

Lowe's Calculation of the 8pm DR

Run 2 hrs 10'minutes Speed 20.95 knots…Course 265 True…
GMT 8-48 5-50pm ship Lat. 42°-00'N… .Long. 47°-00.0'W. (The Corner)
D. Lat. 00°-03.9'S .D.Long. 01°-00.0'W,
GMT 10-58pm -8pm ship Lat. 41°-56.1'N .. Long. 48°-00.0'W.

8pm and the position of the turn had not been calculated, then Lowe
assumed that *Titanic* had turned exactly at *The Corner* as planned, and
since he knew the coordinates of *The Corner* and the course steered between
there and 8pm, all he needed was a speed and we have already seen that
was 20.95 Knots. If as he said, Lowe calculated the 8pm DR according to
the average speed pf 20.95 knots then he would have given his captain an
8pm DR position of: 41°-56.1'North 48°-00.0'West.

Carpathia Calculations.

Turn position - 12-35 am April 15

Arguments:
Course: Distress position to *Carpathia* turn position = S52E. Distance to
steam 58 miles.
Titanic Distress position Lat.   41° 46.0 N   . Long. 50° 14.0 W.
                        D.Lat.   35.7 N. D.Long 1° 01.0 E.

Carpathia - 00-35 am. April 15 41° 10.3 N.   49° 13.0 E.

<u>Message: *Carpathia* to *Olympic* - April 15.</u>

"*Carpathia.*"

"*Captain Olympic - 7.30 G. M. T. 41.15 north longitude 51.45 west. Am steering south 87 west true, returning to New York with Titanic passengers.*

"*ROSTRON.*"

"*Carpathia.*"

From the above : if *Carpathia's* clocks were initially1 hour 50 minutes FAST of EST. then they were 3 hours 10 minutes SLOW of GMT. Consequently the unadjusted time on *Carpathia* would have been 7-30 pm minus 3 hrs. 10 min. = 4-20 pm on the afternoon of April 15, 1912. Therefore, since the course being steered is given and we know *Carpathia* would have been making about 14 knots, we can deduce that at Noon that day,

<u>*Carpathia* Noon Position for April 15, 1912 Calculation</u>

<u>Arguments:</u> Course- 4-20pm position to Noon April 15 = North 87 East
              Distance to steam 14 knots x 4 hours 20 minutes = 60.2miles.

Turn Position at 4-20 pm April 15:   Lat. 41° 15.0'N.   Long. 51° 45.0'W.
                                      D.Lat. <u>3.1' N</u>   D.Long <u>1° 20.5' E.</u>
Carpathia -Noon, April 15, 1912   Lat <u>41° 18.1' N.</u>   Long <u>50° 24.5'W.</u>

When the Noon position was obtained, *Carpathia's* clocks would have been adjusted to correspond to the Noon Longitude. Consequently, they would have been 3 hours 22 minutes SLOW of GMT and 1 hour 38 minutes FAST of EST. Which - incidentally - was exactly the same as the clocks on *Titanic* when she hit the iceberg.

If *Carpathia* was at 50° 25 West at Noon, and she turned westward when she was clear of the south end of the pack ice and on the longitude of 50° West, then she did so at or very near to 10-40 am when on Latitude 41° 19 North.

Since she left the *Californian* at the wreck site at 9 am and steered south to clear the ice, then her departure latitude was, allowing for initial acceleration, at or near to latitude 41°-40 North. This alone destroys the idea of there being a south-setting current present in the area.

Titanic Distress position Calculations

Throughout the years there have been many ingenious - even plausible reasons given as to why two men such as Captain Smith and his Fourth Officer Joe Boxhall made such a bollocks of working the distress signals.

Both men were Extra Masters. The older of the two had almost 50 years experience while the younger was a dedicated Navigator whose daily bread was earned making such simple (to him) calculations/ So what went wrong?

First, let us examine the work of Joe Boxhall. We start with his distress position which we know from the evidence given at both Inquiries and which was the only one accepted and was Lat. 41°- 46.0 north. Lat. 50°-14. '0 West.

However, that would have been where, in Boxhall's opinion, *Titanic* had finally stopped. I will therefore assume that she ran on after hitting the iceberg and stopped a mile to the southward. Consequently, to calculate Boxhall's run at full speed until *Titanic* hit the ice berg, I will use the ice berg impact position of Lat 41°-47.0 North Long. 50°-13'.0West.

Now that we have an end of run position. I will choose a start position which we know was unaltered time. In this case, the correct 8pm DR position on the evening of April 14.

However, how can this be done? I hear you ask. *How can the proper 8pm DR be calculated and verified?*

As we have seen earlier, the ship's clocks were to be retarded by 47 minutes. This amount would have been shared 24 minutes and 23 minutes. We also know that Boxhall assumed *Titanic* was making 22 knots from the last known position taken before 8 pm that evening, so we can use a speed of 22 knots. He also

assumed she was making a course of 266°True. Consequently, if Boxhall also assumed that the full clock change had been made before the ship hit the iceberg, then his run time from 8pm that evening was 4 hours 47 minutes.

This means that he would have used a run distance of 4 hours 47 minutes x 22 knots,,, which equals 105.2 nautical miles.

With the foregoing information, and running in reverse from where iceberg and ship met, we can then calculate a DR position for *Titanic* at 8 pm that evening.

The distress position calculated by Boxhall would not have been the position where Titanic hit the ice berg; it would be the position where she finally came to rest, and where potential rescuers would head for. This being so, then we must also do a bit of assuming too. In this case, we will assume that Boxhall allowed about a mile south and west from where the ship hit the berg to where she finally stopped - his distress position. Consequently:

Boxhall's berg position:	Lat. 41°-47.0' N..	Long.50°-13.0'W.
Run 086°True x 105.2m.	D.Lat. 7.3'N -	D.Long. 2°-21.0'W.
8pm DR position	Lat. 41°-54.3' N	Long. 47°-52.0'W

So what did Boxhall really do wrong? At the Inquiries, he said he used a course of 266°True and an estimated average speed of 22 knots from the evening stellar position to calculate his distress position. However, we do not know what that position was - only that they used the sextant observations of no less than 6 stars to determine it. That alone would guarantee a high degree of accuracy in the position obtained. But all is not lost.

If we accept the result of the previous calculations regarding the true 8 pm DR position are reasonable, then since 3rd Officer Pitman said the ship was right on the prescribed track at about 7-38 pm when these observations were made, we can deduce a fairly accurate position for the position that Boxhall used to calculate his Distress position by running back for 22 minutes on the reverse track for say 7 miles. Let's do it!

Calculated 8 pm DR position Lat. 41°-54.3 North. Long. 47°-52.0 West.

Run: 7 miles on 085°T   D.Lat. <u>0.6 North</u>.   D.Long. <u>9.5 East.</u>

7-38 pm stellar position   <u>Lat. 41°-53.7 North   Long. 47° -42.5 West.</u>

Having established a position for Boxhall's start point and having an approximate position for where he thought *Titanic* hit the ice, and knowing the course and speed he used, we can get a very good idea of the steaming time Boxhall used in his calculation.

7-38 pm stellar position   Lat. 41°-53.7 North   Long. 47°-42.5 West.

Boxhall's impact position: <u>Lat. 41°-47.0 North   Long. 50°-13.0 West.</u>

                              <u>D.Lat. 6.7 South D.Long. 2°-30.5 West.</u>

The foregoing equates to a course made good of 266.5 T. for a distance steamed of 112 miles. At 22 knots, that would have taken 5 hours 6 minutes steaming time.

Since Boxhall used GMT, his start time would have been 10-36 pm GMT and his impact time would have been 3-43 am GMT. However the Time of impact was recorded as 3 am GMT.

(iv)

<u>Relevant Ice Reports concerning ice reported immediately before and after the disaster.</u>

   1.   <u>*SS* Trautenfels …Ice Report</u>

      <u>April 14 - SS Trautenfels …42.01 N 50.06 W 41.40 N 50.22 W.</u>

      "5.40am heavy field ice was encountered which extended for a distance of 30m and made it necessary for the steamer to run in a southwesterly direction for 25m to clear it.

   2.   <u>*SS* Mesaba….Ice Report</u>

      <u>April 14 - SS Mesaba….42.00 N 50.00 W 41.35 N 50.30 W.</u>

At 2pm, "passed another field of pack ice with numerous bergs intermixed, and extended from 4 points on the starboard bow to abeam on the port side. Had to steer about 20 miles south to clear it. Ice seemed to be one solid wall of ice, at least 16 feet high, as far as could be seen. In latitude 41 35' north longitude 50 30 west, we came to the end of it, and at 4 P.M. we were able to again steer to the westward. Saw no more ice after this. Weather clear and bright."

3. - SS Californian.....Ice Report

"April 14 - SS Californian...42.05 N 50.07 W.

"10.20 pm Encountered field ice, about 5 miles wide, stretching north and south; also icebergs."

Perhaps the most significant Ice Report was one filed retrospectively at the US Hydrographic Office sent by the SS Parisian, in which her captain reported:

"April 14, 4:30 P.M., latitude 41 55' N., longitude 49 02' W., passed first iceberg.

8 P.M., latitude 41 42' N., longitude 49 55' W., passed last iceberg."

The highlighted position in that report is only 2 miles southwestward of where the wreck of *Titanic* now lies.

Significantly, 4 hours later, *Titanic* would have been just north of that location - had *Parisian's* captain transmitted that as a warning at the time, you might not be reading this now.

As for the eastern extent of the Ice Field? Captain Rostron of the *Carpathia* told his questioners on Day 1 of the US Inquiry:

"the first iceberg we saw was at a quarter to 3. In the morning, [when it was full daylight] *about two or three miles from the position of the "Titanic's" wreckage we saw a huge ice-field extending as far as we could see, N.W. to S.E."*

(v)

Copies of the Incident Reports made by the 2nd Officer and Apprentice Deck Officer to Captain Lord of the *Californian.*

2nd Officer Stone's report.

"*S.S. Californian At Sea,*   (18 April, 1912)

Captain Lord, Dear Sir,,

At your request I make the following report of the incidents witnessed by me during my Watch on the Bridge of this Steamer from midnight April 14th - 4 a.m. of the 15th. On going up to the bridge I was stopped by yourself at the wheelhouse door, and you gave me verbal orders for the Watch. You showed me a steamer a little abaft of our Star-beam and informed me she was stopped. You also showed me the loose field ice all around the ship and a dense icefield to the southward. You told me to watch the other steamer and report if she came any nearer and that you were going to lie down on the chartroom settee. I went on the bridge about 8 minutes past 12, and took over the Watch from the Third Officer, Mr. Groves, who also pointed out ice and steamer and said our head was E.N.E. and we were swinging. On looking at the compass I saw this was correct and observed the other steamer S.S.E dead abeam and showing one masthead light, her red side-light and one or two small indistinct lights around the deck which looked like portholes or open doors. I judged her to be a small tramp steamer and about five miles distant.

The Third Officer then left the bridge and I at once called the steamer up but got no reply. Gibson, the Apprentice, then came up with the coffee at about 12:15. I told him I called the steamer up and the result. Gibson thought at first he was answering, but it was only his masthead lamps flickering a

344

little. I then sent Gibson by your orders to get the gear all ready for streaming a new log line when We got under weigh again. At 12:35 you whistled up the speaking tube and asked if the other steamer had moved. I replied 'No' and that she was on the same bearing and also reported I had called him up and the result.

At about 12:45, I observed a flash of light in the sky just above that steamer. I thought nothing of it as there were several shooting stars about, the night being fine and clear with light airs and calms. Shortly after I observed another distinctly over the steamer which I made out to be a white rocket though I observed no flash on the deck or any indication that it had come from that steamer, in fact, it appeared to come from a good distance beyond her. and all white in colour. I, at once, whistled down the speaking tube and you came from the chartroom into your own room and answered. I reported seeing these lights in the sky in the direction of the other steamer which appeared to me to be white rockets. You then gave me orders to call her up with the Morse lamp and try and get some information from her. You also asked me if they were private signals and I replied, 'I do not know but they were all white.' You then said: 'When you get an answer let me know by Gibson.' We were also swinging slowly all the time through S. and at 1:50 were heading about W.S.W. and the other steamer bearing S. W. x W. At 2:00 a.m. the vessel was steaming away fast and only just her stern light was visible and bearing S.W. ½ W. I sent Gibson down to you and told him to wake you and tell you we had seen altogether eight white rockets and that the steamer had gone out of sight to the S.W. Also that we were heading W.S.W. When he came back he reported he had told you we had called him up repeatedly and got no answer, and you replied: 'All right, are you sure there were no colors in them,' and Gibson replied, 'No, they were all white.' At 2:45 I again whistled down again and told you we had seen no more lights and that the steamer had steamed away to the S.W. and was now out of sight, also that the rockets were all white and had no colours whatever.

We saw nothing further until about 3:20 when we thought we observed two faint lights in the sky about S.S.W. and a little distance apart. At 3:40 I sent Gibson down to see all was ready for me to prepare the new log at eight bells. The Chief Officer, Mr. Stewart, came on the bridge at 4 a.m., and I gave him a full report of what I had seen and my reports and replies from you, and pointed out where I thought I had observed these faint lights at 3:20. He picked up the binoculars and said after a few moments: 'There she is then, she's all right, she is a four-master.' I said, 'Then that isn't the steamer I saw first,' took up the glasses and just made out a four-masted steamer with two masthead lights a little abaft our port beam, and bearing about S., we were heading about W.N.W. Mr. Stewart then took over the Watch and I went off the bridge.

Yours respectfully, (signed) Herbert Stone Second Officer"

Deck Apprentice James Gibson's Report *. Thursday, April 18th, 1912*

"Dear Sir,

In compliance with your wishes, I hereby make the following statement as to what I saw on the morning of April 15th, 1912:

It being my watch on deck from 12 o'clock, I went on the bridge at about 15 minutes after twelve and saw that the ship was stopped and that she was surrounded with light field ice and thick field-ice to the Southward. While the Second Officer and I were having coffee, a few minutes later, I asked him if there were any more ships around us. He said that there was one on the Starboard beam, and looking over the weather cloth, I saw a white light flickering, which I took to be a Morse light calling us up. I then went over to the keyboard and gave one long flash in answer, and still seeing this light flickering, I gave her the calling up sign. The light on the other ship, however, was still the same, so I looked at her through the binoculars and found it was her masthead light flickering. I also observed her port sidelight and a faint glare of lights on her afterdeck. I then went over to the Second Officer and remarked she looked like a tramp steamer. He said that most probably she was, and was burning oil lights. This ship was then right abeam.

At about 25 minutes after twelve I went down off the bridge to get a new log out and not being able to find it, I went on the bridge again to see if the Second Officer knew anything about it. I then noticed that this other ship was about one and a half points before the beam. I then went down again and was down until about five minutes to one. Arriving on the bridge again at that time, the Second Officer told me that the other ship, which was then about 3 ½ points on the Starboard bow, had fired five rockets and he also remarked that after seeing the second one to make sure that he was not mistaken, he had told the Captain, through the speaking tube, and that the Captain had told him to watch her and keep calling her up on the Morse light. I then watched her for some time and then went over to the keyboard and called her up continuously for about three minutes. I then got the binoculars and had just got them focused on the vessel when I observed a white flash apparently on her deck, followed by a faint streak towards the sky which then burst into white stars. Nothing then happened until the other ship was about two points on the Starboard bow when she fired another rocket.

Shortly after that, I observed that her sidelight had disappeared, but her masthead light was just visible, and the Second Officer remarked after taking another bearing of her, that she was slowly steering away towards the S.W.

Between one point on the Starboard bow and one point on the Port bow I called her up on the Morse lamp but received no answer. When about one point on the Port bow she fired another rocket which like the others burst into white stars. Just after two o'clock she was then about two points on the Port bow, she disappeared from sight and nothing was seen of her again. The Second Officer then said, "Call the Captain and tell him that the ship has disappeared in the S.W., that we are heading W.S.W. and that altogether she has fired eight rockets." I then went down below to the chartroom and called the Captain and told him and he asked me if there were any colors in the rockets. I told him that they were all white. He then asked me what time it was and I went on the bridge and told the Second Officer what the Captain had said. At about 2:45 he whistled down to the Captain again but I did not hear what was said.

At about 3:20 looking over the weather cloth, I observed a rocket about two points before the beam (Port), which I reported to the Second Officer. About three minutes later I saw another rocket right abeam which was followed later by another one about two points before the beam. I saw nothing else and when one bell went, I went below to get the log gear ready for the Second Officer at eight bells.

Yours respectfully, (Signed) James Gibson,

Apprentice"

SOURCES

- wrecksite.eu.
- archives.gov/publications/prologue/2000/fall/us-canada-immigration-records-1.html
- searlecanada.org/volturno/volturno97.html
- theshipslist.com
- Dr. Paul Lee. - *Titanic* Navigation and Ice Reports"
- encyclopedia-titanica.org
- cimorelli.com
- *Titanic* AuthorSenan Molon
- Titanicinquiry.org.
- Hansard.
- Nicholls's Seamanship & Nautical Knowledge.
- Reed's Table of Distance
- Nicholls's Concise Guide Vol. 2
- Pursey - Merchant Ship Stability -
- oceancurrents.rsmas.miami.edu/atlantic/slope-jet.html
- Meteorology for Seamen -
- Last - but not least....Google!